PRAISE FOR *BEYOND THE BORDER*

'This book by Mr Justice Richard Humphreys is both timely and enlightening and, most important, in a non-political way explains excellently the parts of the Agreement that have been misunderstood. The author gives a comprehensive overview of the main events over the past twenty years and deals with the challenges ahead in a way that is helpful to all involved in this debate. What we have in this book is an understanding of the implications of the Agreement now for the short and long term, taking account of the constitutional parameters. As the debate on a New Ireland evolves, this book will be an essential read to understand clearly the central policy issues to be dealt with.'

Bertie Ahern, former Taoiseach

'In his Foreword to Dr. Richard Humphreys' book *Countdown to Unity* (published in 2009) the former Attorney General of Ireland, the late Rory Brady SC, observed that reconciliation of the tension between the right to self determination and the reality of political life on the island of Ireland was to be found in the policy of 'consent' and he described how *Countdown to Unity* carefully and eruditely analysed this fundamental precept.

Some nine years later, Mr. Justice Humphreys, in *Beyond the Border*, provides a likewise learned and reasoned analysis of the challenges to the principle of 'consent' against the changed political and legal landscape in 2018. He explains, for example, in the context of the debate about a border poll, that any aim to secure unity by a 'given date' can only be aspirational rather than be made a legally effective requirement, as to do so would be fundamentally inconsistent with the principle of consent which forms the basis of the Good Friday Agreement and its antecedent legal framework.

In *Beyond the Border* Mr. Justice Humphreys gives an insightful analysis of historical, political and legal factors which have shaped and continue to influence the Good Friday Agreement. It is required reading for all those interested in law, politics and government, the challenges faced by Brexit and the operation of international agreements.

Perhaps most importantly, I would commend *Beyond the Border* to all those on both sides of the Irish sea who continue to work tirelessly to uphold the achievements of the Good Friday Agreement.'

Conleth Bradley SC, author of Judicial Review

'Compulsory reading. Written in a style accessible to a broad readership, Humphreys has demonstrated an encyclopedic knowledge in his eloquent navigation from the Good Friday Agreement to the implications of Brexit. This fine book is a blueprint for uniting the peoples of this island.'

Elaine Byrne, columnist, Sunday Business Post

'At this critical time in our history, when Brexit raises challenges for the island of Ireland, this publication brings us, step by step, through the nuts and bolts of the Good Friday Agreement. It addresses concerns arising from the collapse of devolved government in Northern Ireland, and presents possible options for the future. Even if you do not agree with the author's hypotheticals for the future, this is a remarkable source of relevant information. It is a significant publication in the search to maintain peace, highlighting the importance of a functioning Northern Ireland, and a partnership for peace on both a North/South and an East/West axis, while stressing the necessity for equality and parity of esteem.

Bringing civil conflict to an end has always been ~~...~~ compromise being required from all parties. Follow~~...~~ maintaining a healthy civil society, despite ~~...~~ leadership, accompanied by insight. It is i~~...~~ carefully researched and clearly written a~~...~~ f interest to historians, politicians, lawyers ~~...~~ he island of Ireland. Given the long view ~~...~~ ge of his hypotheticals, it is likely to remai~~...~~ come.'

Susan Denham, former Chief Justice

'An in-depth and substantial publication on the peace process. In light of Brexit, this is a timely study of the legal parameters and implications of the Belfast Agreement.'

Martina Fitzgerald, RTÉ Political Correspondent

'This book expertly analyses the complexities of the Good Friday Agreement. The author displays considerable scholarship and a deep understanding of the issues. The book is a major contribution to the understanding of the legal obligations arising from the Good Friday Agreement.'

Paul Gallagher SC, former Attorney General

'Irish judges used to think it was enough to simply assert that a united Ireland was a constitutional imperative. Mr. Justice Humphreys is not so arrogant. In this meticulous analysis of the Good Friday Agreement, he faces hard questions squarely. Among them: does the Republic really know what to do if a united Ireland is carried by a majority that's even smaller than the Brexit one; how would a future Oireachtas cope with a million new voters who claim British citizenship? Both polities on the island will benefit from his insights.'

Eoghan Harris, columnist, Sunday Independent

'Richard Humphreys has authored a timely and challenging analysis of the implications of the Good Friday Agreement and Brexit for the future of Ireland, north and south, and for the aspiration for Irish unity. His objective but engaging study of the prospects for change in the constitutional status of Northern Ireland ... will serve as an authoritative guide to the obstacles and challenges inherent in a constitutional rapprochement between the parts and traditions of Ireland ...

This study should be read in every part of Ireland and by all those in the islands who care for reconciliation and progress in the spirit of Thomas Davis ... An excellent and much-needed work.'

Michael McDowell SC, former Tánaiste and Attorney General

'This scholarly but very readable book by Richard Humphreys is a timely and important contribution to the debate on Brexit and its implications for the two jurisdictions on the island, viewed through the prism of the Good Friday Agreement.

It is a follow-on from the excellent *Countdown to Unity* (2009), which itself examined the legal aspects (as well as implementation and non-implementation) of the agreement brokered two decades ago. This book provides a form of sequel, updating all that has happened since: 17 suspensions in all; the power-sharing institutions in abeyance for a year and a half.

The core of this new book is the potentially momentous change in the constitutional status of Northern Ireland that will occur after Brexit is implemented. Mr Justice Humphreys examines, in an even-handed and disinterested manner, the implications of Brexit for the Good Friday Agreement, for human rights and for the question of Irish unity ... It is a fascinating, insightful and accessible work.'

Harry McGee, political correspondent, The Irish Times

'This scholarly but hugely accessible book should be required reading for everyone with an interest in the future of Ireland, north and south. The analysis is hugely insightful and will give politicians and policy makers in Ireland and Britain much to ponder in a post-Brexit world.'

Kevin Rafter, Head of the School of Communications,
Dublin City University

'Mr Justice Humphreys has sought to apply a rigorous even-handed logic in analysing what these issues mean now for the Irish people and the EU ... by highlighting [these] misunderstandings with the spirit of logic, he renews our focus towards treating the Agreement as a mandate of the people to make devolution work.'

John Rogers, former Attorney General

BEYOND
THE
BORDER

Richard Humphreys is a Judge of the Irish High Court. He is a graduate of UCD and the King's Inns and holds a PhD in Law from Trinity College Dublin. As a government adviser in 1996 he attended the launch of Multi-Party negotiations in Stormont that ultimately led to the Good Friday Agreement. From 1997 to 2015 he was a practising barrister and in 2015 was appointed to the High Court. This is his third book.

BEYOND

THE

BORDER

THE GOOD FRIDAY AGREEMENT AND IRISH UNITY AFTER BREXIT

RICHARD HUMPHREYS

MERRION
PRESS

For all victims of violence related to the conflict in Ireland – their legacy must be a peaceful and accommodating future.

First published in 2018 by
Merrion Press
An imprint of Irish Academic Press
10 George's Street
Newbridge
Co. Kildare
Ireland
www.merrionpress.ie

9781785372056 (Paper)
9781785372063 (Kindle)
9781785372070 (Epub)
9781785372087 (PDF)

British Library Cataloguing in Publication Data
An entry can be found on request

Library of Congress Cataloging in Publication Data
An entry can be found on request

Interior design by www.jminfotechindia.com
Typeset in Minion Pro 11/15 pt

Cover design by River Design
Cover front: Northern Ireland Parliament and Government
building in Stormont, Belfast (Nahlik/Shutterstock.com).

Contents

Foreword

The Good Friday Agreement of 1998 was a watershed moment in Irish and British history. Overwhelmingly supported by the electorate of Northern Ireland and Ireland, the Agreement created an interlocking set of principles and structures designed to develop a peaceful partnership between the different traditions and conflicting political ambitions robust enough to consign conflict to history. A new future beckoned based on parity of esteem, equality, mutual respect, shared government in Northern Ireland and intergovernmental collaboration on the North–South and East–West axes. Over its twenty years of operation, the Agreement has proved to be encouragingly resilient in the face of many difficulties but there can be little doubt that it now faces a particularly testing period with the collapse of the devolved government in Northern Ireland and the United Kingdom's withdrawal from the European Union. These very issues lend an urgency to refocusing attention on the structure and principles which underpin the Agreement and on the imperative this generation has and owes to past and future generations to ensure it continues to be the lodestar which guides us steadily on the path to peace and reconciliation. The institutions created by it are intended to withstand and provide a safe space for ongoing debate and deliberation on the constitutional choices available to the people of Northern Ireland. They also form the template as much for the shape of Northern Ireland's political structures within the United Kingdom as within a united Ireland as Mr Justice Richard Humphreys' timely and useful book asserts. He argues that a devolved assembly where the various traditions must work together is, under the Agreement, a permanent feature of the landscape, that the validity, equality and mutual respect of the different traditions are enduring commitments, regardless of whether the constitutional situation remains as it is or changes. This raises uncomfortable questions.

Mr Justice Humphreys pursues a number of issues which have been overlooked up to now given this reality and which commend themselves to further investigation by the relevant governments, political parties and the constituencies which make up the public in Ireland and the United Kingdom, jurisdictions whose collegial relationship has been transformed in recent years. This is an area often fraught with fears, and suspicions, but the author is to be commended for exploring these sensitive issues without engaging in political comment or favouring any particular shade of political opinion. His focus is on the Agreement: what it means and what the practical implications are of the spirit and letter of the principles contained in it. It is clear that some aspects of the Agreement have not been understood and assimilated, and, insofar as he seeks to address some of these misconceptions, in a non-political and non-partisan spirit, I believe this is a necessary corrective to the debate. He also highlights how a renewed focus on what is required by the Agreement can provide new perspectives with which to make devolution work. While setting out what the Agreement means, and outlining options for progress within those parameters, he wisely leaves all consequent decisions to the political process. To that extent, it is a book which strives for scrupulous fairness and impartiality in what is usually a hotly contested political space where resentment gets in the way of the calm reasoning that this debate would benefit greatly from.

Mr Justice Humphreys, in this thoughtful and excellent work, carefully lays out the sometimes uncomfortable implications of accommodating all traditions. His is a vision for Northern Ireland as a place at peace, where North/South relationships develop unforced and organically over time as has been happening naturally and imperceptibly since 1998 but with manifest, tangible benefits for all. In his view, constitutional change, if it were to happen, would evolve in the context of progressing partnership rather than sudden political rupture. The old language of winners and losers is redundant in such a vision. It is about choosing the best future for all of us in an egalitarian culture of good neighbours and not simply a flag.

Dr Mary McAleese
8th President of Ireland, 1997–2011
April 2018

Preface

This book seeks to discuss and explain the implications of the Good Friday Agreement in relation to any possible future change to the constitutional status of Northern Ireland. It is clear that there remains misunderstanding on many sides as to what the Agreement means. This book is an endeavour to explain the Agreement and its implications. It is not meant to be a political work in any sense. It is written in a personal and academic capacity. It does not argue for or indeed against Irish unity; obviously there are many weighty arguments on both sides which must be left to political debate. Nor does it even seek to encourage debate about a change in the constitutional status of Northern Ireland. The empirical fact is, however, that unity is currently being discussed, and that discussion is hampered by a certain amount of misconception about what the Agreement involves. This book, therefore, is an attempt to explain the Agreement and its implications, and to set out the legal and constitutional parameters. There is, of course, scope for political judgement within those parameters, as long as the constraints of the Agreement itself are acknowledged. Within those constraints, my intention is to leave any judgements on political issues to the political realm.

This book grew out of my 2009 book, *Countdown to Unity*, which, in turn, developed out of research I began in 2003 for my Ph.D. thesis. My interest in the area was stimulated by having had the privilege of attending, at the outer edge of the Irish delegation, the opening and early sessions of the phase of multi-party talks that began in Stormont in 1996. Those talks ultimately evolved into the process that delivered the Good Friday Agreement two years later.

Since the previous book was published by Irish Academic Press in 2009, there have been significant changes in the constitutional situation. The June 2016 decision by the people of the UK to withdraw from the European Union has created a new context for discussion of the implications of the Good Friday Agreement for possible constitutional outcomes. In addition, the collapse of the Northern Ireland Executive in January 2017 marked a step back for the implementation of the Agreement.

The previous book provided some stimulation for the August 2017 Report of the Oireachtas Joint Committee on the Implementation of the Good Friday Agreement. That report, prepared with the assistance of rapporteur Senator Mark Daly, was a development which made a renewed look at the implications of the Agreement more timely. The 2017 report seems to have taken up where the 2009 book left off; but a lot has changed in the meantime, particularly in terms of difficulties with implementing devolution. That situation changes the context and the emphasis.

Overall, I have attempted to outline the implications of the Agreement and identify principles from it which are offered in the hope of contributing to a shared understanding of the constitutional space within which a debate about alternative futures can be pursued in as accommodating a manner as possible. Finally I should note that any views expressed do not reflect on any actual or potential litigation and are, in the forensic context, 'subject to hearing argument'.

Richard Humphreys
April 2018

Acknowledgements

I would like to record my thanks to all those who assisted me with my original work on this issue for my Ph.D. thesis in Trinity College, Dublin, with the previous book and with the present one. I am particularly grateful to Dr Mary McAleese, Former President of Ireland, for her very kind Foreword. Her monumental commitment towards building relationships across the divide on the island of Ireland makes it a huge privilege to have had her encouragement in outlining the need for accommodation that is mandated by the Agreement. Rebecca Halpin was heroic enough to review successive drafts with her usual exceptional diligence; as always, without her help I would have been in severe difficulty. Conor Graham, Fiona Dunne, Myles McCionnaith and all of the team at Merrion Press have been wonderful publishers and have supplied just the right mixture of carrot and stick to get me moving on delivering the manuscript. Heidi Houlihan did wonderfully thorough copy-editing. Thanks also to Peter O'Connell Media, and to Fionbar Lyons for the index. I am very grateful to all those who looked at some or all of the draft, including the energetically multi-talented former Attorney General Paul Gallagher SC and the prolific Conleth Bradley SC. Seán Mac Cárthaigh also very kindly lent an observant eye and afforded some characteristically mordant observations. Thanks also to those who shared their thoughts on some of the issues, including Ruth Taillon, Director of the Centre for Cross-Border Studies. John Larkin QC, Attorney General of Northern Ireland, one of the island's leading public intellectuals, drew my attention to some legal academic matters and I am very grateful to him for that. Gwen Allman of The Company of Books provided helpful practical feedback. Nicole Scannell-O'Leary, Carmel-Deirdre Humphreys and Eve Humphreys have provided valued encouragement and assistance throughout.

Chapter 1

The Architecture of the Agreement

10 April 1998 saw the adoption of the Good Friday Agreement, also known as the Belfast Agreement. It took the form of two separate documents: a multi-party agreement as a political document was adopted by the talks' participants, and a legally binding international treaty, the British-Irish Agreement, was signed between the two governments. The relationship between those two documents should be clarified at the outset. The British-Irish Agreement, the legally binding treaty, provides that: 'The two Governments affirm their solemn commitment to support, and where appropriate implement, the provisions of the Multi-Party Agreement.'[1]

Thus, while the political agreement is not in itself enforceable as between the political parties, except to the extent that there is legislation to that effect, the two governments are legally obliged to support and 'where appropriate' implement the multi-party agreement in its entirety. That does not mean that every aspect of the multi-party agreement requires legislative implementation. While a great deal of it has been incorporated in legislative form, some elements have not – for example, the declaration of support made by the parties is not buttressed by an ongoing legal mechanism to determine whether any particular party is in breach of that declaration.

In certain respects, the Agreement has been amended or not implemented. As far as the amendment in 2006 by the St Andrews Agreement is concerned, or the clarification by the 2004 interpretative declaration, which we will come to, those amendments were specifically agreed to by the two governments and so are a legitimate and lawful adjustment of the British-Irish Agreement, even without the consent of all or any of the political parties.

Insofar as the Agreement has not been implemented – without the consent of both governments – that seems to be potentially a breach of the Agreement. The Northern Irish Attorney General, John Larkin, draws attention[2] to references in Strand One of the Agreement to the Northern Ireland assembly being 'capable of exercising executive and legislative authority', that it 'will exercise full legislative and executive authority' in respect of devolved matters and that 'the Assembly ... will be the prime source of authority in respect of devolved responsibilities'. These references are at variance with the classic constitutional understanding that 'the supreme executive power of these kingdoms is vested by our laws in a single person, the king or queen'. Thus, the Northern Ireland Act 1998 provides that:

(1) The executive power in Northern Ireland shall continue to be vested in Her Majesty.

(2) As respects transferred matters, the prerogative and other executive powers of Her Majesty in relation to Northern Ireland shall ... be exercisable on Her

Majesty's behalf by any Minister or Northern Ireland department.[3]

But it seems that this can readily be filed under the heading of a drafting matter. The fact that the multi-party agreement did not deem it necessary to spell out the full UK constitutional theory does not mean that the UK is in breach of the Agreement by not recognising the Northern Irish institutions as a source of power independent of the Crown. This is particularly so where the point is one of theoretical nicety rather than of practical significance, and where the Irish side has, so far, raised no issue in this regard.

In short, the fact that the multi-party agreement has been varied and has not been implemented in every respect by legislation does not take from the principle that the commitment to support that agreement embodied in the British-Irish Agreement is legally binding in the absence of any further treaty between the two governments to the contrary. By way of example, a central commitment of the Agreement, in the strongest terms possible, is the requirement of equal respect for the two traditions. Yet this specific commitment has not been given statutory form (other than in specific contexts, such as the declaration required by police constables[4]). That does not mean that it is irrelevant, or that the UK in all its manifestations is not required to uphold parity of esteem if the Northern Irish parties do not. Indeed, it may be that the absence of such legislation could amount to a breach of the Agreement if the commitment to parity of esteem is not otherwise being upheld. That may be a pertinent issue at the present time following the breakdown of the executive in 2017.

The text of the multi-party agreement is set out under a number of different headings: a declaration of support, constitutional issues, the various strands of relationships, rights, safeguards and equality, security and justice related issues, and validation, implementation and review.

Declaration of Support

The declaration of support with which the Agreement begins acknowledges the principle of mutual respect. It firmly establishes a parity of esteem between the two traditions:

> 2. [W]e firmly dedicate ourselves to the achievement of reconciliation, tolerance, and mutual trust, and to the protection and vindication of the human rights of all.

> 3. We are committed to partnership, equality and mutual respect as the basis of relationships within Northern Ireland, between North and South, and between these islands ...

> 5. We acknowledge the substantial differences between our continuing, and equally legitimate, political aspirations. However, we will endeavour to strive in every practical way towards reconciliation and rapprochement within the framework of democratic and agreed arrangements. We pledge that we will, in good faith, work to ensure the success of each and every one of the arrangements to be established under this agreement. It is accepted that all of the institutional and constitutional arrangements – an Assembly in Northern Ireland, a North/South Ministerial Council, implementation bodies, a British-Irish Council and

a British-Irish Intergovernmental Conference and any amendments to British Acts of Parliament and the Constitution of Ireland – are interlocking and interdependent and that in particular the functioning of the Assembly and the North/South Council are so closely inter-related that the success of each depends on that of the other.

Constitutional Issues

Under the heading 'Constitutional Issues', an agreement to provide for self-determination by agreement between a majority in both parts of the island is endorsed:

1. The participants endorse the commitment made by the British and Irish Governments that, in a new British-Irish Agreement replacing the Anglo-Irish Agreement, they will:

(i) recognise the legitimacy of whatever choice is freely exercised by a majority of the people of Northern Ireland with regard to its status, whether they prefer to continue to support the Union with Great Britain or a sovereign united Ireland;

(ii) recognise that it is for the people of the island of Ireland alone, by agreement between the two parts respectively and without external impediment, to exercise their right of self-determination on the basis of consent, freely and concurrently given, North and South, to bring about a united Ireland, if that is their wish, accepting that this right must be achieved and exercised with and subject to the

agreement and consent of a majority of the people
of Northern Ireland;

(iii) acknowledge that while a substantial section of
the people in Northern Ireland share the legitimate
wish of a majority of the people of the island of
Ireland for a united Ireland, the present wish of a
majority of the people of Northern Ireland, freely
exercised and legitimate, is to maintain the Union
and, accordingly, that Northern Ireland's status
as part of the United Kingdom reflects and relies
upon that wish; and that it would be wrong to
make any change in the status of Northern Ireland
save with the consent of a majority of its people;

(iv) affirm that if, in the future, the people of
the island of Ireland exercise their right of self-
determination on the basis set out in sections (i)
and (ii) above to bring about a united Ireland, it
will be a binding obligation on both Governments
to introduce and support in their respective
Parliaments legislation to give effect to that wish.

The 'Constitutional Issues' section went on to record
an agreement to rigorous impartiality and to continued
recognition of the right of people in Northern Ireland to
British citizenship, saying that the participants endorsed
the decision of the governments to:

(v) affirm that whatever choice is freely exercised
by a majority of the people of Northern Ireland,
the power of the sovereign government with
jurisdiction there shall be exercised with rigorous

impartiality on behalf of all the people in the diversity of their identities and traditions and shall be founded on the principles of full respect for, and equality of, civil, political, social and cultural rights, of freedom from discrimination for all citizens, and of parity of esteem and of just and equal treatment for the identity, ethos, and aspirations of both communities;

(vi) recognise the birthright of all the people of Northern Ireland to identify themselves and be accepted as Irish or British, or both, as they may so choose, and accordingly confirm that their right to hold both British and Irish citizenship is accepted by both Governments and would not be affected by any future change in the status of Northern Ireland.

Draft clauses were set out, to be included in both British legislation and the Irish Constitution. The UK legislation would provide as follows:

1. (1) It is hereby declared that Northern Ireland in its entirety remains part of the United Kingdom and shall not cease to be so without the consent of a majority of the people of Northern Ireland voting in a poll held for the purposes of this section in accordance with Schedule 1.

(2) But if the wish expressed by a majority in such a poll is that Northern Ireland should cease to be part of the United Kingdom and form part of a united Ireland, the Secretary of State shall lay before Parliament such

proposals to give effect to that wish as may be agreed between Her Majesty's Government in the United Kingdom and the Government of Ireland.

This was given effect to in the Northern Ireland Act 1998. The legislative commitment is simply a requirement to lay proposals before parliament in the event of a border poll resulting in a vote for unity. A statute cannot specifically commit parliament to enact a further statute. The Act went on to say:

1. The Secretary of State may by order direct the holding of a poll for the purposes of section 1 on a date specified in the order.
2. Subject to paragraph 3, the Secretary of State shall exercise the power under paragraph 1 if at any time it appears likely to him that a majority of those voting would express a wish that Northern Ireland should cease to be part of the United Kingdom and form part of a united Ireland.
3. The Secretary of State shall not make an order under paragraph 1 earlier than seven years after the holding of a previous poll under this Schedule.

Provisions to be inserted into the Irish Constitution included the entitlement to ratify the British-Irish Agreement, provision for cross-border bodies and extra-territorial jurisdiction, and reworded Articles 2 and 3 of the Constitution.

Article 2
It is the entitlement and birthright of every person born in the island of Ireland, which includes its islands

and seas, to be part of the Irish nation. That is also the entitlement of all persons otherwise qualified in accordance with law to be citizens of Ireland. Furthermore, the Irish nation cherishes its special affinity with people of Irish ancestry living abroad who share its cultural identity and heritage.

Article 3
1. It is the firm will of the Irish nation, in harmony and friendship, to unite all the people who share the territory of the island of Ireland, in all the diversity of their identities and traditions, recognising that a united Ireland shall be brought about only by peaceful means with the consent of a majority of the people, democratically expressed, in both jurisdictions in the island. Until then, the laws enacted by the Parliament established by this Constitution shall have the like area and extent of application as the laws enacted by the Parliament that existed immediately before the coming into operation of this Constitution.

2. Institutions with executive powers and functions that are shared between those jurisdictions may be established by their respective responsible authorities for stated purposes and may exercise powers and functions in respect of all or any part of the island.

The Three Strands

The Agreement considered the 'totality of relationships' relating to Northern Ireland in three strands:

- Strand One, relating to matters internal to Northern Ireland.

- Strand Two, North/South matters.
- Strand Three, matters relating to Britain and Ireland as a whole (East/West matters).

Under Strand One, the Agreement provided for a 108-member assembly to 'exercise full legislative and executive authority' in respect of devolved functions. A number of safeguards were provided for, including incorporation of the European Convention on Human Rights (ECHR), a possible Bill of Rights for Northern Ireland, a Human Rights Commission and an Equality Commission.[5]

Key decisions had to be taken on a cross-community basis; that is either by parallel consent from both traditions or 60 per cent support including at least 40 per cent of each tradition. A 'petition of concern' could trigger the need for cross-community support, if thirty assembly members so required.[6] Executive authority was to be discharged by a First Minister and Deputy First Minister, elected jointly on a cross-community basis, and up to ten ministers.[7]

Continued UK sovereignty was emphasised by the express statement that the 'power [of the Westminster parliament] to make legislation for Northern Ireland would remain unaffected'.[8] Generally, the UK parliament's role would be to legislate for non-devolved issues and to ensure that the UK's international obligations are met in respect of Northern Ireland. In UK constitutional practice (the 'Sewel convention'), the Westminster parliament does not normally legislate for a devolved matter without the consent of the devolved legislature, by way of a legislative consent motion, but ultimately 'The United Kingdom Parliament retains authority to legislate on any issue, whether devolved or not.'[9]

A consultative Civic Forum was to be established.[10] It should be noted that the Stormont House Agreement was later to envisage that this would be reconfigured as a 'civic advisory panel' on a far more compact basis.[11]

Strand Two of the Agreement, the North/South dimension, envisaged a North/South Ministerial Council to bring together both executives,[12] including by way of establishment of North/South implementation bodies on agreed areas for co-operation.[13]

The Agreement provided that the assembly and the Oireachtas would consider developing a joint parliamentary forum, bringing together equal numbers from both sides 'for discussion of matters of mutual interest and concern'.[14] Likewise, consideration was to be given to the establishment of an independent consultative forum to represent civic society on both sides of the border.[15]

The parliamentary body was set up on 4 July 2012 in a watered-down form as the North/South Inter-Parliamentary Association.[16] It has ceased to function with the collapse of devolution. The North/South civic consultative forum has never been established. These North/South parliamentary and civic forums were supported by the All-Party Oireachtas Committee on the Constitution in 2002:

> The committee strongly endorses the proposal in paragraph 18 of Strand Two of the Good Friday Agreement that the Northern Ireland Assembly and the Oireachtas should 'consider developing a joint parliamentary forum, bringing together equal numbers from both institutions for discussion of matters of mutual interest and concern ...
>
> We also support the establishment of an independent consultative forum 'representative of civil society,

comprising the social partners and other members with expertise in social, cultural, economic and other issues', as mooted in paragraph 19. Both [this and a parliamentary forum] could make a major contribution to dialogue and mutual understanding between North and South.[17]

Strand Three of the Agreement, dealing with East/West issues, provided for three new institutions:

(i) a British-Irish Council, to be established under a new British-Irish Agreement to provide for representatives of the sovereign and devolved governments within the UK, as well as the Channel Islands and Isle of Man.

(ii) The Agreement encouraged the elected institutions of the members of the British-Irish Council to develop interparliamentary links, 'perhaps building on the British-Irish Interparliamentary Body'.[18] This was taken up, and that body evolved to become the British-Irish Parliamentary Assembly, consisting of members of the UK and its member parliaments/assemblies, including those of the crown dependencies, as well as the Oireachtas.

(iii) A British-Irish Intergovernmental Conference (BIIGC) was to be established to bring together the British and Irish governments to promote bilateral co-operation.

The Agreement provided that:

In recognition of the Irish Government's special interest in Northern Ireland and of the extent to which issues of mutual concern arise in relation to Northern Ireland, there will be regular and frequent meetings of the Conference concerned with non-devolved Northern Ireland matters, on which the Irish Government may put forward views and proposals. These meetings, to be co-chaired by the Minister for Foreign Affairs and the Secretary of State for Northern Ireland, would also deal with all-island and cross-border co-operation on non-devolved issues.[19]

The implication, therefore, is that where devolution is not operating, the British-Irish Intergovernmental Conference acts as a forum in which the Irish government can put forward its views and proposals on any matters relating to Northern Ireland. That is presumably what the Taoiseach conveyed by his comment in November 2017 that:

As I have done at previous meetings, I said to Prime Minister May that the Government could not accept a return to direct rule as it existed prior to the Good Friday Agreement and that if Sinn Féin and the DUP failed to form an administration, the Government I lead would expect the Good Friday Agreement to be implemented without them.

That means convening the British-Irish Intergovernmental Conference, as if nothing is devolved then everything is devolved to that conference.

I indicated to her I would seek a meeting in the new year of the British-Irish Intergovernmental Conference so British and Irish Ministers could meet to plot a way forward for Northern Ireland in the absence of the elected representatives in Northern Ireland being able to form an administration.[20]

The Taoiseach clarified these remarks in December 2017, by saying that: 'The Good Friday Agreement speaks of a British-Irish governmental conference, which is not joint rule because obviously the legislative powers remain at Westminster, but it does involve real and meaningful involvement of the Irish Government.'[21]

It is possibly worth adding the gloss that direct rule 'as it existed prior to the Good Friday Agreement' is not hugely different from the position where the Irish government can put forward views and proposals, because that was so under the Anglo-Irish Agreement of 1985. Direct rule pre-1985 was, it must be emphasised, quite different from direct rule since then. In March 2018, Tánaiste and Minister for Foreign Affairs and Trade Simon Coveney told the Dáil of his discussions with Secretary of State Karen Bradley on this issue:

> I told Ms Bradley that I would like her to consider a British-Irish Intergovernmental Conference. I felt it would be appropriate at this stage to have that structure enacted so both Governments could formally discuss the various options they need to consider around a budget for Northern Ireland, how we take our next steps getting a devolved Government back up and running in Northern Ireland and other practical issues that can and should be raised on an east–west basis between the two Governments. I have not yet had a response to this proposal.[22]

Unionist reaction to these comments has been to reject the idea that non-devolved matters included internal matters where devolution had ceased to function, with unionist commentator Newton Emerson contributing a particularly inaccurate piece to that effect in March 2018, calling this an 'extraordinary blunder' and 'tearing the agreement up'.[23] In an earlier piece, Emerson went even further, suggesting that:

> the agreement's mechanism for such meetings is the British-Irish Intergovernmental Conference ... Far from being triggered by a collapse of Stormont, it is only meant to operate in parallel with Stormont – both represent two of the three interlocking strands of the agreement, with the third being the North–South Ministerial Council ... The agreement says that in the absence of devolution, the conference cannot operate at all. When devolution is operating, BIIGC's remit is restricted to bilateral relations and powers that are not devolved, and only then to discussing those powers, not exercising them. The UK retains full sovereignty.[24]

On sovereignty, he is clearly right. On the lack of status of the British-Irish Intergovernmental Conference, not so. The North/South Ministerial Council, as a 'Strand Two' North/South body, is dependent on there being a functioning assembly.[25] But the Intergovernmental conference is a 'Strand Three', East/West body, and operates independently of whether devolution is functioning or not. Similarly, the other main East/West body, the British-Irish Council, has met continuously despite periods of no government in Stormont. To prove the point, the British-Irish Intergovernmental Conference has previously met on many occasions during Stormont suspension. For example, the assembly was suspended between October 2002 and May 2007, and in that period the Conference met seventeen times, on:

1. 22 October 2002[26]
2. 18 December 2002[27]
3. 20 May 2003[28]
4. 2 July 2003[29]
5. 18 September 2003[30]
6. 22 January 2004[31]
7. 21 April 2004[32]
8. 7 July 2004[33]
9. 15 December 2004[34]
10. 2 March 2005[35]
11. 27 June 2005 (summit-level meeting between heads of government)[36]
12. 19 October 2005[37]
13. 1 February 2006[38]
14. 2 May 2006[39]
15. 25 July 2006[40]
16. 24 October 2006[41]
17. 26 February 2007[42]

It is simply a misconception to suggest that the Conference falls when the assembly falls. It is true that the Declaration of Support states that:

> it is accepted that all of the institutional and constitutional arrangements – an Assembly in Northern Ireland, a North/South Ministerial Council, implementation bodies, a British-Irish Council and a British-Irish Intergovernmental Conference and

any amendments to British Acts of Parliament and
the Constitution of Ireland – are interlocking and
interdependent and that in particular the functioning
of the Assembly and the North/South Council are so
closely inter-related that the success of each depends
on that of the other.[43]

But that is not the same thing as saying that if the assembly
ceases to function all other bodies also cease to function.
Acts of Parliament and the Irish Constitution are mentioned
in this respect as well, and it can hardly be the case that the
Constitution falls away (and we revert to the old Articles
2 and 3) every time the assembly is deadlocked. All that is
committed to is that the 'success' of the Conference and
other arrangements 'depends on that of' the assembly,
and vice versa. That may well be so, but it does not mean
that it is not lawful for those other institutions to operate.
The language in relation to the North/South Ministerial
Council is significantly stronger – that 'one cannot
successfully function without the other'. Emerson simply
misunderstands the Agreement in this respect. The separate
idea that the British-Irish Intergovernmental Conference
cannot discuss devolved matters if there is no functioning
devolution is also misconceived. If devolution has ceased
to operate, then the exclusion for devolved matters from
the functions of the Conference can hardly be said to be
operative. There is no error in the interpretation of the
Agreement that underlies the point made by Tánaiste
Coveney. But misunderstandings continue. DUP leader
Arlene Foster went even further again:

In keeping with the principle of consent and the
three-stranded approach it is not appropriate for the

> Irish Prime Minister to outline future political steps relating to Northern Ireland and a resumption of talks ... Whilst we will work with the Irish government on appropriate issues, the political process is an internal matter and should be taken forward by Her Majesty's Government.[44]

Unfortunately, this is clearly incorrect having regard to the text of the Agreement. The British-Irish Intergovernmental Conference is specifically given the following function: 'The Conference will contribute as appropriate to any review of the overall political agreement arising from the multi-party negotiations but will have no power to override the democratic arrangements set up by this Agreement.'[45]

Rights, Safeguards and Equality of Opportunity

Turning to the section headed 'Rights, Safeguards and Equality of Opportunity', the Agreement provided for incorporation in law of the ECHR, and of a specific set of rights, including the right 'to seek constitutional change by peaceful and legitimate means'.[46] A Northern Ireland Human Rights Commission was to be established by Westminster legislation,[47] as well as a statutory Equality Commission.[48] The Irish government was to consider incorporation of the ECHR also, and to establish an Irish Human Rights Commission.[49]

Of some importance, the Irish government was also to 'continue to take further active steps to demonstrate its respect for the different traditions in the island of Ireland'. There was also to be a joint committee of representatives of the two human rights commissions.[50] Commitments were made regarding linguistic diversity in relation to Irish and Ulster Scots, and specifically:

> 4. In the context of active consideration currently being given to the UK signing the Council of Europe Charter for Regional or Minority Languages, the British Government will in particular in relation to the Irish language, where appropriate and where people so desire it:
> - take resolute action to promote the language;
> - facilitate and encourage the use of the language in speech and writing in public and private life where there is appropriate demand;
> - seek to remove, where possible, restrictions which would discourage or work against the maintenance or development of the language.[51]

Security and Justice Matters

The Agreement went on to deal with matters concerned with the peace process – decommissioning, security, and policing and justice. An independent commission was to make recommendations for future policing arrangements,[52] and for a review of the justice system.[53] Provisions for the accelerated release of certain prisoners were also provided for.

Validation, Implementation and Review

Under the heading of 'Validation, Implementation and Review', the two governments agreed to sign a new British-Irish Agreement replacing the 1985 Anglo-Irish Agreement.[54] Referenda were to be held on 22 May 1998,

North and South. In those referenda, 71 per cent of people in the North voted to support the Agreement, as did 94 per cent of people in the South. While the Agreement is not without flaws, and indeed has had its critics both at the time and since, it is fair to suggest that, as an empirical proposition, nothing has been put forward as an alternative that stands any realistic prospect of commanding greater support.

Chapter 2

The Evolution of the Agreement

In this section, we will discuss how the text of the Agreement has evolved and been supplemented by a series of further implementing agreements since it was adopted.

The First Assembly: 1998–2003

The first assembly was elected on 25 June 1998. Unionists won 58 seats out of 108 (an absolute majority of 53 per cent), nationalists 42 (38.8 per cent) and others 8. Designates for First and Deputy First Ministers were appointed, but the executive did not take office until 2 December 1999. Thereafter, the executive was suspended on four occasions; in 2000, in August and September 2001 and October 2002 onwards.[1]

The Northern Ireland Act 1998 was enacted on 19 November 1998 and represents one of the most significant modern constitutional laws of Northern Ireland. John Larkin, Attorney General for Northern Ireland, in referring to sections 1(1) and 1(2) of the Northern Ireland Act 1998 has observed that 'Northern Ireland is the only region of the UK equipped with a constitutional departure lounge, no possibility of a return journey, and an electoral lock on the entrance to the departure lounge.'[2] The Act sets out the current status of Northern Ireland in the UK and allows for a united Ireland by consent of a majority following a border poll. The provisions allowing the Secretary of State to call a border poll by Order also specifically provided that:

4. (1) An order under this Schedule directing the holding of a poll shall specify –
    (a) the persons entitled to vote; and
    (b) the question or questions to be asked.

(2) An order –
    (a) may include any other provision about the poll which the Secretary of State thinks expedient (including the creation of criminal offences); and
    (b) may apply (with or without modification) any provision of, or made under, any enactment.[3]

In December 1998, political agreement was reached between the First Minister designate, David Trimble, and the Deputy First Minister designate, Seamus Mallon, regarding the organisation of Departments and the establishment of North/South implementation bodies and other matters for North/South co-operation.[4]

On 8 March 1999, the two governments signed four agreements supplementing the British-Irish Agreement of April 1998. The new agreements provided for the establishment of six North/South implementation bodies, a North/South Ministerial Council, a British-Irish Council and a British-Irish Intergovernmental Conference. The Minister for Foreign Affairs, David Andrews, described the signature of the Agreements as 'a very important milestone in the implementation of the Agreement'.[5] At the same time, the Department of Foreign Affairs described the agreements establishing the North/South Ministerial Council, the British-Irish Council and the British-Irish Intergovernmental Conference as being 'of a purely technical character' and as providing that these institutions will be constituted and will operate in accordance with the provisions of the Good Friday Agreement.[6] However, the Department went on to describe the Agreement establishing the six implementation bodies as 'more substantial' and as resulting 'from intensive negotiations with the British Government, in consultation with the Northern Ireland parties, following on from the political agreement on the identity of these bodies reached on 18 December 1998'.[7] The Department noted that each of the four agreements would enter into force on the date of entry into force of the British-Irish Agreement itself, and that legislation before the Oireachtas would be necessary regarding the agreement establishing the implementation bodies.[8] On 8 March 1999, the two governments entered into a further agreement to resolve any problems in relation to the implementation bodies agreement:

> the Governments acknowledge that it is essential to avoid any problems which may arise from differences in the laws of the two jurisdictions as they apply to the implementation bodies established by their Agreement of 8 March 1999. For this purpose:
>
> (i) the Attorneys-General in the two jurisdictions, or such other representatives as each Government may

designate, as appropriate, will consult and co-operate as necessary in order to address any problems which may arise concerning the interpretation and application of such laws to the bodies and will report within six months of the entry into force of the Agreement on whether additional steps should be taken.

(ii) In the event of problems arising from differences in the laws of the two jurisdictions which impede the proper functioning of any of the implementation bodies, the two Governments will consult and cooperate as necessary with a view to taking all appropriate steps to restore harmony.[9]

In April 1999, the Independent Commission for the Location of Victims' Remains was established by agreement between the two governments.[10] The publication of the Patten report on policing took place in September 1999,[11] and, separately, further efforts continued to resolve outstanding issues that remained following the Good Friday Agreement. These were eventually overcome in December 1999, and the executive took office, with the British-Irish Agreement coming into force simultaneously alongside the commencement of the changes to the Irish Constitution.

The day prior to the coming into force of the British-Irish Agreement, Taoiseach Bertie Ahern told the Dáil that 'the new Articles 2 and 3 encapsulate our modern understanding of constitutional republicanism. The last traces of irredentism are gone. The nation is defined in the most open, inclusive and pluralist manner possible, without coercion.'[12] The Taoiseach said that he could not envisage a situation, 'even where the functions of the Agreement had been interrupted for a considerable time', in which the parties or the people would wish to revert to the previous wording of Articles 2 and 3, which, he said, 'were put in place as a form of protest against the legitimacy of partition, after all the safeguards of the 1920/1 Settlement had been cast aside'.[13]

It is not entirely clear which safeguards the Taoiseach had in mind. Insofar as the provisions of the Government of Ireland Act 1920, which provided for all-Ireland institutions, were cast aside, they were cast aside by agreement between the two protagonists under the 1921 Anglo-Irish Treaty, rather than unilaterally disregarded by the British. The safeguards of the 1921 Treaty, such as the Boundary Commission, were not so much cast aside but proved to be illusory having regard to the fact that the Irish side seemed to have missed the point that the Treaty made clear that the 'wishes of the inhabitants' were subject to 'economic and geographic conditions'[14] and not the other way around. Those 'safeguards' too were set aside by international agreement. In concluding the speech, Taoiseach Ahern said that:

the setting up of the North/South Ministerial Council and implementation bodies is of particular importance to us. It is not only a reinstatement of an essential element missing from the implementation of the 1921 Settlement. It is also the logical culmination of the initiative on North–South co-operation begun on our side by Seán Lemass and Jack Lynch.

It should, however, be noted that the 1921 Treaty only made minimal, purely enabling provisions for North/South executive cooperation,[15] so it is not really some sort of lost legacy from 1921 of which Ireland was deprived until 1998.

The Agreement came into force on 2 December 1999, and inaugural meetings then took place for the North/ South Ministerial Council,[16] the British-Irish Council,[17] the British-Irish Intergovernmental Conference[18] and other institutions established by the Agreement.

Ongoing political difficulties and issues related to decommissioning and paramilitary activity led to a collapse of the executive on 12 February 2000. In the absence of any legislative provision for suspension, and indeed in the absence of any such provision from the Good Friday Agreement, the Westminster parliament legislated for a suspension of the devolved institutions by enacting the Northern Ireland Act 2000. The fact that there was felt to be a need to bring in the 2000 Act did highlight a central and persistent difficulty of the Good Friday Agreement arrangement; namely, the problem of a satisfactory fall-back provision in the event of the executive not functioning. While there was some complaint at the time that the unilateral nature of the 2000 Act was in breach of the Agreement, that difficulty was perhaps impliedly acknowledged by a later agreement to repeal the Act.

In March 2000, a review of Criminal Justice in Northern Ireland was published. Devolution was restored on 30 May 2000. In November 2000, the UK parliament enacted legislation renaming the Royal Ulster Constabulary as the Police Service of Northern Ireland[19] and creating a Northern Ireland Policing Board and district policing partnerships. Difficulties continued, however, and the assembly was suspended, twice, in 2001.

2001 – Weston Park Agreement

On 1 August 2001, the two governments entered into the 'Weston Park Agreement',[20] a series of proposals to address policing, normalisation, the stability of the institutions and decommissioning, including proposals to facilitate the functioning of the North/South institutions.

In February 2002, Westminster legislation extended the amnesty period for arms decommissioning, up to February 2007 at the latest. In April 2002, the two governments entered into a new international agreement on police co-operation in the light of the Patten reforms and the new policing environment in Northern Ireland.[21] In July 2002, Westminster legislation was enacted regarding the Northern Irish justice system.[22] It established a Public Prosecution Service for Northern Ireland, a Chief Inspector of Criminal Justice in Northern Ireland and a Northern Ireland Law Commission (which has since fallen into abeyance). It provided that the Attorney General of England and Wales would cease to be Attorney General for Northern Ireland, and that a specific office holder would be appointed jointly by the First and Deputy First Minister.[23] The Attorney General would then appoint a Director of Public Prosecutions for Northern Ireland.[24] The Act provided that the royal coat of arms would not be displayed in any courtroom or outside any court, except effectively where this had already been done prior to the legislation.[25] It also extended legislation regulating the flying of flags on public buildings to include court-houses.[26]

A further suspension of this assembly occurred in October 2002, following a DUP motion on 8 October 2002, expressing concern at the implications of a raid on the Sinn Féin Offices at Parliament Buildings on 4 October 2002, and of the arrest of three Sinn Féin members on spying charges (one of whom, Denis Donaldson, was subsequently murdered following the dropping of the proceedings and his identification as an informant to the British government).

2002 – Agreement on Continuation of North/ South Bodies

Following the suspension of the Northern Ireland assembly on 15 October 2002, the British and Irish governments entered into a further agreement by means of an exchange of letters dated 19 November 2002, which were designed to allow the continued functioning of the North/South bodies in the absence of the assembly and Northern Executive. The letters between the Irish Minister for Foreign Affairs, Brian Cowen, and the British Ambassador, Sir Ivor Roberts, referred to an intention 'to protect and maintain the achievements of the British-Irish Agreement and Multi-Party Agreement, and to ensure the continuation of the necessary public function performed by the Implementation Bodies during the period of temporary suspension of the Assembly, and pending its restoration'.[27]

The agreement proposed that decisions of the North/South Ministerial Council on policies and actions relating to the implementation bodies, Tourism Ireland Ltd or their respective functions should be taken by the two governments, and that no new functions should be conferred on the implementation bodies.[28] The agreement goes on to provide that in the implementation bodies' agreement, any reference to a Northern Ireland Minister shall be construed as a reference to the relevant Northern Ireland Department, and any reference to the assembly shall be construed as a reference to the parliament of the United Kingdom.[29] The agreement only applies to the suspension commencing in 2002 under the Northern Ireland Act 2000 and not to any possible further future suspensions. The 2000 Act has since been repealed, and the 2002 agreement, therefore, does not seem to have any ongoing meaning. No similar agreement seems to have been entered into to cover the period of the non-functioning executive since 2017. Presumably the thinking is that no such agreement is necessary as non-functioning is distinct from a suspension situation.

In March 2003, the UK parliament legislated to provide for the following assembly elections to be held in May of that year.[30]

2003 – Joint Declaration

On 1 May 2003, the two governments published a Joint Declaration dealing with normalisation, policing and justice, and rights, equality, identity and community.[31] Additionally, a draft agreement relating to monitoring and compliance was published,[32] as well as proposals in relation to so-called 'on the runs' (i.e., republicans still being sought for extradition, imprisonment or questioning).[33]

In addition, the Joint Declaration dealt with the issue of the restoration of the political institutions, which were described as 'the democratic core of the Agreement'.[34] The Joint Declaration drew attention to the provision[35] in the Agreement envisaging that the Northern Ireland assembly and the Oireachtas should consider developing a joint parliamentary forum.[36] Among the initiatives considered by the Joint Declaration was the devolution to the restored assembly of responsibility for policing and justice matters.[37] This analysis also contemplated the possible establishment of a North/South implementation body related to justice and policing following such devolution.[38] The declaration committed both governments to the establishment of a new independent body to monitor and report on the carrying out of commitments relating to the ending of paramilitary activity and the programme of security normalisation.[39]

On 15 May 2003, the Westminster parliament legislated to allow for the postponement of the assembly elections, which had been due to take place that month.[40] Legislation was enacted by the Westminster parliament in September 2003 to give effect to the agreement on monitoring and to provide for consequential exclusion or censure of politicians where necessary.[41] The formal agreement between the two governments setting up the Independent Monitoring Commission was signed on 25 November 2003.[42] The Commission was not expressly envisaged by the Good Friday Agreement – a point of objection for republicans – but rather was designed to police the commitments on activities of paramilitary groups and security normalisation by the British government. In the zero-sum logic that sometimes applies in Northern Ireland, some unionists objected to it by reference to the role of the Irish government in the process. The Agreement provided for a power to determine breaches of the pledge of office:

(1) The Commission may consider a claim by any party represented in the Northern Ireland Assembly:

(a) that a Minister, or another party in the Assembly, is not committed to non-violence and exclusively peaceful and democratic means; or

(b) that a Minister has failed to observe any other terms of the pledge of office; or that a party is not committed to such of its members as are or might become Ministers observing the other terms of the pledge of office.

(2) Insofar as a claim under paragraph 1(b) relates to the operation of the institutional arrangements under Strand One of the multi-party Agreement, the claim shall be considered only by those members of the Commission appointed by the British Government ...[43]

The agreement establishing the commission was later terminated with effect from March 2011,[44] as was the agreement establishing the Independent International Commission on Decommissioning.[45]

The Second Assembly: 2003–2007

Following the November 2003 election,[46] the DUP and Sinn Féin emerged as the largest parties representing unionism and nationalism/republicanism respectively, displacing the UUP and the SDLP.[47] Sixty unionists were elected. Nationalist representation remained at 42 out of 108 (as before), and others amounted to 6: a unionist gain at the expense of others, in the polarised atmosphere of a suspended executive.

Following this, a review of the Agreement got underway, and a plenary meeting of the review was held at Parliament Buildings, Stormont, on 3 February 2004. In his opening remarks to that meeting, the Minister for Foreign Affairs Brian Cowen stressed that:

As the Secretary of State outlined, it is the two Governments' view that the fundamentals of the Agreement must remain in place. The review is about the operation of the Agreement ... the Good Friday Agreement is both an international treaty and a part of the Irish Constitution. It will come as no surprise to anyone here, therefore, when I say that we take its provisions very seriously.[48]

He went on to say that the fundamentals of the Agreement were not up for negotiation and that, without being prescriptive, the fundamentals would, in his view, include the constitutional principle of consent, partnership government in Northern Ireland on an inclusive basis, the interlocking institutions of the Agreement including its North/South and East/West dimensions, the entrenchment of human rights and equality for all, the removal of the use and threat of paramilitary violence, the normalisation of security arrangements and the consolidation of the new policing and criminal justice arrangements.

2004 – Agreed Declaration on Citizenship under the Agreement

In the context of proposed changes to the Irish law and Constitution to tighten qualification for citizenship, the Irish government responded to criticisms that such change was in breach of the Agreement[49] by agreeing an interpretative declaration with the United Kingdom government in April 2004, which provided that:

the two Governments hereby give the following legal interpretation: that it was not their intention in making the said Agreement that it should impose on either Government any obligation to confer nationality or citizenship on persons born in any part of the island of

Ireland whose parents do not have sufficient connection with the island of Ireland: and therefore the two Governments declare that proposal to amend Article 9 of the Constitution of Ireland so as to provide that a person born in the island of Ireland, which includes its islands and seas, who does not have, at the time of his or her birth, at least one parent who is an Irish citizen or is entitled to be an Irish citizen, is not entitled to Irish citizenship or nationality, unless otherwise prescribed by law, is in accordance with the intention of the two Governments in making the said Agreement and that this proposed change to the Constitution is not a breach of the said Agreement or the continuing obligation of good faith in the implementation of the said Agreement.[50]

It was further provided that the rights of all persons referred to in the provisions of the Agreement[51] would be preserved by legislation.[52] In short, the 'declaration' asserted that their intention in 1998 was not to impose an obligation to confer citizenship on persons born in Ireland who did not have any other sufficient connection with the island of Ireland. The declaration paved the way for the referendum on the 27th Amendment to the Constitution on 11 June 2004, which curtailed the constitutional right to acquire citizenship on the basis of birth in Ireland. This was followed up with a statutory provision restricting such citizenship with effect from 1 January 2005.[53]

2004 – 'Comprehensive Agreement' Following Leeds Castle Talks

In July 2004, a letter was issued to political parties jointly by Secretary of State Paul Murphy and Minister for Foreign Affairs Brian Cowen outlining details the arrangements for of the resumption of talks in September 2004.[54] Talks took place on 1 September 2004, and subsequently on 16 to 18 September 2004, at Leeds Castle. On 8 December 2004, further negotiations ended without agreement. Despite this failure, the two Prime Ministers then published the draft Comprehensive Agreement,[55] which would have involved decommissioning of all weapons, an agreement that the IRA would instruct its members not to endanger the Agreement, confirmation of decommissioning including photographs, a Sinn Féin Árd Fheis to decide on support for new policing arrangements, devolution of criminal justice and policing powers to the assembly and re-establishment of the institutions by agreement.[56]

The December 2004 proposals involved the introduction into the British parliament of legislation to amend a number of aspects of the Northern Ireland Act 1998 and related legislation, which would also provide for the removal of the power of suspension.[57] Devolution of policing powers would also take effect by means of primary legislation.[58] Emergency legislation would be introduced immediately to establish a Shadow Assembly in December 2004,[59] to be followed in January 2005 by the enactment of necessary legislation amending existing legislative arrangements on Strands One to Three.[60] Detailed proposed changes to the operation of the Agreement, including changes to the Northern Ireland Act 1998, were set out. These included proposals to enhance collectivity and accountability, including the agreement of a draft programme for government and budget, which would have to be approved by the assembly on a cross-community vote.[61]

In a key change, the appointment of First Minister and Deputy First Minister, previously to be made jointly, was now to be decoupled, and these were to be nominated separately by the nominating officers of the largest and second largest parties respectively.[62] There would be an Institutional Review Committee of the assembly, to keep the operational aspects of the Strand One institutions under virtually permanent review, and there was an explicit commitment to repeal the Northern Ireland Act 2000.

Proposals by both governments for changes in Strands Two and Three were also set out, including a proposal that the Northern Ireland Executive and the Irish government would, under the auspices of the North/South Ministerial Council, appoint a review group to examine objectively the efficiency and value for money of the existing implementation bodies and 'the case for additional bodies and areas of co-operation within the NSMC where mutual benefit would be derived'.[63] Any changes to existing arrangements would require the endorsement of the assembly and the Oireachtas. The executive would encourage the parties in the assembly to establish a North/South Parliamentary Forum, bringing together equal numbers from the Oireachtas and the assembly. In addition, the executive would support the establishment of an independent North/South Consultative Forum appointed by the two administrations and representative of civil society.[64]

Under Strand Three, the two governments would facilitate the establishment of a Standing Secretariat for the British-Irish Council, and would encourage the Oireachtas, the British parliament and the relevant elected institutions in the British and Irish islands to approve an East/West Inter-Parliamentary framework which would embrace all their interests, following consultation with the British-Irish Inter-Parliamentary Body.[65] The proposals went on, unusually, to set out the text of draft statements to be made by the DUP, Sinn Féin, the Independent International Commission on Decommissioning (deference being paid to the independent position of this body by the use of the phrase 'elements for an IICD statement'[66]) and – most unusually – a draft statement to be issued by the IRA. Presumably because it is an offence to 'publish' any 'document ... issued by or emanating from an unlawful organisation or appearing to be so issued or so to emanate',[67] the two governments sought to fudge what was being done by using square brackets, publishing the proposed IRA statement under the heading '[IRA] Statement'.[68]

The proposals, as they themselves noted, emerged from a process of dialogue, primarily with the DUP and Sinn Féin. The SDLP was quick to express reservations not only about the manner in which these proposals were put together, but also about their content, which they described as an agreement which 'weakens the principles and protections of the real Agreement – The Good Friday Agreement'.[69] Chief among the SDLP objections was the scrapping of the joint election of the two First Ministers. The SDLP also singled out the change to the previous arrangement that no party could veto the other parties' ministerial appointments, and the new requirement that any party that did not vote to approve an executive could not take seats in it.[70] Taoiseach Ahern, speaking at the Seventh British-Irish Council in the Isle of Man in May 2005, said: 'The review of the Good Friday Agreement was politically accepted by everyone, including the DUP on December 8th ... we've had the review and the review is finished.'[71]

However, the precise accuracy of this statement seems to be in doubt in the sense that the proposals do not seem to have been agreed to by all parties.

A further historic step in the process was the announcement by the IRA of the formal end to its armed campaign at 4.00 pm on Thursday, 28 July 2005.[72]

2006 – Armagh Joint Statement

As events moved into 2006 without a restoration of the institutions, the two governments published so-called 'Plan B' proposals,[73] which, in new language, referred to the governments' 'joint stewardship of the process'. (In 2017, nationalists were to point to the 'joint stewardship' language to incorrectly suggest that this involved joint authority. It does not.[74]) The two governments set out broadly what would happen if the parties failed to restore devolution – an end to funding and the radical notion of an active implementation of the Agreement including 'a step-change in advancing North–South co-operation'.

> 10. If restoration of the Assembly and Executive has to be deferred, the Governments agree that this will have immediate implications for their joint stewardship of the process. We are beginning detailed work on British-Irish partnership arrangements that will be necessary in these circumstances to ensure that the Good Friday Agreement, which is the indispensable framework for relations on and between these islands, is actively developed across its structures and functions. This work will be shaped by the commitment of both Governments to a step-change in advancing North–South co-operation and action for the benefit of all.

11. The British Government will introduce emergency legislation to facilitate this way forward. It will set out clearly the limited timescale available to the Assembly to reach agreement. In parallel with the recalling of the Assembly, we will engage intensively with the parties to establish the trust necessary to allow the institutions not only to function but to flourish. There is a great deal of work to be done. The Governments will do all in their power to restore the institutions and return devolved Government to those elected by the people of Northern Ireland. But the final decisions are for the parties. We hope they will seize the opportunity to move forward.[75]

The assembly was recalled for 15 May 2006, with a proposed final six-month deadline to elect a functioning executive by November 2006.[76] A 'preparation for government' committee of the assembly began work on the steps required to restore devolution.

In May 2006, Westminster legislated to provide for a non-legislative fixed-term assembly (consisting of the same members as the Northern Ireland assembly) to prepare for restoration of devolution. That legislation also provided for repeal of the power to suspend, which had been contained in the 2000 Act.[77]

2006 – Joint Statement and Work Plan

On 29 June 2006, the two governments published a Joint Statement by Taoiseach Bertie Ahern and Prime Minister Tony Blair,[78] which referred to a deadline of 24 November 2006 for restoration of devolution, and separately published a Work Plan and indicative timetable for restoration of devolution.[79] The endgame of that Work

Plan is of considerable interest in the post-2017 situation. It is as follows:

Either
November
Parties and Governments make final preparations for restoration of the institutions.

- W/B [week beginning] 20 November: last opportunity to amend Standing Orders and introduce Emergency Bill (on changes to the institutions) at Westminster following all-party agreement to restore devolution.
- 24 November: last opportunity for selecting FM/DFM [First Minister/Deputy First Minister] and Executive and affirming pledge of office. By midnight Secretary of State notifies Presiding Officer of intention to make a Restoration Order [effective on Monday 27 November].
- W/B 27 November: Ministers arrive at Departments. Executive meets.

Or
November
- 24 November: Salaries and allowances for MLAs and financial assistance to parties stop.

December
- BIIGC [British-Irish Intergovernmental Conference] at Prime Ministerial-Summit level to launch new British Irish partnership arrangements.

The joint statement also provided that: 'we also took the opportunity today to review progress on new partnership arrangements that would need to be put in place to ensure our effective joint stewardship of the Good Friday Agreement in the event that devolution does not take place by 24 November. This work continues.'[80]

In July 2006, Westminster legislation was enacted to provide for, among other things, devolution of policing and justice functions[81] – a task that was to require a considerable amount of further legislation before it happened four years later. The legislation also extended the amnesty period for decommissioning from 2007 to 2010.[82] July 2006 also saw a further international agreement between the two governments to extend the scope of the EU programmes' implementation body to cover future programmes.[83]

2006 – St Andrews Agreement

All-party talks were convened at St Andrews in Scotland in 2006, resulting in an agreement on 13 October 2006. Under the St Andrews Agreement, there were to be a number of changes to the Good Friday Agreement institutions.[84] Progress towards devolution of criminal justice and policing was provided for. A series of measures to advance human rights, equality and issues relating to victims were set out.[85] There would be a Victims' Commissioner for Northern Ireland and a forum on a possible Bill of Rights. An Irish Language Act was to be introduced, as well as support for development of Ulster Scots. A financial package for the newly restored executive was also envisaged, as well as a timetable for the restoration of devolution. The St Andrews Agreement provided that 'in the event of failure to reach agreement by the 24 November we will proceed on the basis of the new British-Irish partnership arrangements to implement the Belfast Agreement'.[86]

The changes to the Good Friday Agreement included a statutory ministerial code, referral of matters to the executive, amendments to the pledge of office, and repeal of the legislation that had provided for the power to suspend the institutions. Changes were also made in relation to Strands Two and Three, including progressing the North/South parliamentary and civic forums and East/West parliamentary co-operation.

The St Andrews Agreement involved a timetable to devolution combined with confirming republican adherence to the policing institutions and some adjustments to the detail of the Northern Ireland Act 1998. UK legislation was enacted in November 2006 to give effect to the Agreement.[87] This created a transitional assembly to prepare for restoration of devolution,[88] and included provision for a Northern Irish minister for justice and policing. Importantly for future purposes, it added a new provision regarding the promotion of minority languages:

(1) The Executive Committee shall adopt a strategy setting out how it proposes to enhance and protect the development of the Irish language.

(2) The Executive Committee shall adopt a strategy setting out how it proposes to enhance and develop the Ulster Scots language,[89] heritage and culture.

(3) The Executive Committee – (a) must keep under review each of the strategies; and (b) may from time to time adopt a new strategy or revise a strategy.[90]

Former Foreign Affairs Minister Dermot Ahern has commented:

There was always an understanding that the British government agreed to an inclusion and commitment to an Irish Language Act ... But the quid pro quo would be that there would be reciprocal attention given to the whole issue of Scots-Irish.[91]

The Third Assembly: 2007–2011

The Second Assembly ended never having operated a functioning executive. The Third Assembly was elected on 7 March 2007. It consisted of 55 unionists, 44 nationalists and 9 others.[92]

On 22 March 2007, the two governments agreed[93] on an amendment to the 1998 British-Irish Agreement in order to give effect to the St Andrews Agreement, as follows:

Article 1
The two Governments re-affirm their solemn commitment as contained in the British-Irish Agreement to protect, support and where appropriate implement the provisions of the Multi-Party Agreement.

Article 2
The two Governments affirm their solemn commitment to support, and where appropriate implement, the alterations to the operation of the institutions established under the British-Irish Agreement agreed at St Andrews and as set out in the Annex to this Agreement.

On 27 March 2007, UK legislation was enacted to extend the date for restoration of devolution to May 2007.[94] In accordance with this timetable, devolution was restored on 8 May 2007. On 24 May 2007, Westminster legislation was enacted providing for a Northern Ireland minister responsible for policing and justice.[95] In March 2009, more detailed UK legislation was enacted to provide for a department with policing and justice functions.[96]

2010 – Hillsborough Castle Agreement

The Hillsborough Castle Agreement of 5 February 2010 set out measures on a number of problematic issues. Further legislation was envisaged on parades. A working group was proposed to improve executive functioning and delivery. Outstanding executive business was to be progressed, and a further working group was to progress matters outstanding from St Andrews. The agreement would pave the way for devolution of policing and justice functions. Financial commitments for Northern Ireland were also contemplated. Justice and police powers were eventually devolved on 12 April 2010.

On 1 May 2010, the two governments entered into an agreement on criminal justice[97] which involved a structure for North/South Ministerial Meetings on Criminal Justice Co-Operation[98] as well as a Working Group on Criminal Justice Co-operation at official level.[99] This effectively replaced a previous similar agreement of 2005.[100]

The Fourth Assembly: 2011–2016

The Fourth Assembly was elected on 5 May 2011. It returned 56 unionist members (51.8 per cent), 43 nationalists (39.8 per cent) and 9 others. This represented a net gain of one seat for unionism from nationalism.

A minor adjustment to the cross-border bodies agreement was made in September 2011 in an exchange of notes between Minister Eamon Gilmore and Ambassador Julian King, to take into account new Irish departmental structures.[101]

Talks led by US diplomat Richard Haass and Prof. Meghan O'Sullivan, which included the issues of flags and emblems, parades and dealing with the Troubles-related legacy, ended with a draft text but without agreement in December 2013,[102] although it was felt that the draft proposals formulated would be of use in later talks,[103] and indeed this proved to be the case.

In March 2014, Westminster legislation was enacted providing for disqualification of MPs and TDs from the assembly and allowing the assembly to enact legislation altering its own size.[104] The Act also extended the life of any given assembly from four to five years.[105] In addition, it provided for procedures for the appointment of the Justice Minister.

2014 – Stormont House Agreement

Following on from the Haass proposals, the Stormont House Agreement of 23 December 2014 provided for a Commission on Flags, Identity, Culture and Tradition, which was ultimately established in June 2016.[106] The Commission has been dealing with issues such as the possible regulation of bonfires and the flying of the Union flag on public buildings. In that regard, Sinn Féin has said:

> Our policy, on flags on public buildings is that of equality or neutrality ie for to fly both national flags or no flag to be flown at all in line with the concept of parity of esteem and recognition, as outlined in the Good Friday Agreement of both main identities, Irish, British or both.[107]

The Stormont House Agreement went on to provide for regulation of parades,[108] and set out specific measures to deal with legacy issues. These included an Oral History Archive, and measures on victims, including a pension for victims. There was to be a Historical Investigations Unit to take forward investigations into outstanding Troubles-related deaths.[109] An Independent Commission on Information Retrieval (ICIR) was to be established. An international agreement to do so was signed on 15 October 2015.[110] The agreement establishing the ICIR would come into force following ratification,[111] which would involve the enactment of relevant legislation.[112] That legislation has yet to materialise. An Implementation and Reconciliation Group would oversee these developments. These victims' measures have yet to be implemented,[113] a matter of serious concern to the Victims and Survivors Commissioner.[114]

Significant changes were made to the Strand One institutions, including a reduction in the size of the assembly and executive, and in the number of government Departments. Constitutional changes under the Stormont House agreement included a provision entitling parties to opt out of government and to take part in a formal opposition. The agreement provided for quarterly reviews and six-monthly progress reports on implementation.

A compact civic advisory panel was envisaged to replace the Civic Forum.[115] However, it could be contended that the civic dimension of the Agreement is a key element in bringing disparate communities together, and it is not immediately easy to see how a far smaller panel can do this more effectively than the wider Forum envisaged by the Agreement.

There was language about 'the need for respect for and recognition of the Irish language in Northern Ireland, consistent with the Council of Europe Charter on Regional or Minority Languages'.[116] A lack of consensus on a Bill of Rights was noted, in which context: 'the parties commit to serving the people of Northern Ireland equally, and to act in accordance with the obligations on government to promote equality and respect and to prevent discrimination; to promote a culture of tolerance, mutual respect and mutual understanding at every level of society'.[117]

2015 – 'A Fresh Start' Agreement

Difficulties in implementing the Stormont House Agreement and ongoing concerns about paramilitarism, which destabilised the executive, then led to a further round of talks in 2015 culminating in A Fresh Start – the Stormont Agreement and Implementation Plan of 17 November 2015, which included provisions on tackling paramilitarism, financial matters, welfare and tax issues, financial support from the governments and implementation of the Stormont House Agreement.

The 2015 Fresh Start Agreement provided for measures to tackle paramilitarism and organised crime, including a Joint Agency Task Force between police and customs North and South,[118] which was subsequently established.[119]

An international body was to be set up to report on ending paramilitarism.[120] A subsequent international agreement between the two governments formally established the body as the Independent Reporting Commission on 13 September 2016, and this was followed by UK[121] and Irish[122] legislation.

Provision was also made by the Fresh Start Agreement for financial reforms, welfare and tax issues, and financial support. A civic advisory panel was to be set up with only six members, limited to consideration of only two issues per year.[123] Ultimately, this is a far cry from what was originally envisaged by the Agreement in terms of a civic forum. The Centre for Cross-Border Studies has been critical of the lack of structure for meaningful civic engagement:

> This long list of failed or inadequate proposals and arrangements for the inclusion of civic voices in the political process both reveals a core problem with politics (rather than with political institutions) and suggests a possible alternative for a Northern Ireland voice in UK–EU negotiations ...

> Northern Ireland political arrangements include a long list of failed attempts to establish a meaningful forum for the inclusion of civic voices from outside the toxic bi-polar model of political relationships. Despite the fact that consecutive political agreements have provided for such fora (where civic views could be considered in relation to key social, cultural and economic issues), problems have been encountered with each of those.[124]

It would be hard to disagree with the proposition that the watering-down of the Civic Forum was a major deviation from the 1998 Agreement. Perhaps a more considered look at the pros and cons of involving the wider civic society through a broadly-based Forum, with a North/South counterpart, in the manner envisaged in 1998, could be worthwhile.

In the wake of the Fresh Start Agreement, the First Minister Peter Robinson stood down as DUP leader on 18 December 2015. He was succeeded in both roles by Arlene Foster. Legislation was introduced at Westminster, enacted on 4 May 2016, to give effect to the Stormont Agreement and Implementation Plan.[125]

The Fifth Assembly: 2016–2017

The Fifth Assembly was elected on 5 May 2016. Again, 56 unionists were elected (51.8 per cent), but only 40 nationalists (37 per cent), as well as 12 others – a net gain of 3 for others from nationalism. Taking advantage of the Stormont House Agreement, the SDLP, UUP and Alliance opted out of government and formed an official opposition.

Shortly after the assembly was elected, the Brexit referendum took place on 23 June 2016. A clear majority of voters in Northern Ireland supported remaining in the EU, 56 per cent to 44 per cent. All major parties supported remain, other than the DUP. The majorities for remain in Northern Ireland, Scotland and Gibraltar (and indeed Greater London) were, of course, outweighed by a majority for leave across England and Wales. We will discuss the implications of Brexit for discussions of Irish unity in a later chapter.

The executive lasted only eight months. Deputy First Minister Martin McGuinness resigned in the context of the controversy over the Renewable Heat Incentive (RHI) Scheme. Other issues became mixed up in the resignation decision, as discussed below. A judge-led inquiry into the RHI scheme was announced on 24 January 2017 but, before its work got underway, the controversy precipitated a further election.

The Sixth Assembly: 2017 Onwards

The Sixth Assembly was elected on 2 March 2017. Pursuant to the Stormont House Agreement, this was the first election to the reduced-size chamber, now at 90 members rather than 108. However, the composition of the assembly significantly changed. Unionism now only carried 40 seats, or 44.4 per cent, the first time in the history of Northern Ireland that it had lost its absolute majority. That loss of a majority is in itself a huge staging post towards possible altered constitutional futures for the island. Nationalism returned 39 members (43.3 per cent), only 1 less than unionism. Others numbered 11. To compound the shock, the DUP returned only 28 members, 2 less than the 30 required to trigger a petition of concern. Thus, it lost its right to block legislation on its own, as it can no longer invoke the procedure for cross-community support without the help of other members. To put this seismic change into context, one would need to compare it with the first election to the Northern Irish House of Commons in 1921. At that election, 40 unionists were elected and 12 nationalists, a unionist supermajority of 76.9 per cent to 23.1 per cent. Within a century – and in Ireland one has to think in terms of centuries – that gap has closed to touching distance.

The new context where neither bloc has an absolute majority, and where thus the balance of power lies with 'others', puts a very new emphasis on the 'petition of concern', which is now, to an extent, a mechanism for deadlock rather than counter-majoritarian protection. Newton Emerson's view is that:

What has become redundant at Stormont is not powersharing but vetoes – the petition of concern at Assembly level and the ability of either main party to bring government down at Executive level.

These vetoes were very much intended as protections from majoritarianism in a Northern Irish context. In a new era without majorities, all they do is let both sides block each other, frustrating any possible consensus.[126]

The Sixth Assembly failed to elect an executive, with disagreement ultimately centring on four major issues:

- the unresolved RHI controversy
- Irish language legislation
- matters relating to victims, including funding for legacy inquests into Troubles-related deaths[127]
- marriage equality legislation.

On 27 April 2017, the Westminster parliament enacted amending legislation[128] to extend (on a one-off basis) from 14 to 108 days the period for election of a First Minister and Deputy First Minister.[129]

Matters were further complicated by a snap UK General election on 8 June 2017, which resulted in the loss of all Westminster seats for the SDLP and the UUP, as well as the loss of the Conservative government majority at Westminster. The UK government was then compelled to enter into a Conservative–DUP confidence and supply agreement on 26 June 2017, to facilitate the formation of a minority government at national level. While the agreement provided for continued adherence to the Good Friday Agreement, it also provided for the ongoing commitment of the Conservative Party to Northern Ireland remaining part of the UK. The dependence of the UK government on one actor in the Northern Irish scene, the DUP, is seen by some as potentially limiting the options that are likely to be pursued to achieve political progress in the Northern Irish context. An application to seek leave for judicial review of the confidence and supply agreement was dismissed in October 2017.[130]

In the absence of a functioning assembly, in November 2017, the Westminster parliament voted through a budget for Northern Ireland up to 31 March 2018.[131]

Talks to resolve the impasse between the DUP and Sinn Féin ended without agreement in February 2018. The issue of Irish language legislation was particularly contentious and, in that regard, Sinn Féin suggested that they had reached an 'accommodation with the leadership of the DUP' who then 'failed to close the deal' with their membership.[132] A draft text has been made available on Eamonn Mallie's website[133] which would have resolved the relevant issues as follows:

- there would be three bills on language, one setting out general principles and two separate Acts dealing with corresponding provisions on Irish and Ulster Scots
- same sex marriage was to be left to the assembly[134]
- legacy issues were not mentioned[135]
- the objection to First Minister Foster continuing in the light of the RHI affair was not mentioned.[136]

In the aftermath of the breakdown of discussions, the DUP called for direct legislation to impose a budget to allow Northern Ireland departments to function (which is what happened), whereas SDLP leader Colum Eastwood stated 'we can't allow this British government or this DUP to think that they are going to govern Northern Ireland on their own. That cannot be allowed to happen.'[137]

In one sense, there is nothing particularly new about the Westminster parliament legislating for Northern Ireland, particularly in the absence of devolved institutions. This has been happening since the Agreement was adopted and is a consequence of the UK's sovereignty over Northern Ireland, as recognised by the Agreement itself. That power to legislate is, however, subject to two important constraints: first, the right of the Irish government to put forward views and proposals, including on Strand One issues, and second, the requirements of rigorous impartiality imposed by the Agreement itself.

The DUP's position as of March 2018 was to seek the establishment of a shadow assembly to sit at Stormont until devolution is restored, to scrutinise legislation and Westminster ministerial actions.[138]

As of March 2018, the Alliance Party was calling for action on a range of fronts:

[O]nly fully inclusive multi-party talks, chaired by an independent facilitator, can re-establish trust between the parties and hold them to account, privately and publicly, for their actions. They also provide the only prospect of delivering an inclusive Executive.

We have proposed transitional Assembly arrangements, running in parallel with the talks, as a step towards the restoration of full devolution ...

By reconstituting Assembly Committees, MLAs can start to do the job we were elected to do: to give advice and guidance, scrutinise departmental spending and planning, and develop policy and legislation. Plenary sessions would allow us to progress legislation, via Committee Bills or Private Member's Bills.

The formation of a cross-party Brexit committee would give NI a voice in the discussions which are shaping our future, whilst the re-constitution of the Policing Board would restore the oversight required to maintain public confidence and accountability in policing ...

We have also proposed that Westminster legislate for key devolved matters such as the Irish language and equal marriage which have become a barrier to restoration, erasing some red lines and changing the dynamics of the talks process.

Indeed, this week, the first steps will be taken to introduce a private members bill on Equal Marriage at Westminster. While it has a long way to go yet, it is a major step forward towards the day when LGBT couples in NI will finally be able to say 'I do' and get the same recognition and respect under the law as any other married couple. My only regret is that yet again it is Westminster and not Stormont delivering on LGBT rights and equality.

Finally, we have identified reserved matters which Westminster should also progress including, crucially, reform of the petition of concern. That would ensure a restored Assembly could deal effectively with other social policy and equality issues and preventing any one party frustrating the will of the electorate.

The planned Government consultation on the enabling legislation to implement the Stormont House Agreement on legacy, the funding of legacy inquests and the implementation of a pension for the seriously injured should also now proceed without further delay.[139]

The Sinn Féin position, as articulated by Mary Lou McDonald in March 2018, was that:

Any proposed shadow Assembly would mark a retreat from powersharing and the leadership needed to restore the Good Friday Agreement framework. It would be an unacceptable step backwards, lacking credibility.

The onus is now on the two governments to act and through their joint stewardship to remove the obstacles to restoring the political institutions.

Both governments must now convene the British-Irish Intergovernmental Conference to find a way to implement outstanding agreements and to fully respect the rights of citizens to marriage equality, to language rights and the funding of legacy inquests.

Direct rule is not an option. It was a failure in the past and would be so again.

It's time to face the real challenge to deliver citizens' rights and to re-establish the institutions of the Good Friday Agreement.[140]

The SDLP's Colum Eastwood proposed the following:

I am calling on the Irish and British governments, as part of the intergovernmental conference, to agree a package of legislation and implement it. I believe that package should include much of the draft accommodation that was agreed between the DUP and Sinn Féin. This package would include legislation for an Irish language Act and an Ulster Scots Act. It should include the establishment of legacy bodies and the release of inquest monies. I am also proposing that it should also include the reform of the petition of concern so that marriage equality can finally be brought to the North.

If these two parties couldn't bring the deal over the line then the two governments should do it for them. That positive forms part of their governmental duty as guardians and guarantors of the agreement. ... The unionist and nationalist peoples of Ireland can retreat from each other or we can choose to work, live and govern together. As John [Hume] himself would say, the problem hasn't changed, therefore the solution hasn't changed. Despite all the difficulties ahead, the Good Friday agreement remains the solution to secure the interests of all our futures. Twenty years on, now is not the time to abandon it – now is the time to defend it.[141]

The UUP have rejected the Intergovernmental Conference idea,[142] and leader Robin Swann has called for UK government intervention:

The Secretary of State has to take decisive action. The Government must consider all options including a voluntary coalition or a Grand Council type Assembly. If that means Direct Rule Ministers temporarily bringing legislative proposals to the committees for scrutiny in order to ensure a role for locally elected politicians, then so be it.

What is clear is that Sinn Féin cannot be allowed to block progress any longer. They have a mandate but they have 27 seats out of 90 and 28 per cent of the vote. They cannot be allowed to dictate to the rest of us. They don't take their seats in Westminster by choice, if they don't want to take their seats in the Assembly then they should no longer be allowed to stop those of us who do.[143]

Chapter 3

The Challenge of Brexit

The Good Friday Agreement presupposes continued EU membership. Indeed, one of the North/South bodies is specifically devoted to implementing EU programmes. However, presupposing membership is not the same thing as requiring membership, and, despite voting to remain in the EU, Northern Ireland finds itself having to submit to the overall majority for a leave vote within the UK as a whole. As it was put by Prof. Jonathan Tonge:

> The [Good Friday] Agreement assumes continuing EU membership for both the UK and Ireland but binds neither explicitly to maintaining that membership. [A] 2016 Belfast High Court case[1] ... ruled that there was nothing in the Good Friday Agreement to prevent the triggering of Article 50. That High Court in Belfast declared in October 2016 that it would be an over-statement to suggest that EU membership was a constitutional bulwark central to the Good Friday Agreement, which would be breached by notification of Article 50. This, the Court asserted, would be to 'elevate ... [EU membership] over and beyond its true contextual position'. In its January 2017 verdict, the

UK Supreme Court[2] ... upheld the Belfast High Court position: the principle of consent for constitutional change contained in the Good Friday Agreement referred to whether Northern Ireland remained in the UK or unified with the rest of Ireland. It did not refer to EU membership or withdrawal.

He went on: 'By far the most probable scenario is that the continuing cooperative bilateralism between the UK and Irish governments will allow the necessary rewriting and deletions required of Strand Two of the Good Friday Agreement.'[3]

The logic of this analysis is that there will be a separate bilateral British-Irish international treaty alongside the withdrawal agreement between the EU member states and the UK. That bilateral agreement will amend the British-Irish Agreement and the agreements regarding North/South bodies, in order to accommodate Brexit.

At the time of writing, the terms for Brexit remain unclear. Key staging-posts to date and into the future include the following:

- 23 June 2016 – Brexit vote
- 24 January 2017 – UK Supreme Court decision in Miller, Agnew and McCord cases that legislation is required to issue a notification of intention to withdraw from the EU
- 16 March 2017 – UK legislation enacted allowing for notification of withdrawal
- 29 March 2017 – Article 50 notification issued triggering the process of withdrawal from the EU[4]
- 29 April 2017 – European Council includes support for the Good Friday Agreement in its guidelines for

Brexit negotiations;[5] there was a declaration that a united Ireland can be part of the EU in its entirety

- 8 June 2017 – UK general election – followed by Conservative confidence and supply agreement with DUP
- 19 June 2017 – official start of Brexit negotiations
- 13 July 2017 – publication of European Union (Withdrawal) Bill, UK legislation to give legal effect to Brexit
- 28 February 2018 – European Commission publishes draft withdrawal agreement, containing a Protocol on Ireland/Northern Ireland [6]
- 19 March 2018 – EU and UK negotiators publish a partial agreement on the text of the withdrawal agreement, including agreement in principle to a backstop protocol avoiding a hard border, unless any alternative is agreed[7]
- October 2018 – EU deadline for finalisation of withdrawal agreement, commencement of ratification period[8]
- 30 March 2019 – Brexit takes effect, start of transitional period
- 31 December 2020 – end of transitional period
- 1 January 2021 – full disengagement from the EU.

Re-incorporation of Northern Ireland Post-Unity, Post-Brexit

The April 2017 European Council meeting adopted the following Statement to the Minutes (published after the minutes were approved at the June meeting):

The European Council acknowledges that the Good Friday Agreement expressly provides for an agreed mechanism whereby a united Ireland may be brought about through peaceful and democratic means; and, in this regard, the European Council acknowledges that, in accordance with international law, the entire territory of such a united Ireland would thus be part of the European Union.[9]

Following the April meeting,[10] the Irish government stated: 'The Government is pleased that the European Council statement of 29 April highlights the paramount importance of continuing to support and protect the achievements, benefits and commitments of the Peace Process, and states EU Treaties would apply to the entire territory of a united Ireland, if brought under the Good Friday Agreement.'[11]

This proposed declaration was supported by the Joint Committee on the Implementation of the Good Friday Agreement in its 2017 report:

Brexit has implications for the principle of consent. In this respect, the Committee welcomed the important declaration made by the European Council on 29 April 2017 in respect of the possibility of a future united Ireland being entitled to full automatic EU membership, without the need for any separate accession process:

As the Committee with responsibility for overseeing the implementation of the Good Friday Agreement, the importance of including explicit references to the need to uphold all aspects of the Good Friday Agreement in the EU's negotiating guidelines cannot be overstated. While an important achievement, this is just the beginning of long and complex negotiations and there is no room for complacency. The Committee underlines the necessity of the Good Friday Agreement being kept to the fore at all times in the forthcoming negotiations. The additional declaration secured by the Government which allows for the entire territory of any future united Ireland being legally part of the EU is also strongly supported by this Committee.[12]

Current Terms of Draft Withdrawal Agreement

The draft Withdrawal Agreement published on 28 February 2018 includes a Protocol on Ireland/Northern Ireland which contains a number of key proposals relevant to the constitutional future of the island. While objections were initially raised, the British government subsequently accepted the inclusion of a backstop in the Withdrawal Agreement if nothing better is agreed, as reflected in a later, partially agreed text published in March 2018.[13] The Commission's draft preamble says that the signatories make the agreement:

> RECOGNISING that it is necessary to address the unique circumstances on the island of Ireland in order to ensure the orderly withdrawal of the United Kingdom from the Union;

> AFFIRMING that the Good Friday or Belfast Agreement of 10 April 1998 between the Government of the United Kingdom, the Government of Ireland and the other participants in the multi-party negotiations (the '1998 Agreement'), which is annexed to the British-Irish Agreement of the same date (the 'British-Irish Agreement'), including its subsequent implementation

agreements and arrangements, should be protected in all its parts; ...

RECOGNISING the need to respect the provisions of the 1998 Agreement regarding the constitutional status of Northern Ireland and the principle of consent;

DESIRING to create a common regulatory area on the island of Ireland in order to safeguard North–South cooperation, the all-island economy, and protect the 1998 Agreement;

HAVING REGARD to the devolution arrangements between the United Kingdom and Northern Ireland in relation to the common regulatory area;

RECOGNISING that Irish citizens in Northern Ireland, by virtue of their Union citizenship, will continue to enjoy, exercise and have access to rights, opportunities and benefits, and that this Protocol should respect and be without prejudice to the rights, opportunities and identity that come with citizenship of the Union for the people of Northern Ireland who choose to assert their right to Irish citizenship as defined in Annex 2 of the British-Irish Agreement 'Declaration on the Provisions of Paragraph (vi) of Article 1 in Relation to Citizenship';

NOTING that Union law has provided a supporting framework to the provisions on Rights, Safeguards and Equality of Opportunity of the 1998 Agreement.[14]

The March text is colour coded – green as agreed, yellow as agreed as to the objective, and white as not agreed.

These recitals are coded yellow in the March version, meaning agreed as to the objective although not as to the precise text.[15] Dealing with rights of individuals, the draft provides:

> 1. The United Kingdom shall ensure that no diminution of rights, safeguards and equality of opportunity as set out in that part of the 1998 Agreement entitled Rights, Safeguards and Equality of Opportunity results from its withdrawal from the Union, including in the area of protection against discrimination as enshrined in the provisions of Union law listed in Annex 1 to this Protocol, and shall implement this paragraph through dedicated mechanisms.

> 2. The United Kingdom shall continue to facilitate the related work of the institutions and bodies pursuant to the 1998 Agreement, including the Northern Ireland Human Rights Commission, the Equality Commission for Northern Ireland and the Joint Committee of representatives of the Human Rights Commissions of Northern Ireland and Ireland.[16]

Again, this is coded yellow in the March 2018 version.

The draft protocol goes on to provide for the continuation of the Common Travel Area with Ireland; coded green in the March 2018 version, meaning agreed.[17] The protocol establishes a 'backstop' arrangement, consisting of a common regulatory area on the island of Ireland with a view to avoiding any hard border:

> A common regulatory area comprising the Union and the United Kingdom in respect of Northern Ireland is

hereby established. The common regulatory area shall constitute an area without internal borders in which the free movement of goods is ensured and North–South cooperation protected in accordance with this Chapter.[18]

This is coded white, meaning it is not agreed text as of March 2018.

But, crucially, the March 2018 partial agreement includes the following:

With respect to the DRAFT PROTOCOL ON IRELAND/NORTHERN IRELAND, the negotiators agree that a legally operative version of the 'backstop' solution for the border between Northern Ireland and Ireland, in line with paragraph 49 of the Joint Report, should be agreed as part of the legal text of the Withdrawal Agreement, to apply unless and until another solution is found. The negotiators have reached agreement on some elements of the draft Protocol. They further agree that the full set of issues related to avoiding a hard border covered in the draft reflect those that need to be addressed in any solution. There is as yet no agreement on the right operational approach, but the negotiators agree to engage urgently in the process of examination of all relevant matters announced on 14 March and now under way.[19]

Provision is made, in the February 2018 text, for North/ South cooperation to continue (coded green, agreed):

1. Consistent with the arrangements set out in Articles 4 to 7 of this Protocol, and in full respect of Union law, this Protocol shall be implemented and applied so

as to maintain the necessary conditions for continued North–South cooperation, including in the areas of environment, health, agriculture, transport, education and tourism, as well as energy, telecommunications, broadcasting, inland fisheries, justice and security, higher education and sport. In full respect of Union law, the United Kingdom and Ireland may continue to make new arrangements building on the provisions of the 1998 Agreement in other areas of North–South cooperation on the island of Ireland.[20]

The draft provides for continued jurisdiction of the Court of Justice of the EU in respect of EU bodies regarding these arrangements and continued direct effect of certain acts of EU bodies (coded white, not agreed).[21] The draft also provided for the possibility of a future alternative agreement if the backstop arrangements in the protocol could be improved upon later (coded green, agreed):

Should a subsequent agreement between the Union and the United Kingdom which allows addressing the unique circumstances on the island of Ireland, avoiding a hard border and protecting the 1998 Agreement in all its dimensions, become applicable after the entry into force of the Withdrawal Agreement, this Protocol shall not apply or shall cease to apply, as the case may be, in whole or in part, from the date of entry into force of such subsequent agreement and in accordance with that agreement.[22]

The backstop would have effect from 1 January 2021, at the end of the transitional period (30 March 2019 to 31 December 2020).

The Challenges of Brexit

The challenges of Brexit threaten to rupture a whole suite of arrangements and presuppositions that have existed on the island in the forty-five years since the UK and Ireland joined together on 1 January 1973. We will examine some of these in turn.

The Invisible Border

The Centre for Cross Border Studies has made the point that even a border that remains invisible may not be what it was before Brexit.

> There is a complex relationship between the visibility and openness of borders. Each affects the other in ways that vary for different groups of people, and depend on practices of border enforcement. No visible physical infrastructure at the post-Brexit border would not in itself mean it retains its previous degree of openness.

> The UK-Ireland border is historically constituted through the crisscrossing of at least four different border regimes: the Common Travel Area (CTA), EU membership, the Belfast/Good Friday Agreement, and UK devolution arrangements.[23]

The Irish perspective has been articulated in this way:

> The Irish Government's position is that the removal of security infrastructure as part of post-conflict normalisation, combined with shared membership of the European Union, including participation in

the Single Market, ha[s] resulted in the effective disappearance of any border on the island of Ireland. This most tangible gain from the Peace Process has allowed commercial, political and social relationships to develop and thrive across the island.

Additionally, both the Irish and British Governments have indicated their strong desire to maintain operation of the Common Travel Area following the UK's withdrawal from the EU. While at that point, the UK will be free to establish its own rules and procedures, Ireland will continue to fully uphold its obligations as an EU Member State, including as regards the free movement of EU citizens within the EU. [24]

In Tánaiste Simon Coveney's words:

We hoped the UK electorate wouldn't vote for it. But it did, by a narrow margin. And now we are determined to ensure that, no matter what else, Ireland-UK relations do not suffer as a consequence. This involves protecting perhaps the greatest UK-Ireland achievement of recent times: the Good Friday agreement of 1998. The agreement removed barriers and borders – both physically, on the island of Ireland; and emotionally, between communities in Ireland and between our two islands.[25]

As we have seen, the draft Withdrawal Agreement now provides a mechanism to avoid a hard Brexit, to which the UK has agreed in principle if nothing better can be negotiated.[26]

Divergent Rights Protections

Prof. Chris McCrudden commented in October 2017 that:

> When it was concluded, the GFA clearly presupposed that both Ireland and the United Kingdom would be members of the European Union – no one even contemplated the idea that one of them might leave the EU, a view endorsed by the UK Supreme Court in Miller [*R. (Miller) v. Secretary of State for Exiting the European Union*,[27] the case that required parliamentary approval for Brexit]. This significantly affected the way in which rights in the GFA were dealt with. This, in turn, affected the framework of the Northern Ireland Act 1998 and, indirectly, the wider UK devolution settlement. Whilst the EU was never conceived as the sole guarantor of rights in Northern Ireland, rights deriving from the EU are, nevertheless, an important dimension of the post-GFA architecture.[28]

In the *Miller* case, the UK Supreme Court decided not only that parliamentary approval to trigger Brexit was required, but also addressed important devolution issues regarding Northern Ireland. The Court decided in summary:

(i)   the Northern Ireland Act 1998 and the other devolution statutes had been enacted on the assumption that the United Kingdom would be a member of the European Union, but they did not require the United Kingdom to remain so;

(ii) relations with the European Union were reserved to the United Kingdom Government and Parliament;

(iii) the decision to withdraw from the Union was not a function of the Secretary of State for Northern Ireland under the Northern Ireland Act 1998;

(iv) the principle that there would be no change in the constitutional status of Northern Ireland without the consent of a majority, under the 1998 Act, only applied to the right to determine whether to remain part of the United Kingdom or to become part of a united Ireland; and

(v) the Northern Ireland Assembly and the other devolved legislatures did not have a veto as to whether the United Kingdom should withdraw from the EU.

Prof. McCrudden and Prof. Daniel Halberstam have further suggested that the UK Supreme Court missed the opportunity in the *Miller* litigation to address head-on the adverse implications of triggering Brexit for the Good Friday Agreement. They suggest that while the UK Supreme Court in *Miller* provided a robust defence of parliamentary authority and a nuanced understanding of the constitutionally grounded relationship between the UK and the EU, when it came, however, to examining parliamentary sovereignty in Northern Ireland, the Court deployed 'a very traditionalist' and 'rather blunt' approach 'at odds with what is required to accommodate Northern Ireland's evolving constitutional development, potentially undermining the Belfast-Good Friday Agreement.'[29]

Their analysis of the *Miller* case is interesting on a number of levels, including their condemnation of the haste with which the UK Supreme Court dealt with the matter, given their view that the British government was 'woefully under-prepared' for Brexit;[30] as well as the fact that the devolution issues were shunted to the sidelines and only 'severely truncated amounts of time'[31] afforded to the parties arguing those issues. 'There was a strong impression among many present that the devolution issues were dealt with largely as an afterthought by the Court … It might be thought that this is not the way in which arguably the most important constitutional case affecting Northern Ireland since its foundation should be decided.'[32] The impression was that the real issue was parliamentary sovereignty vs. royal prerogative, and anything else was a 'side-show' and 'distinctly unwelcome', resulting in a 'distinctly English constitutional debate'. Northern Irish, Scottish and Welsh counsel 'were making arguments that were clearly outside the London-based legal interpretative community that dominated the public arguments, and subsequently became hegemonic'.[33] The Supreme Court's treatment of the Northern Irish issues in particular was 'cursory'.[34] It sidestepped the issues and misrepresented the submissions made: 'the Court dramatically simplified the arguments put to them'.[35] What makes these complaints particularly interesting is that Prof. McCrudden was one of the counsel in *Miller* whose devolution arguments had been thus sidelined. The authors' pessimistic conclusion was:

> The Court's approach to the arguments presented from Northern Ireland in *Miller* leave[s] one to wonder whether much academic and political thinking in and about Northern Ireland on these issues is fundamentally at odds with the understanding of the most senior members of the judiciary in the UK. A necessary, but of course not sufficient, condition for future stability in Northern Ireland is a rethinking of the British constitutional underpinnings of the

relationship between Britain and Ireland, one which explicitly transcends what appears to be the existing legal orthodoxy and limits the doctrine of Parliamentary sovereignty (in the Northern Ireland context at least). It would, of course, be an irony of the highest order if the clearest and most robust articulation of the fundamental nature of that doctrine was also the cause of its demise.[36]

In January 2018, solicitor Michael Farrell also wrote of the risks of loss of rights protections in the event of Brexit.[37] The Joint Committee of Human Rights Commissions has also expressed concerns.[38] Now, as we have seen, the February 2018 draft text does include strong protections for the retention of rights, although this has yet to be finally agreed. The Centre for Cross Border Studies, reporting in January 2018, highlighted a number of risks to rights protections:

> Rather than through physical checks at the geographical borderline, control of the border after Brexit will be exercised through legislative changes and administrative processes that regulate citizenship- and socio-economic rights and entitlements ...

> All citizens will be affected by such changes, regardless of their nationality.

> The continued openness of the UK-Ireland border to the movement of different categories of people after Brexit cannot be deduced or guaranteed on the basis of the progress achieved through the EU-UK Brexit negotiations so far.

Leaving the European single market and customs union means that checks on all kinds of movement through the UK-Ireland border will be necessary

… Equally damaging is the potential for creating a differentiation of citizens' rights and entitlements between Irish and British citizens within Northern Ireland. There has been no discussion to date in relation to the rights of Northern Ireland-born citizens who choose not to exercise their right to an Irish passport.

The Charter of Fundamental Rights and the Human Rights Act of 1998 protect a number of citizens' and human rights in Northern Ireland, while the European Convention on Human Rights is embedded in the Good Friday Agreement to safeguard the work of the democratic institutions in Northern Ireland. Plans to withdraw from or repeal any or all of these protections undermines the equivalence of a rights regime north and south of the UK Ireland border and the ability for structured North-South co-operation.[39]

Paul Daly, Kirsty Hughes and Kenneth Armstrong have identified possible mechanisms for protecting existing rights in British law post-Brexit, but essentially suggest that the most appropriate mechanism would be one that gives protection against implied repeal such as by preserving the European Communities Act 1972 for the purposes of upholding rights under the withdrawal agreement or providing a similar mechanism akin to the Human Rights Act 1998.[40]

The Risk of Divisions

The very fact of Brexit, no matter how sensitively handled, creates the risk of a significant psychological, cultural and legal barrier along the border. Duncan Morrow, former head of the Community Relations Council, commented in relation to improved community relations that 'Brexit puts all of this at risk, because it is framed as putting up barriers, moving away from common values and rules and ending common membership of a shared project.'[41] Similarly, Dennis Kennedy has commented:

> inevitably, we will end up with a physical border, which, however soft, will involve some degree of control of goods and persons ... But damaging as the return of any such border might be, there remains a more important border that has been hardening as the physical one has been disappearing. This is the divide between identities, between nationalist and unionist, between Irishness and Britishness, as politicians on both sides have chosen to distort those identities.[42]

McCrudden and Halberstam comment that the effect of EU membership North and South has been 'reducing the significance of sovereignty and national identity'.[43] Such considerations perhaps also explain the phrase once used by Former Taoiseach Charles J. Haughey about a united Ireland in the context of a united Europe; or in other words, that joint membership of the EU by Ireland and the UK had abolished much of the significance of the border. Magnifying the effect of the jurisdictional divergence now being put in place is the markedly different voting patterns on Brexit of the two communities – 89 per cent of nationalists were 'remainers' as against only 35 per cent of unionists.[44] Thus, as described by Prof. Tonge, 'the binary divide is being reinforced in Northern Ireland by Brexit'.[45]

Creating an Incentive to Undermine the Agreement

It has certainly been suggested by some unionist opinion that the collapse of the executive is related to the uncertainty created by Brexit. Lord Trimble's view in December 2017 was that:

> The real reason why the border has become such an issue is that Sinn Féin is trying to exploit Brexit to break up the UK. And the whole reason Sinn Féin collapsed Northern Ireland's assembly is because its leaders realised that if they were serving in British institutions – and the Northern Ireland Assembly is a British institution – it would be much harder for them to do this.[46]

Indeed, the very perception that Brexit is being used to push the case for a united Ireland seems, from one point of view, to be undermining the exploration of possible solutions that might help in managing Brexit constructively, such as enhancing North/South co-operation. This is one of many potential ironies of the post-Brexit situation.

The Risk of Repeal of the Human Rights Act

There seems little doubt but that repeal of the UK Human Rights Act 1998 has been an objective of many interested parties on the leave side of the equation, once Brexit is out of the way. Indeed, some such interests have been associated with a three-step programme – Brexit, then repeal of the Human Rights Act, and ultimately denouncing the ECHR itself. Prof. Tonge again:

> Secession from the EU may embolden those in the UK Conservative Government seeking to replace adherence to the ECHR with a UK Bill of Rights. Again, this would be at odds with the Good Friday Agreement, in which the British government committed to 'complete incorporation into Northern Ireland law of the ECHR, with direct access to the courts, and remedies for breach of the Convention' ... and retreat from this pledge may be subject to legal challenge.[47]

In February 2015, Minister Frances Fitzgerald wrote to her UK counterpart stating that 'while a domestic Bill of rights could complement incorporation [of the ECHR], it could not replace it', otherwise there could be 'serious consequences for the operation of the Good Friday/Belfast Agreement'.[48] There does not seem to have been any substantive reply to this from the British side.

In 2016, English Attorney General Jeremy Wright stated that rather than having any 'quarrel with the content' of the ECHR, 'it is the way in which that document is applied that gives us difficulty'.[49] Discontent with the latter may lead to pressure, if the Human Rights Act is repealed, to withdraw from the ECHR itself. To the extent that Brexit might lend succour to such developments, there are clearly implications for the Agreement settlement. The Brexit backstop protocol seems to have sought to anticipate and forestall some of those developments. Ultimately, however, it should be emphasised that de-incorporation of the ECHR without the consent of the Irish government would clearly be in breach of the Agreement. Replication of the wording of the ECHR without linkage and reference to the European Convention itself and the principles established in its case law would almost certainly amount to de-incorporation for this purpose.

Attitudes to a United Ireland

The other significant effect of Brexit would be to change the perception of the pros and cons of a united Ireland. Taoiseach Varadkar has suggested that Brexit 'creates risks for the union itself'.[50]

A possibly surprising straw in the wind is a December 2017 poll (sponsored by the GUE/NGL group of the European parliament, to which Sinn Féin belongs), which showed a majority vote for remaining in the EU through a united Ireland rather than leaving the EU with a hard Brexit by remaining in the UK, by 47.9 per cent to 45.4 per cent.[51] Bill White, managing director of LucidTalk polling, which carried out the poll, commented:

> These election results show the unionist vote running at slightly less than 50% (on average), the nationalist/republican vote at about 40%–42% (again on average), and the Alliance/Green/Others vote at about 10%–11% …

> I would suggest that 60% pro NI-in-the-UK is the minimum unionists should be aiming for in such a NI border poll – anything less (and particularly less than 55%) would be de-stabilising and result in the NI border issue remaining 'on the agenda', with the

pro-United Ireland camp pushing for another border poll within a short period.

In terms of this last point, just look at Scotland – their referendum result was 55% to 45%, which in independence referendum terms is a pretty close result, and it's this sort of narrow result that allows the argument to be kept alive – and in Scotland the independence argument and discussion is still going.[52]

As it has been put by economist Paul Gosling: 'It would take a very optimistic Brexit supporter to believe leaving the EU will be good for Northern Ireland.'[53] Matt Carthy, Sinn Féin MEP, took up this theme:

Brexit is creating an entirely new dynamic in the debate on Irish Unity.

The prospect of the North of Ireland being removed from the European Union against the will of the people who live there, and a reinforcing of the border, has brought the issue of Irish unity firmly to the centre of the political agenda.

The prospect of having one part of this island inside the EU and another outside it is illogical to anyone with a concern for the economic, political or social future of a country.

In one clear signal of changing times, 82,000 residents in the North sought an Irish passport in 2017, an increase of almost 20%.[54]

Colum Eastwood, SDLP Leader, commented:

> While others were waving banners, the SDLP made
> the prospect of a successful unity referendum much
> more possible because a Border poll is no longer solely
> the project of Irish nationalism but of pro-European
> internationalism ... A unity referendum now has
> a much broader reach, offering us a return to the
> European Union as a sovereign country. That's the
> kind of progress that's made by MPs who turn up for
> work, not just wine receptions and lobbying lunches.[55]

The implications of Brexit for attitudes to unity may depend
on the type of Brexit involved. The logic of the republican/
nationalist position is that a hard Brexit would stoke a
public demand to re-enter the EU through unification with
Ireland. In the zero-sum logic associated with Northern
Ireland, some unionist opinion has alternatively argued
that a likely soft Brexit would enhance a united Ireland
identity by separating Northern Ireland from the island
of Britain: 'a scenario in which Northern Ireland in effect
stays in the customs union and single market [which] would
then necessitate a border in the Irish Sea ... would be the
biggest move towards a united Ireland since 1921.'[56] On
that logic, of course, Brexit would also have to be regarded
as the biggest own goal scored by unionism since 1921.

Chapter 4

The Implications of the Agreement for the Discussion of Irish Unity

Reconciliation Does Not Require Nationalists to Cease to be Nationalist

A unionist response to any question of discussing a united Ireland might be that the Agreement copper-fastens British rule in Northern Ireland and that discussion of unity is an impertinence and a defiance of the Agreement. An alternative argument from agnosticism might be that unity is so far-fetched and fanciful as to not be worth discussing.

The response to the objection against discussing the issue is simple. The Agreement itself acknowledges the legitimacy of both sets of aspirations for the political future of the island. The Agreement specifically protects 'the right to seek constitutional change by peaceful and legitimate means'.[1] The nationalist aspiration is expressly acknowledged. Indeed, it is written into the Irish Constitution that the 'firm will' of the people of Ireland is to achieve unity by peaceful means and by consent.[2] Given that the aspiration is clearly recognised as legitimate by the Agreement, it is simply a misunderstanding for unionism to claim that there is any breach involved in arguing for peacefully pursuing or even considering the issue of unity.

The agnostic argument is harder to answer, if only because cynical rejection of the relevance of any proposition will always command a substantial audience. It was alluded to by Deaglán de Bréadún in suggesting that discussion of unity may be simply 'a curiosity'.[3] But an answer to this argument is that the debate on unity has already begun. Indeed, it has been underway for a long time. As an empirical observation, one could legitimately comment that there is much to suggest that the debate is going to continue and intensify.

The Good Friday Agreement embodies radical concepts of a parity of esteem between the two perspectives on the ultimate constitutional issue, and a radical equality of rights as between the two communities. Reflecting on these concepts and principles has major implications for future constitutional arrangements for the island of Ireland. Certainly, a purely nationalist, 'four green fields', version of a united Ireland is out of the question. The Agreement mandates an inclusive and pluralistic vision for any future constitutional arrangements. It is up to Irish nationalism and republicanism to internalise the Agreement's vision of inclusiveness in the pursuit of their constitutional objectives. Indeed, some commentators may even take the view that there is a disconnect for some between a stated or ostensible objective of reunification and an attachment to the approach that has failed to recognise the equality of both traditions, an approach which, to some, has somehow been seen as acceptable thus far.

The legitimacy of the aspiration for a united Ireland means that, by definition, it is legitimate to discuss or advocate for a united Ireland, just as it is also legitimate to advocate for a United Kingdom. When Tánaiste Simon Coveney spoke of the desirability of seeing a united Ireland in his lifetime, Arlene Foster responded by saying 'Why then did Simon use this moment in time to talk about his aspiration for a United Ireland in his political lifetime? I think that's quite aggressive.'[4] But the Agreement itself recognises that aspiration as legitimate – indeed, as the firm will of the Irish people. That does not mean that it is necessarily desirable, still less obligatory, for anyone to pursue that objective, either at this particular point in time or at all – and here we are firmly in the realm of political debate which can safely be left to politicians. But one might ask is it any more aggressive to advocate for a united Ireland than for a United Kingdom, as the DUP–Conservative agreement does? Reciprocity and parity of status of the two aspirations is the key principle here. Dr Mike Burke comments:

> Given that Mervyn Gibson, the Grand Secretary of the Orange Order, finds it insulting and offensive when people try to persuade him to support a united Ireland,[5] and that well-known unionist economist Graham Gudgin views talk of a united Ireland as a form of political harassment,[6] the chances of satisfying the conditions of [a suggested] veto [on discussing unity without unionist consent] are remote.[7]

John Wilson Foster has commented:

> I have always said that the road to a united Ireland should not have a signpost and that [those] who desire it should trust in cultural evolution and the fullness of time.

Instead, and despite the fact that until recently intercommunity social relations were the most amicable I have ever seen them, events have taken an ominous turn. During the recent and deplorable Troubles, the social centre held and the business, professional and academic classes rubbed along quite well.

Now because of the determination of a minority of educated republicans smelling meat, the faultline is threatening to run upwards, through the academy and professions. Pan-nationalism now looks cultural, not just political, and might even become social. If the upward fracture continues, we will be in serious trouble.[8]

Following some comments from Taoiseach Varadkar about the aspiration to unity with a degree of cross-community support, the DUP and UUP objected to the issue being articulated at all.[9] Former Prime Minister Blair dismissed complaints about comments made by Taoiseach Varadkar and similar views articulated by Tánaiste Coveney regarding their aspiration for a united Ireland, stating:

Well, they're perfectly entitled to say that. The Good Friday Agreement allows the nationalist aspirations to be recognised. But it doesn't change the basic point, of course, that Northern Ireland remains part of the UK as long as a majority of people there want it. What this whole Brexit thing does is obviously it puts pressure on the Union. It's bound to put pressure on the Union. I think long-term it will put pressure on the Union in respect of Scotland if we end up with a hard Brexit.[10]

In one sense, it does few favours to those of a unionist persuasion to pretend that the nationalist aspiration does not exist, and it seems better and more honest to acknowledge that clearly in a spirit of open dialogue. But the possibility of unity is not just a problem for unionists. Indeed, given the need to reflect the British dimension within a new 32-county context, the prospect of unity poses perhaps a particular challenge to republicans, as well as to the partitionist mindset that pervades much of the Southern landscape.

The Agreement Anticipates a Pathway to Unity

Of course, the Agreement does more than acknowledge the legitimacy of the nationalist aspiration. It sets out a clear constitutional pathway to a united Ireland by consent. Drawing on the language of the Downing Street Declaration of 15 December 1993, the participants endorsed the commitment made by the British and Irish governments to new principles for constitutional change regarding Northern Ireland. These included agreement by the two governments to:

> [R]ecognise that it is for the people of the island of Ireland alone, by agreement between the two parts respectively and without external impediment, to exercise their right of self-determination on the basis of consent, freely and concurrently given, North and South, to bring about a united Ireland, if that is their wish, accepting that this right must be achieved and exercised with and subject to the agreement and consent of a majority of the people of Northern Ireland.[11]

The two Governments went on to:

> [A]ffirm that, if in the future, the people of the island of Ireland exercise their right of self-determination … to bring about a united Ireland, it will be a binding obligation on both Governments to introduce and support in their respective Parliaments legislation to give effect to that wish.[12]

Any one of these elements would be radical – all elements taken together are exceptionally so. In these terms, the Agreement expressly recognises the legitimacy of the aspiration to unity and precisely how it is to be achieved.

The Test for Unity is 50 Per Cent + 1

The Agreement puts front and centre the principle of equal respect between the two traditions. That has many uncomfortable consequences. The most obvious one is that nationalism is not to be viewed as inherently inferior to unionism. That means that the test for a united Ireland must correspond to that required for a United Kingdom, subject to the rider that agreement is also required in a referendum in the South.

The test for a United Kingdom is the support of 'a majority' – in a democracy that is 50 per cent + 1 of those present and validly voting. That consent will remain effective even if it is a bare majority of one. On the principle of equal and reciprocal respect, the test for a united Ireland cannot be any more difficult. 50 per cent + 1 of those present and validly voting in referenda North and South is legally sufficient to trigger Irish unity. Generally, people who say that one cannot coerce hundreds of thousands of unionists into a united Ireland have no real problem with coercing hundreds of thousands of nationalists into a United Kingdom. If one takes equal respect seriously, one has to accept the consequences of a reciprocal test.

Beyond that, we are in the realm of political debate. It may well be appropriate for those who favour a unity outcome to seek as much support for Irish unity as possible above a bare majority, but that is in the realm of the (to those actors) desirable rather than the legally necessary.

An important document in this respect is 'The British Response to Sinn Féin Request for Clarification [of the Joint Declaration on Peace: The Downing Street Declaration]', a Statement by the Northern Ireland Office issued on 19 May 1994.[13] This document related to the corresponding provisions of the Downing St Declaration that prefigured the constitutional commitments of the Agreement. That clarification contains the following question, posed by Sinn Féin through the Irish government, and the response of the UK government.

Q.4. The British Government says, in the Downing Street Declaration, 'that they will uphold the democratic wishes of a greater number of the people of Northern Ireland'. What is the British Government's precise definition of 'a greater number of the people of Northern Ireland' and how would this be measured in practical terms?

Comment
The wish of a greater number of the people of Northern Ireland would be determined by a numerical majority of those validly voting in a poll fairly and explicitly organized for this purpose. Provision for such a poll is

made in section 1 of the Northern Ireland Constitution Act 1973.

This crucial clarification is not referenced in the completely misconceived discussion in Kelly's *The Irish Constitution*[14] to the effect that the meaning of 'a majority of the people' is 'not clear' and '[i]t might mean a simple majority of those voting on the day ... Alternatively it could mean a majority of all those on the electoral register.' This unfortunately entirely overlooks the context of the Agreement, its history and its balance between the traditions, not to mention its express language. The Constitutional Issues section agrees the text of language to be inserted in British legislation as follows: 'It is hereby declared that Northern Ireland in its entirety remains part of the United Kingdom and shall not cease to be so without the consent of a majority of the people of Northern Ireland *voting* in a poll held for the purposes of this section ... [emphasis added].'[15]

That 'majority' means 'majority ... voting' is expressly stated on the face of the Agreement itself, a point unfortunately not mentioned in Kelly's *Constitution*. The Good Friday Agreement would never have come into existence if there had been any suggestion by anyone involved, which there was not, that a majority on the electoral register was required. Furthermore, it is not explained what would happen if there was a border poll which resulted in a vote for continued union, but the votes in favour of continued union were less than a majority on the register. The Constitutional Issues section of the Agreement provides that 'whatever choice is freely exercised by a majority of the people',[16] rigorous impartiality will apply. There is no suggestion there that a majority means one thing for the union and another thing for unity. Again, the completely erroneous suggestion in Kelly's *Constitution* can be filed, alongside the notion of 'unionist consent', under the heading of misconceived ideas that would rig the system against the nationalist aspiration in a way that fundamentally undermines parity of esteem.

Moving beyond this particular error, one might think that it would be much better if sceptics about the thesis of a united Ireland could simply argue against unity on the merits, rather than suggest that the Agreement does not mean what it means. Such misconceptions are not without consequences in that they could embolden certain sections of loyalist/unionist opinion to resist the implementation of the Agreement if and when the time comes. Hence clarification is more than simply a matter of correcting blunders in academic analysis. It is an attempt to support an agreed understanding of the framework for constitutional debate and constitutional sequencing that might reduce the temperature of what will be a fraught situation.

Taoiseach Varadkar said in October 2017:

I wouldn't like us to get to the point whereby we are changing the constitutional position in Northern Ireland on a 50pc plus one basis ...

One of the best things about the Good Friday Agreement is that it did get very strong cross-Border support – that's why there was 70pc for it.

I don't think that there would be a 70pc vote for a united Ireland in the morning, for example, or anything remotely to that. And I really think we should focus on making the agreement that we have work.[17]

In the light of the clear wording of the Agreement, it seems these comments must be taken as speaking to what is desirable rather than what is legally necessary. It is a misunderstanding that the latter is being referred to that led to one commentator's suggestion that 'Leo Varadkar has torn up the Belfast Agreement in unionism's favour'.[18] For example, there is clearly not 70 per cent support for a United Kingdom – does that make such an option illegitimate? Clearly not. So, the legitimacy of a united Ireland based on a simple majority cannot be called into question either. Of course, it is perfectly appropriate to seek a broader consensus before any individual actor might wish to advocate for any particular change in a border poll, and one should see comments such as the Taoiseach's in that light.

In the febrile atmosphere of Northern Irish politics, one also has to make allowances for the fact that what people say is not necessarily what other people hear. For example, one immediate response to the Taoiseach's remarks, from loyalist controversialist Jamie Bryson, was:

> Mr Varadkar also went [on] to allude to a potential figure of a 70% vote in a referendum for a constitutional change to take place. If the Irish Government are serious about reassuring the unionist community that they are not launching a covert attempt to wedge Northern Ireland out of the United Kingdom, then why don't they provide consent for an amendment to the Belfast Agreement that would positively reflect the Irish Prime Minister's position in relation to the requirement for a figure of 70% in a referendum on Irish unity? This change to the treaty could be made by the consent of the British and Irish Government.

> The treaty ... is an entirely separate matter to the 1998
> Northern Ireland Act, which wrote devolution into law
> at Westminster in the wake of the Belfast Agreement.
> Such a positive step by the Irish Government, which
> would reflect their quite sensible position in relation to
> a border poll, would undoubtedly provide reassurance
> to many unionists.[19]

That Bryson contemplated an amendment of this nature to
the Good Friday Agreement over the heads of the parties
to the multi-party agreement, or to the Northern Ireland
Act 1998 over the heads of everyone except unionists
and the UK government, shows perhaps how little the
Agreement is really understood by some commentators.
Of course, one could also comment that if 70 per cent
support for a United Kingdom is also to be required on
a reciprocal basis, then the union is indeed under mortal
threat. Bryson's intervention highlights how important a
precise understanding of the Agreement is, because any
misapprehensions can only add to the risks of the situation
if and when unity draws closer.

Fintan O'Toole makes the point that a majority vote in
the South cannot be taken for granted: 'southerners have
no interest in inheriting a political wreck, or becoming
direct participants in a gory sequel, Troubles III: the Orange
Strikes Back. They will not vote for a form of unity that
merely creates an angry and alienated Protestant minority
within a bitterly contested new state.'[20] He goes on to
suggest:

> In the context of Ireland's future, 50 per cent + 1 is
> not, as Adams claims, 'what democracy is about'. That
> kind of crude, tribal majoritarianism is precisely what

the Belfast Agreement is meant to finish off. Again, the new article 3 of the Constitution is a good guide: 'It is the firm will of the Irish nation, in harmony and friendship, to unite all the people who share the territory of the island of Ireland, in all the diversity of their identities and traditions ...' Harmony, friendship, diversity, multiplicity, a unity not of territory but of people – not: 'We beat you by one vote so suck it up and welcome to our nation.' Irish democracy has to be 'about' the creation of a common polity in which minorities of different kinds can feel fully at home. We're not remotely there yet – on either side of the Border.

Pushing for a Border poll in which a majority of one vote would solve all our historic problems is as pointless as it is delusional. The ultimate cause of Irish unity is being very well served as things stand – by its sworn enemies. Its friends can serve it best by working to create a Republic of equals that might be worth joining.[21]

The point that the parity of esteem envisaged by the Agreement requires creating an island of equals on both sides of the border is valid and is one we will review in a later chapter. But even taking that point as well made, a focus on the problems of 50 per cent + 1 for unity overlooks equivalent problems the other way. Dr Mike Burke has noted the increasing attempts to challenge the 50 per cent + 1 rule thus:

The verbal barrage against the 50 percent + 1 threshold was overwhelming. Commentator Andy Pollak scorned the logic of a 'demographic arithmetic' that 'creeps over the fateful 50 per cent mark,' warning that it was 'old, ugly nationalism by numbers.' Sean Donlon, former Secretary General of the Department of Foreign Affairs, agreed with Pollak and said 'reunification by numbers is neither desirable nor achievable.' He rejected the prospect of 'unity by numbers and without consent.' Former Taoiseach Bertie Ahern said any GFA-mandated poll 'was not for some kind of a sectarian vote or a day that the nationalists and republicans could outvote the unionists and loyalists.' Fintan O'Toole mocked the 50 percent + 1 rule as 'crude, tribal majoritarianism.' This outbreak of acute but selective arithmophobia is breathtaking in its hypocrisy. Ever since partition, and explicitly since 1973, majority support of the people in the north was sufficient to keep the north within the UK. The 50 percent + 1 rule was acceptable when it served the interests of Union, as it does even today. That a majority in the north continue to support the Union is seen by many as the democratic mainspring of the northern regime. But the moment majority support is meaningfully applied to the prospects of Irish unity, the beauty of democracy becomes the horror of the old, the ugly, the undesirable, the sectarian, the crude and the tribal.

If a northern majority, understood as 50 percent + 1, is not enough to win a poll for Irish unity, then what kind of majority do these proposals require? Pollak wants a majority to include 'some significant element of unionist consent.' Ahern suggests that a border poll is meant for a time when people in the north – 'of all traditions' – would consent to a united Ireland. O'Toole says a united Ireland is dependent on a united north: 'Forcing a million unionists into a new Irish state without their consent is in nobody's interest.' Similarly, Tom Kelly states: 'The principle of consent cannot be set aside. Nearly one million hearts and minds within the unionist community are not convinced about the benefits of a united Ireland.'[22]

Lord Kilclooney's view on the test is representative:

Assuming … there was a 50.1% in favour of a united Ireland, in no way would one dare have a united Ireland. Because the reality on the ground in Northern Ireland is there would be civil war. You cannot force Northern Ireland out of the UK by a 1% majority. Can you imagine the loyalists in Belfast taking it quietly? I couldn't.[23]

While one can, of course, understand the point being made, that is not how parity of esteem or consent under the Agreement works; unless it be the case that if unionism won the border poll by a tiny margin it would also accept that it could no longer keep Northern Ireland in the UK by 1 per cent. That is the issue. The test has to be reciprocal – otherwise talk of parity of esteem is hot air. Strangely, many people who object to unity by 50 per cent + 1 normally have no difficulty with union with Britain on a 50 per cent + 1 basis, or indeed to Brexit on a 52–48 per cent basis. In such cases, one generally finds statements relating to how that is what democracy is all about. And, more fundamentally, to come to that question, the genius of the Agreement was to overcome majoritarianism in everything except the ultimate constitutional issue where 50 per cent + 1 was the only equal and reciprocal tie-breaking answer available, apart perhaps from the option of joint authority that the Agreement did not pursue. Democracy as envisaged by the Agreement involves power sharing, inclusion, rights, equality and counter-majoritarianism across the board, except on the constitutional status of Northern Ireland. So, the concept that 'that is what democracy is about' has to be taken in the context of a vast web of counter-majoritarian protections stitched-in at every level of the Agreement's architecture.

That being said, one can still recognise the crudeness of the simple majority test. The only answers to that are to make Northern Ireland work as a self-contained entity that respects both traditions, so that the constitutional issue does not matter so much and would make virtually no difference in practice; combined with a lengthy period of co-operation between the two governments so that any eventual transition of formal sovereignty would be slow, gradual and imperceptible.

A related problem with the arguments made by the opponents of the 50 per cent + 1 rule is that there is no other natural exit point after which sovereignty would move exclusively to the Irish side. If sovereignty does not shift on the basis of 50 per cent + 1 support for unity, why should it shift on the basis of 52.5 per cent or 55 per cent support? In the final analysis, the 50 per cent + 1 rule is the only mechanism for determining sovereignty which is based on a logical and equal principle, and, in any event, is legally enshrined in the Agreement. But rather than provide for 100 per cent transfer of control of Northern Ireland to the Irish side on the basis of a 50 per cent + 1 vote, the 'offering' prepared by nationalist Ireland in advance of a border poll could include the voluntary proposal of a lengthy transitional period of joint authority (that is, joint management), over the initial few decades of the transition. Such a managed transition – initially within UK sovereignty and subsequently within Irish jurisdiction – might provide a less fraught and, in the end, more flexible transitional mechanism to avoid the abrupt discontinuities of the 50 per cent + 1 approach of the Good Friday Agreement, especially if coupled with an ongoing consultative and cultural role in Northern Ireland for the British state thereafter.

There is No Requirement for Unionist Consent to Unity

The constitutional commitments of the Agreement acknowledge that the right of self-determination will be exercised by agreement between 'a majority' of the people on each side of the border. There is a crucial difference between 'a majority' in this context, which means a numerical majority present and validly voting, and the phrase 'the majority', which at time of writing, in the Northern Irish context, is generally identified with the unionist community. There is no requirement for consent of 'the majority' and absolutely no requirement for 'unionist consent' to Irish unity, if for no other reason than that there is no requirement for nationalist consent to a United Kingdom.

The lack of reciprocity that flows from the 'unionist consent' notion is problematic; unless, that is, one believes that unionism is an inherently superior position – a posture incompatible with the parity of esteem put front and centre in the Agreement. Furthermore, it is a meaningless test because, by definition, unionism is about preserving the union. Unionism will never consent to ending the union without ceasing to be unionism. Thus, a demand for unionist consent guarantees permanent failure of the nationalist constitutional project. As Burke puts it: 'Once again, the conditions placed on winning the poll ensure that it will be lost.'[24]

A perhaps unguarded comment from Sinn Féin President Gerry Adams, of all people, that unionist 'assent or consent'[25] would be required to bring about a united Ireland was rejected as incompatible with this threshold,[26] as were similar comments from unionist politicians. The SDLP declared even-handedly: 'the threshold for a united Ireland cannot be any higher than for a United Kingdom'.[27] Reunification will occur 'if in a referendum a majority in the North votes for one'.[28]

Talk of consent and vetoes may have a semantic dimension. Yes, at one level the pre-Good Friday Agreement statutory requirement of no unity without the consent of the Northern Irish parliament amounted to a 'unionist veto', but only in practice as opposed to in theory. In theory, there was nothing stopping Stormont from voting for unity. Likewise, at present, the requirement for the consent of 'a majority' gives unionism, on current conditions, a right to say no. But those current conditions could change, and if unionism ended up in a minority position it would no longer have that right on its own, without support from others to get over the 50 per cent + 1 barrier. Sean Donlon wrote, in August 2017, that:

> It is not helpful, and almost certainly not true, to say, as Mary Lou McDonald said on June 9, that 'we are in the endgame as far as partition is concerned'. Does she ever stop to think about unionist consent? In 1998 in a referendum which Sinn Féin supported, 71 per

cent of voters in Northern Ireland and 94 per cent
of voters in this jurisdiction endorsed the need for
that consent. Harping on about the end of partition
as if consent was irrelevant will not help to unlock
unionists.[29]

I read that comment as referring to unionist consent in
the sense of the empirical fact that unionists currently
constitute 'a majority'. If unionism were no longer a
majority, the issue of majority consent (which the Good
Friday Agreement included) and unionist consent (which it
did not) would no longer coincide, and the point made by
Donlon would no longer hold.

From another point of view, somewhat more sceptical
about the Good Friday Agreement, Burke has argued as
follows:

> Consent is a sham, for at least two reasons. First,
> referring to the unionist veto as the principle of
> consent puts a democratic façade on the anti-
> democratic ethos of partition. That is, it hides – and
> is usually meant to hide – the sectarian, seditious and
> coercive origins of the northern regime. Second, it
> disguises a fundamental inequality central to unionism
> even today: that unionists are and should be treated
> as superior to nationalists.
>
> The term 'unionist veto' unmasks both those
> pretensions of the 'consent principle' by highlighting a
> negative and illegitimate power of blocking. The veto
> was used to partition the country by thwarting the
> movement towards unified self-government that had
> indisputable democratic support on the island. And the

veto privileged unionism over nationalism by giving a unionist minority the power to frustrate the express wishes of the nationalist majority.[30]

Taking the latter two points, the first is a more overarching appeal to a nationalist historical narrative that goes back to the origins of partition. However, the acceptance of the Good Friday Agreement in referenda must mean that such concerns are water under the bridge. The second point made, though, is fundamental – both traditions must be treated with equal respect. But, in a number of respects, much political narrative and practice treats unionism as superior to nationalism. The notion of 'unionist consent' is one example, as is the resistance to acknowledging that the test for Irish unity must be reciprocal to that for a United Kingdom. Burke points out that seeking to impermissibly offer some form of enhanced veto above and beyond what the Good Friday Agreement provides does few favours to unionism:

> There are real dangers in trying to encourage reconciliation by assuring unionists their constitutional future is protected by some kind of revitalized veto that undermines the rights of an anticipated nationalist majority.

> This kind of reasoning gives little incentive to unionists to engage [in] the process of reconciliation. Granting them the power to impede constitutional change will encourage unionists to remain steadfast in support of the constitutional status quo. They will have no reason even to consider any reconciled constitutional alternatives.

> There is another danger, more pertinent to my
> purpose here, to promoting a reconciliation founded
> on enhancing unionism's veto ... proposals for a
> specifically unionist veto are based on a hierarchy of
> constitutional rights that subordinates nationalism to
> unionism. That is, such proposals tend to reinforce
> unionists' sense of superiority, which is itself one of
> the primary obstacles to reconciliation.[31]

Ultimately, any ambiguity or loose references to a
supermajority will be doing Northern Ireland no favours
because it can only embolden loyalist resistance aimed at
thwarting the will of a majority – a resistance to a democratic
majority decision that could take calamitous forms if given
breathing space and credibility. Hence, providing emphatic
clarity on the test involved is not just a question of clearing
up academic misconceptions. It is a pivot on which any
peaceful transition depends. If there is a feeling that Dublin
does not have the will to insist on a transfer of sovereignty
following a simple majority in a border poll, that can
only set the scene for tragic consequences. To avoid such
repercussions, it is best for all concerned if the clear position
of the Agreement was firmly understood.

There is No Arbitrary Date for a Border Poll

The only border poll to date took place in March 1973.
Boycotted by nationalists, it resulted in 99 per cent support
for the United Kingdom. Subsequent to the adoption of
the 1998 Agreement, there have been intermittent calls for
such a poll to be re-run. The UK government has discretion
to hold such a poll at any time: 'The Secretary of State may
by order direct the holding of a poll ... on a date specified

in the order.' Contrary to one commentator's view, it is not 'a literal breach of the agreement' to hold a 'speculative border poll'.[32] But such a poll is only obligatory if a formal test is met: 'the Secretary of State shall exercise the power [to call such a poll], if at any time it appears likely to him that a majority of those voting would express a wish that Northern Ireland should cease to be part of the United Kingdom and form part of a united Ireland'.[33]

Thus, there can be no arbitrary dates for such a poll, still less any arbitrary requirements such as that the British government set a date for withdrawal from Northern Ireland. Any aim to secure unity by a given date can only be an aspiration rather than being made a legally effective requirement, as to do so would be fundamentally inconsistent with the principle of consent at the heart of the Agreement and the law preceding it. There was much comment on a possible poll for the 100th anniversary of the Easter Rising in 2016. That date came and went without constitutional incident. Brexit has stimulated further such demand, with Sinn Féin calling for a poll within five years,[34] and the SDLP, for example, having called for such a poll after the Brexit negotiations concluded.[35] Secretary of State Theresa Villiers responded:

> The Good Friday Agreement is very clear that the circumstances where the secretary of state is required to have a border poll is where there is reason to believe there would be a majority support for a united Ireland …
>
> There is nothing to indicate that in any of the opinion surveys that have taken place.[36]

More recent SDLP language has possibly softened somewhat. According to a September 2017 *Irish Times* report:

> New SDLP deputy leader Nichola Mallon has warned that rushing to a Border poll where Irish unity is not clearly mapped out is 'an absolute recipe for disaster' that could result in violence.
>
> ...
>
> She said she would like a Border poll to be called 'when it can be won' and not during the Brexit process, as this would play on people's fears.
>
> 'You need to show people clearly what they are voting for,' she said.
>
> 'Just calling a Border poll and getting your 50 [per cent] plus one is an absolute recipe for disaster. And I honestly believe and fear that it will actually erupt in violence.'[37]

Ultimately, the point remains that a border poll under the Agreement is not necessarily there to test public opinion or mark the progress of nationalism. It is only required to be called if the UK government reasonably thinks it will result in a 50 per cent + 1 or more vote for a united Ireland. Short of the Secretary of State forming such an opinion, the decision whether to hold a poll or not is a discretionary matter for the British government.

From one point of view, the British government might not be doing nationalism any favours with an early border poll anyway. Bill White of LucidTalk polling comments:

Sinn Féin need to be careful as they may get what they ask for and they need to score over 40% in any such referendum for the 'pro United Ireland' side, for that cause to have any hope of surviving with credibility.

Put it this way, if the pro-union side (that is NI in UK) scores 60–70% in a border poll that would effectively kill off the argument for a generation, and remove any possibility of another referendum for many years.[38]

The Agreement Rules Out Joint Sovereignty, Independence or Repartition

The Good Friday Agreement, at its most fundamental level, rules out exotic alternative 'solutions' to the problem of the constitutional status of Northern Ireland, such as joint sovereignty, independence, repartition, or any other alternative, including, in particular, the idea of joint consent – the conception that a majority of both communities would have to consent before a united Ireland could come into existence. That notion is without legal or indeed logical basis. The clear and unambiguous language of the Good Friday Agreement firmly rejects all of these alternative proposals, which would have the effect of undermining the will of the majority of the people of Northern Ireland as expressed in a referendum. The only legally permissible way in which any such alternative solutions could be advanced would be by way of further international agreement between the two sovereign governments.

Independence would, in any event, be a fraught notion given the manner in which dominant political power by the unionist 'majority' during home rule in the six counties was used against the nationalist 'minority'. Repartition, likewise, would be a wholly unequal outcome given that nationalists have been asked to live within the 6-county entity for the past century on the basis of a particular test – the majority wish of that entity. It would be historically contradictory, oppressive of those trapped within new ghettoes, and fundamentally discriminatory to change the rules of the game just as the run of play could be going in a direction that does not suit one position. More fundamentally, it would be a repudiation of the Agreement at a basic level.

If a majority for a united Ireland draws closer, further efforts may be made to unravel the guarantee contained in the Good Friday Agreement that a united Ireland will be given effect to should a majority wish it. Indeed, it is obvious from public discourse that those efforts are well underway. It seems likely that all of the exotic alternatives to the simple right of self-determination referred to in the Agreement will be rolled out in the years to come as the prospect of a nationalist majority in Northern Ireland becomes more likely. Again, one can only suggest that any ambiguity regarding the clear choice of options set out in the Agreement may have serious consequences in stoking resistance and division, if and when the time comes. The best guarantee of peacefully negotiating the issue is for the primacy and clarity of the Agreement to be upheld.

The Northern Irish Attorney General John Larkin has floated in an academic paper a possible argument for repartition. This is based on the observation that the Northern Ireland Act 1998 does not 'define' what 'Northern Ireland' is precisely but only that it includes the associated waters of Northern Ireland:[39]

The absence of definition may be very important when s. 1(1) of the [Northern Ireland Act] 1998 is considered … Section 1(1) of the [Act] provides that Northern Ireland in its entirety remains part of the UK and shall not cease to be so without the consent of a majority of the people of Northern Ireland voting in a poll for that purpose. If Northern Ireland were to be defined by statute in a manner that embraced less territory than the territory that was the 'Northern Ireland' of the 1920 and 1973 Acts [i.e., the Government of Ireland Act 1920 and the Northern Ireland Constitution Act 1973] but was not Northern Ireland in some (hypothetical) later statute, that ('surplus') territory would not fall within s. 1(1) of the [Northern Ireland Act] 1998.[40]

The scenario might thus be that UK legislation could 'expel' nationalist areas into what would effectively be 'Bantustans' (that is, notionally independent territories, artificially created for gerrymandering purposes, if such areas were not incorporated immediately into the South) and could redefine Northern Ireland as a solidly unionist area, within which the principle of consent would operate in perpetual favour of unionism. This argument can be responded to in a number of ways.

Most basically, Larkin is only speaking of the interpretation of the 1998 Act, and not of the interpretation of the Agreement. The fact that the 1998 Act does not stop the UK legislature from enacting future legislation that is in breach of the Agreement does not make such hypothetical legislation permissible in international law terms.

It is clear that any redefinition of Northern Ireland in this way or indeed in any way without Irish consent would be a massive breach of the fundamental international law principle that treaties must be implemented in good faith. The Good Friday Agreement would never have been entered into had there been the faintest suggestion of such a sleight of hand.

It is thus ultimately irrelevant that the Northern Ireland Act 1998 does not 'define' Northern Ireland. The issue here is not what UK legislation articulates, but what the UK's obligations in international law are. There can be no question that 'Northern Ireland' in the British-Irish Agreement means the six counties for a range of reasons, some of which we will shortly come to. And while the 1998 Act does not define Northern Ireland, the 1921 Treaty (which remains in force) indirectly defined 'Northern Ireland' by reference to the Government of Ireland Act 1920,[41] which, in turn, referred to six specific counties and their parliamentary boroughs.[42] The repeal of the 1920 Act cannot affect the meaning of the 1921 Treaty.

The lack of definition of Northern Ireland in the 1998 Act does not seem to be significant. 'Northern Ireland' did not need definition in 1998 to the same extent because it was already an existing entity rather than the new entity that was defined in 1920. It had a relatively clear meaning. The Agreement refers to Northern Ireland 'in its entirety', which is fundamentally inconsistent with the idea that the six counties could be dismembered for the purposes of a unionist gerrymander to thwart a democratic majority. Admittedly, if Northern Ireland left the UK, it would put up questions of maritime jurisdiction and continental shelf division for negotiation again between the two governments. That is more likely to be the reason why Northern Ireland is not precisely defined – one could not pre-empt the precise outcome of such negotiations.

But we do know for sure that Northern Ireland includes the six counties named in the Government of Ireland Act 1920.

The fundamental architecture of the principle of consent is that it operates between the two parts of Ireland – that can only mean as they existed when the Agreement was entered into. That principle ceases to be a principle if it is subject to whatever gerrymandering is put in place from time to time on a unilateral basis by one side only. Indeed, nothing could be further removed from the concept of 'principle' than a one-way system that gives unionism a rigged ticket to eternal constitutional victory. Nothing could be further removed from the parity of esteem and equality between the two traditions that is the centrepiece of the Agreement.

The principle of consent between the two parts of the island is very far from the only part of the Agreement that becomes meaningless if one side reserves the right to redefine the 'part' in question. (Indeed, on this logic, why could the South not temporarily cede the remaining three counties of Ulster to Northern Ireland in order to create a 'majority' for unity in Ulster as a whole?) To take another example, the 'birthright' of the people of Northern Ireland to British and Irish citizenship would be rendered illusory for many people if, say, the south-western four counties of the North were to be lopped off leaving a north-eastern rump statelet. The citizens of those four counties would suddenly find themselves having no entitlement to British citizenship, as they would, on that theory, no longer be part of Northern Ireland. At every level, the Agreement simply breaks down if unilateral repartition were to be accepted as legally permissible. Any good faith interpretation of the

Agreement precludes such an option. Indeed, overall, the Agreement can be viewed as a massive repudiation of unilateralism – particularly the kind of one-sided unilateralism that blighted Northern Ireland for half a century of domination by one community.

The Good Friday Agreement is Intended to Endure after Unity

The status of the Good Friday Agreement after unity goes back to the status of the British-Irish Agreement as a legally binding international treaty. As such a treaty, it cannot be unilaterally changed, and any termination of obligations under the treaty requires the consent of the other government.

The Vienna Convention on the Law of Treaties is an agreement to which both the UK (since 1971) and Ireland (since 2006) are parties. Ireland acceded to the Vienna Convention after signing and ratifying the British-Irish Agreement in 1998–9, and, therefore, the Vienna Convention does not apply to the Irish obligations under the Agreement except to the extent that it is declaratory of international law.[43] The Vienna Convention provides for a number of ways in which obligations under a treaty can be ended:

(a) where the treaty was invalid when made;[44]

(b) where the treaty itself expressly provides for termination;[45]

(c) where the treaty does not expressly so provide but it is established that the parties intended to admit the possibility of denunciation or withdrawal;[46]

(d) where the treaty does not expressly provide for termination but a right of denunciation or withdrawal may be implied by the nature of the treaty;[47]

(e) by consent of all the parties after consultation with the other contracting States[48] which may include acquiescence to a treaty falling into desuetude or obsolescence[49] and including where the consent is to be implied by the states agreeing a later inconsistent treaty;[50]

(f) in the case of a material breach by the other side;[51]

(g) if performance becomes impossible otherwise than due to the state's own wrong;[52]

(h) in the event of a fundamental change of circumstances not originally foreseen;[53]

(i) in the event of the emergence of a new and conflicting peremptory norm of general international law.[54]

In broad terms, the Convention appears to reflect previous state practice. The Good Friday Agreement does not expressly provide for termination; nor can any denunciation clause or intention be properly inferred from it. Previous state practice only allowed 'strictly limited exceptions'[55] where denunciation of a treaty without a denunciation clause was recognised. There is no implied intention that the agreement can be terminated because the vast majority of its provisions are capable of implementation either under a United Kingdom or a united Ireland.

An example of a provision which cannot operate post-hypothetical unity is the statement that the jurisdiction of Westminster would remain unaffected – post-unity this obviously falls away. In that situation, Dublin sovereignty applies.[56] But apart from such necessary modifications there is nothing in the Agreement to the effect that the internal institutions fall away because of unity. If Strand One institutions remain in being, there would be a continued need for Strand Two institutions to co-ordinate the work of the Oireachtas and the devolved institutions. So even Strand Two would not fall away post-unity. Likewise, the Strand Three relationships continue to exist across the two islands and there is no reason why those elements should be regarded as redundant post-unity. Admittedly here, the provision that the Irish government could put forward views and proposals in relation to non-devolved matters[57] would cease to have effect post-unity, but, overall, almost all of the text of the Agreement is capable of being operated in a united Ireland context.

Could it be argued that Britain would have no post-unity interest in Ireland compatible with an intention to have a continuation of the Agreement? The text itself answers that point. It expressly provides for a right to continued British citizenship in perpetuity for the people of Northern Ireland. The governments:

> recognise the birthright of all the people of Northern Ireland to identify themselves and be accepted as Irish or British, or both, as they may so choose, and accordingly confirm that their right to hold both British and Irish citizenship is accepted by both Governments and would not be affected by any future change in the status of Northern Ireland.[58]

Leaving aside other exceptions that clearly do not apply, or the question of the consent of the two governments to discontinuing the Agreement, which is always a possibility (however theoretical), that leaves fundamental change of circumstances. The Vienna Convention provides:

1. A fundamental change of circumstances which has occurred with regard to those existing at the time of the conclusion of a treaty, and which was not foreseen by the parties, may not be invoked as a ground for terminating or withdrawing from the treaty unless:

(a) the existence of those circumstances constituted an essential basis of the consent of the parties to be bound by the treaty; and

(b) the effect of the change is radically to transform the extent of obligations still to be performed under the treaty.

2. A fundamental change of circumstances may not be invoked as a ground for terminating or withdrawing from a treaty:

(a) if the treaty establishes a boundary; or

(b) if the fundamental change is the result of a breach by the party invoking it either of an obligation under the treaty or of any other international obligation owed to any other party to the treaty.[59]

The fundamental change of circumstance exception is very narrow and has been described as a 'codified'[60] version of previous state practice.[61] The International Court of Justice considered the issue in the Fisheries Jurisdiction Case (*UK v. Iceland*):

35. In his letter of 29 May 1972 to the Registrar, the Minister for Foreign Affairs of Iceland refers to

'the changed circumstances resulting from the ever-increasing exploitation of the fishery resources in the seas surrounding Iceland'. Judicial notice should also be taken of other statements made on the subject in documents which Iceland has brought to the Court's attention. Thus, the resolution adopted by the Althing on 15 February 1972 contains the statement that 'owing to changed circumstances the Notes concerning fishery limits exchanged in 1961 are no longer applicable.

36. In these statements the Government of Iceland is basing itself on the principle of termination of a treaty by reason of change of circumstances. International law admits that a fundamental change in the circumstances which determined the parties to accept a treaty, if it has resulted in a radical transformation of the extent of the obligations imposed by it, may, under certain conditions, afford the party affected a ground for invoking the termination or suspension of the treaty. This principle, and the conditions and exceptions to which it is subject, have been embodied in Article 62 of the Vienna Convention on the Law of Treaties, which may in many respects be considered as a codification of existing customary law on the subject of the termination of a treaty relationship on account of change of circumstances.[62]

The principle has never been applied by the International Court of Justice or the Permanent Court of International Justice so as to allow a state to escape treaty obligations,[63] and 'fell into serious disrepute' in the early 20th century. It is clear that this 'change of circumstances' clause, or any state practice on this issue, could not apply to allow the Agreement to lapse in the event of unity; for the very simple reason that Irish unity is not something unforeseen at the time of the 1998 Agreement but specifically referred to and contemplated in the Agreement itself.

More fundamentally still, the governments in the British-Irish Agreement:

(i) recognise the legitimacy of whatever choice is freely exercised by a majority of the people of Northern Ireland with regard to its status, whether they prefer to continue to support the Union with Great Britain or a sovereign united Ireland;

and

(iv) affirm that if in the future, the people of the island of Ireland exercise their right of self-determination on the basis set out in sections (i) and (ii) above to bring about a united Ireland, it will be a binding obligation on both Governments to introduce and support in their respective Parliaments legislation to give effect to that wish.[64]

Thus, not only is the Good Friday Agreement not stated to be applicable only so long as Northern Ireland is part of the union – but rather unity is expressly envisaged. That express statement is incompatible with the idea that the Good Friday Agreement falls away once unity is achieved.

The background to the Agreement supports such a conclusion. In the 1995 Joint Framework Documents, the two governments set out their agreed position:

They agree that future arrangements relating to Northern Ireland, and Northern Ireland's wider relationships, should respect the full and equal legitimacy and worth of the identity, sense of allegiance, aspiration and ethos of both the unionist and nationalist communities there. Consequently, both Governments commit themselves to the principle that institutions and arrangements in Northern Ireland and North/South institutions should afford both communities secure and satisfactory political, administrative and symbolic expression and protection. In particular, they commit themselves to entrenched provisions guaranteeing equitable and effective political participation for whichever community finds itself in a minority position by reference to the Northern Ireland framework, or the wider Irish framework, as the case may be, consequent upon the operation of the principle of consent.[65]

The lack of a denunciation clause in the Agreement is clearly consistent with this explicit statement of prior intention. To infer any such provision is without basis, in any event, but would also contradict that clear prior intention.

Thus, in the absence of any hypothetical future agreement to the contrary, the Good Friday Agreement would continue to be binding in international law following a united Ireland. This is so despite the fact that at least some adjustment will be required in the international treaty that will follow any border poll for unity. Conor Donohue comments in a 2016 academic paper:

The Agreement would remain in force in a united Ireland. There is no sunset clause in the Agreement, and the plain wording of the text implies that it is intended to continue regardless of the North's territorial status. The Agreement states that 'whatever choice is freely exercised by a majority of the people of Northern Ireland', the State exercising sovereignty there is obliged to exercise jurisdiction impartially. This creates an obligation that is clearly intended to continue even in the event of a united Ireland. This intent is also shown through the fact that the Agreement confers on the people of Northern Ireland a right to Irish and British identity and citizenship, regardless of the North's status. As such, unless the parties agree to terminate the Agreement by consent,[66] the Agreement would remain in force.[67]

While not all parties appear to appreciate this point at present, the SDLP has articulated that point for some time. A 2005 SDLP document, *A United Ireland and the Agreement*,[68] sets that out clearly, repeating proposals previously published in 2003.[69] The key message of the document is that: 'In the united Ireland to which we are committed, all the Agreement's principles and protections would endure.'[70]

In terms of the structures of a united Ireland, the SDLP proposed that the assembly would continue 'as a regional Parliament of a united Ireland'. The executive would also continue, as would the Agreement's equality and human rights guarantees, and the right to identify oneself as British or Irish or both and to hold passports accordingly. There was also a pragmatic argument for maintaining the Good Friday Agreement institutions – it would provide certainty and stability and thereby assist in making the case for a united Ireland.

The SDLP also proposed that a referendum on unity should be held once the Agreement's institutions 'have bedded down and are operating stably',[71] a call which has been made at various times (albeit for different reasons) by Sinn Féin, the UUP and the DUP, the document stated. However, in the context of a referendum, the SDLP committed themselves to seeking the agreement of all the island's parties that the Agreement endures regardless of whether one is in a United Kingdom or a united Ireland. The alternative approach, that of not making clear that the Agreement will endure, was dismissed:

> Instead of making clear that the Agreement will endure, Sinn Féin has argued that unionists should negotiate the kind of united Ireland that they want.

> If Sinn Féin expects unionists to conduct such negotiations now, they are misguided. Unionists are most unlikely to negotiate on a united Ireland before a referendum.

> If, on the other hand, Sinn Féin expects negotiations after a referendum, they are also misguided. Winning a referendum will be made much more difficult if voters know nothing of how they will be governed afterwards, other than that there will be negotiations.[72]

Overall, the Agreement is more than just a mechanism for determining which state Northern Ireland will be part of – it is a 'democratic common denominator' between both sections of the community.[73] The document makes no specific argument that the continuation of the Good Friday Agreement would be a legal requirement as matters stand at the moment. The document spelled out some of the consequences of the putting in place of a united

Ireland – instead of sending MPs to Westminster, Northern Ireland would send TDs to Dáil Éireann. Some rebalancing of power between the assembly and the Oireachtas might be required, and constitutional change in Ireland would be necessary to guarantee the future of the assembly as a regional parliament of a united Ireland, to implement all the protections of the Good Friday Agreement to reflect greater pluralism and inclusion, and to guarantee British citizenship to those who wish to have it in the North.[74] However, it might be observed that this latter point is not something that could, in reality, be guaranteed by any amendment to the Irish Constitution, other than to say that it would be lawful for Irish citizens also to hold a second or subsequent nationality. The document also envisaged that unity would bring changes to the Good Friday Agreement itself, but these should be made in the way envisaged by the Agreement, namely through a review. The SDLP argued: 'It is futile talking in high-minded language about unity while at the same time engaging in the sort of underhand actions that put unionists off even the Agreement, never mind the idea of a united Ireland.'[75]

Finally, describing the Agreement as a covenant of honour (referring presumably to the multi-party agreement which is a political agreement, rather than the British-Irish Agreement which is legally binding), the SDLP made the point that the best protection for unionists in a united Ireland would be through the mechanisms of the Agreement: 'For unionists to "smash the Agreement" would be to forego not only their say in the Northern Ireland of today, but their guaranteed position in a future united Ireland.'[76]

At the launch of the document,[77] the Minister for Foreign Affairs Dermot Ahern described the Sinn Féin proposal for a Green Paper as 'a red herring' and the proposal of a 'snake-oil salesman', saying 'we already have a template for Irish unity in the form of the Good Friday Agreement'.[78]

The thesis that there would be practical advantages to preserving the Good Friday Agreement post a united Ireland was also advanced by the unionist commentator Roy Garland, reacting to the November 2003 version of the SDLP proposals, who described them as 'welcome and innovative'.[79] It would fulfil a unionist proposal to 'insist on Northern Ireland remaining an administrative unit, even if Irish unity were achieved', and therefore 'has some potential to appeal to unionists'. Calling for the continuation of East/West links following a united Ireland, including the British-Irish Council, he also commented:

> The crazy notion that Irish is the first language in the South and the remaining exclusively Catholic elements in the Irish Constitution would have to be ditched. The reality of close ties of many kinds between our islands should be given official recognition and in that context perhaps the Irish tricolour might fly freely alongside the Union flag in Dublin and Belfast without causing offence.[80]

Thus, in the absence of any amending agreement, it would be a legal obligation on Ireland to continue to give effect to the Agreement after Irish unity. This simple conclusion has profound consequences for the way in which the whole question of reunification is to be approached. In particular, that means that the strong protections for whichever community does not command a majority within Northern Ireland would endure, in the absence of any further agreement, so as to benefit unionism following a united Ireland. This aspect of the Agreement is the other side of the coin to the fact that the Agreement rejects joint sovereignty, independence, repartition or dual consent of both communities. This dimension perhaps deserves to be highlighted further in that by necessary implication it rules out the prospect of an all-Ireland unitary state, governed exclusively from Dublin.

Pursuant to the provisions of the Good Friday Agreement, the unionist minority can be guaranteed, first of all, that Northern Ireland will continue to exist after a united Ireland as a separate administrative entity with a devolved legislative assembly; secondly, that a devolved executive for the six counties will also be maintained pursuant to the Good Friday Agreement within a united Ireland; and thirdly, that, pursuant to the Agreement, the devolved executive will exercise executive power for Northern Ireland on a cross-party basis. These vital protections for the unionist minority flow from the status of the Good Friday Agreement as a legally binding agreement of indefinite duration, which will endure notwithstanding the existence in the future of a majority in favour of a united Ireland. This also means that the border is permanent – albeit not necessarily as an international boundary, but in the event of unity, as an internal boundary beyond which devolved powers will continue to apply.

This ongoing aspect of the Agreement has yet to be fully appreciated. For example, Matt Carthy, Sinn Féin MEP, said in 2018, 'We need to be open to considering transitional arrangements, which could mean continued devolution to Stormont within an all-Ireland structure.'[81] Unfortunately, this is a misunderstanding of the Good Friday Agreement. As a matter of international legal obligation, the Agreement institutions are permanent. They do not depend on any one party being 'open to considering' them, nor are they 'transitional' arrangements. Stormont is a permanent feature of the landscape under the Agreement, whether within a United Kingdom or a united Ireland.

This legal obligation should be front and centre in any discussion of the issue. It is essentially a game-changing perspective because it significantly lowers the stakes on the constitutional issue, meaning that constitutional transitions could take place gradually with little impact in practice on the functioning of Northern Ireland.

While the New Ireland Forum Report of 1984 discussed a number of models for unity which might be proposed in the context of a future consent sought by peaceful means becoming available, that discussion has been significantly overtaken by the Good Friday Agreement. The Forum discussion considered three options: a unitary state, a federal arrangement or, alternatively, joint sovereignty. A unitary state, as Prime Minister Margaret Thatcher presciently said of that option, is 'out', since it is contrary to the Agreement, which guarantees the six counties as a permanent power-sharing administrative unit. Joint sovereignty is also 'out' for the same reason, again barring any agreement to the contrary. So, anticipating the Good Friday Agreement, Mrs Thatcher got two out of three correct. But the second option, a federal arrangement, is 'in' – it is the constitutional arrangement envisaged by the 1998 Agreement assuming that unity is approved in a border poll.

The precise form of federation, though, could be up for debate. In that hypothesis, one could ask whether, post-unity, the twenty-six counties would also be a separate federal 'province' of a truly federal overall 32-county unit, or whether the basic structure would be a 32-county unit with certain local powers in the 6-county area exercised locally (and therefore not a true federation, but rather a unitary state with a devolved government in a particular locality). That is a matter for political judgement. On the one hand, a natural preference to avoid proliferation of structures (the federal arrangement would require a federal parliament as well as two local parliaments North and South), as well as a possible wish to emphasise the primacy of the 32-county context, could militate against a true federal structure, and in favour of a single national 32-county parliament and government with certain powers devolved to local institutions in the six counties. Since the union with Scotland in 1707, there has been no parliament of England by analogy.

On the other hand, a 32-county Dáil with devolved powers in Stormont would create an Irish 'West Lothian question' – just as Scottish MPs get to vote on local English legislation where English MPs cannot return the favour, that issue would be much more problematic in a smaller parliament where Northern Irish TDs would vote on legislation for the 26 counties, but Southern TDs would have no say on devolved Northern Irish legislation. There are certainly arguments both ways, and no doubt there are other options that could be considered.

Northern Ireland Remains, to an Extent, British in Perpetuity

Conor Donohue comments:

> Should a united Ireland eventuate, this does not mean that the role of the United Kingdom in the North will cease. It will be continued in at least two ways, both

of which will ensure that the interests of unionists are aptly protected. First, the Agreement creates cross-border [that is East/West] bodies and forums, which allow the discussion of matters of mutual concern. As the Agreement will continue in force, these entities, too, will continue to exist ...

Secondly, the people of Northern Ireland will remain entitled to British citizenship. States have a right to invoke the responsibility of another state for wrongful acts done to one of their nationals. Theoretically, the United Kingdom could therefore invoke the responsibility of Ireland for any violations of the right to self-determination, or other fundamental rights, of unionists therein.[82]

Even without any enhanced role for the British government to put forward its views on the non-devolved functions of government relating to Northern Ireland, the Agreement provides for a permanent, ongoing, British identity. With the parties' support, the two governments agreed that they:

(v) affirm that whatever choice is freely exercised by a majority of the people of Northern Ireland, the power of the sovereign government with jurisdiction there shall be exercised with rigorous impartiality on behalf of all the people in the diversity of their identities and traditions and shall be founded on the principles of full respect for, and equality of, civil, political, social and cultural rights, of freedom from discrimination for all citizens, and of parity of esteem and of just and equal treatment for the identity, ethos, and aspirations of both communities.[83]

Thus, the unionist community of Northern Ireland is entitled to Britishness in perpetuity, and the Irish side and all parties are obliged to ensure full respect for that Britishness on the basis of equality. Thus, the British dimension of Northern Ireland is a permanent feature of the constitutional landscape.

It should, perhaps, not be assumed that unionism is immune from change and adaptation. One could, perhaps, ask what a united Ireland, or even full parity of esteem within Northern Ireland, would mean for unionism long-term; perhaps especially if, in decades to come, Scotland were to become even more detached from the UK if not independent or if the role and status of the Crown in the UK were to reduce further. It may be that unionism would evolve towards a broader, more cultural, relationship with the wider Anglosphere. In that context, Irish membership of the Commonwealth could serve as an important bridge. Certainly, the strand of unionism/loyalism that consciously or otherwise defines itself in terms of majority rule, superiority and confrontation would have to examine its raison d'être.

Chapter 5

Bedding Down the Agreement

The 2017 Breakdown of Devolution

The Agreement, as supplemented subsequently, including by the St Andrews Agreement, envisages a series of interlocking institutions and supporting bodies. However, since the breakdown of devolution in January 2017, an assessment of the status of those bodies is dispiriting. A table perhaps best summarises how they are functioning.

Table 1. Bodies Established under the Agreement and Subsequent Agreements

Body	Source	State of Play after January 2017
1. Assembly	Agreement, Strand One	Not functioning
2. Executive	Agreement, Strand One	Not functioning
3. Civic Forum / Civic Advisory Panel	Agreement, Strand One, amended by Stormont House Agreement and A Fresh Start	Forum not functioning Panel never effectively commenced work

Body	Source	State of Play after January 2017
4. North/South Ministerial Council	Agreement, Strand Two	Not functioning
5. North/South implementation bodies	Agreement, Strand Two	Functioning
6. North/South Inter-Parliamentary Association (previously described as North/South joint parliamentary forum)	Agreement, Strand Two, supplemented by St Andrews Agreement	Not functioning
7. North/South independent consultative forum	Agreement, Strand Two	Never established
8. British-Irish Council	Agreement, Strand Three	Functioning
9. British-Irish Parliamentary Assembly (formerly British-Irish Interparliamentary Body)	Pre-dated Agreement but enhanced by Agreement, Strand Three	Functioning
10. British-Irish Intergovernmental Conference	Agreement, Strand Three	Not meeting at political level (as of April 2018)
11. Northern Ireland Human Rights Commission	Agreement, Rights, Safeguards and Equality of Opportunity	Functioning

Body	Source	State of Play after January 2017
12. Equality Commission for Northern Ireland	Agreement, Rights, Safeguards and Equality of Opportunity	Functioning
13. Irish Human Rights and Equality Commission (formerly Human Rights Commission)	Agreement, Rights, Safeguards and Equality of Opportunity	Functioning
14. Joint Committee of the Irish Human Rights and Equality Commission and the Northern Ireland Human Rights Commission	Agreement, Rights, Safeguards and Equality of Opportunity	Functioning
15. Independent Commission for the Location of Victims' Remains	Bilateral agreement, 27 April 1999	Functioning
16. Commission for Victims and Survivors for Northern Ireland	St Andrews Agreement, Annex B	Functioning
17. North/South Ministerial Meetings on Criminal Justice Co-operation	Hillsborough Castle Agreement	Not functioning

Body	Source	State of Play after January 2017
18. Working Group on Criminal Justice Co-operation	Hillsborough Castle Agreement	Not stated
19. Commission on Flags, Identity, Culture and Tradition	Stormont House Agreement	Functioning but may not report prior to restoration of devolution
20. Oral History Archive	Stormont House Agreement	Not established
21. Historical Investigations Unit	Stormont House Agreement	Not established
22. Independent Commission on Information Retrieval	Stormont House Agreement	Not established
23. Implementation and Reconciliation Group	Stormont House Agreement	Not established
24. Joint Agency Task Force	A Fresh Start	Functioning
25. Independent Reporting Commission	A Fresh Start	Functioning

Thus, only around half of the bodies envisaged by the various agreements were actually operating as of April 2018 – and, of course, the most important ones are among the non-functional half. That is a disturbing situation, and indicative of a significant failure of the agreed arrangements.

Making Devolution Work

The fundamental implication of the Agreement is a commitment to make the Northern Irish institutions work through inclusive devolution, irrespective of ultimate constitutional choices. As the Declaration of Support states: 'We pledge that we will, in good faith, work to ensure the success of each and every one of the arrangements to be established under this agreement.'[1]

Not only that, but one can clearly make the case that a functioning Northern Ireland is a prerequisite for meaningful discussion of changed constitutional possibilities. SDLP Leader Colum Eastwood put it this way:

> Nationalism's sneaking regard for the idea of 'a failed political entity' ended with the signing of the Good Friday Agreement. Although many have been slow to grasp the significance of that new state of affairs, people should understand this to be a major departure for Northern Nationalism ...

> We are committed to creating a society with which the South would be happy to integrate. To do so we must accept the new reality of Nationalism. We now have a selfish and strategic interest in making Northern Ireland work.[2]

This point, that Northern Ireland has to be made to work before one can even meaningfully start putting any change in constitutional status on the horizon, was also noted by Prof. John Wilson Foster, from a unionist perspective:

> [T]he SDLP knows, which Sinn Féin either does not know, or knows but perversely ignores, that unless

Northern Ireland develops into a successful devolved government of the United Kingdom, there is no possibility of a united Ireland down the line.

Simply put, the second, should it come about, requires the first. It is no paradox. Only Northern Ireland's success can create the circumstances of persuasion. The idea that the fall of Northern Ireland, or a mechanism of imposed joint authority, or even the withholding of a wholehearted recognition of the devolved jurisdiction, advances the peaceful cause of a united Ireland seems to me a dangerous delusion.[3]

In another piece, he returned to the same theme; that the failure of Northern Ireland is also the failure of future constitutional accommodations:

Prophecy is magical thinking that Sinn Féin practise, the idea that a united Ireland is predestined and thus justifiably to be achieved by any means. It suffocates debate, makes every reform a staging post, and obstructs daily reality from flowing in the direction the stream of consciousness takes us, a direction that might well be towards closer unity on the island were Sinn Féin itself magically to disappear.

It also deliberately diverts energy away from the truer issues that affect us all – education, the economy, health, employment. Instead, human rights, an Irish Language Act, legal pursuit of security forces from the time of the Troubles, are the current issues of choice in the politics of prophecy and endgame.

After all, Sinn Féin is dedicated to the failure of Northern Ireland, a dedication implicit in their refusal to speak the name of the jurisdiction or take their seats in Westminster.[4]

The reference to the 'refusal to speak the name of the jurisdiction' is to the Sinn Féin refusal to use the expression 'Northern Ireland', with only very occasional exception.[5] Such linguistic rigidity is questionable if the aim is to open up new vistas for the future.

Preventing Future Deadlock

Some have seen the breakdown of devolution in 2017 as evidence of the failure of the Good Friday Agreement and have called for the 'last rites' to be performed. Certainly, the Agreement is not beyond criticism. Criticisms have tended to focus on two points: that it 'entrenches sectarianism' and that 'it doesn't work', in particular that there is no clear pathway forward when devolution breaks down. On the first point, it may be that a renewed focus on the inclusive spirit of the Agreement is required to ensure that all voices contribute constructively. On the second point, in the event of breakdown of the Strand One institutions, we return to London rule by virtue of UK sovereignty, with two major conditions: the Irish government having a right to put forward views and proposals through the British-Irish Intergovernmental Conference,[6] and the requirement of rigorous impartiality imposed on the UK government to uphold the rights of all traditions.

And, indeed, in the absence of devolved institutions, the Westminster parliament has had to legislate for Northern Ireland. Not only has it set a budget, but it has also legislated for rates and for the RHI cost-capping scheme up to March 2019. Such legislation 'makes necessary provisions in light of the continued absence of Assembly business, in order to protect and preserve public services and finances'.[7] As it is put in respect of a budget-related Bill, 'Without an Executive to agree a Budget and a sitting Assembly to pass Budget Bills, it falls to [the Westminster] Parliament to legislate to provide authority for expenditure in Northern Ireland.'[8]

On the basic principles of incentives, devolution is more or less guaranteed to collapse any time that either of the largest parties on either side decides that the benefits of deadlock (by way of hypothetical example, by extracting further concessions on one's agenda in the resultant crisis negotiations) outweigh the benefits of continuing in office. That is not a very stable arrangement on which to plan for the future, even if one were to get over any particular deadlock.

This basic difficulty in the Agreement has prompted pessimistic comment, particularly in the context of Brexit where the Agreement has been seen in some quarters as an obstacle. It has been described as 'failed'[9] and seen as an impediment to achieving clean British withdrawal from the EU. Questions that were canvassed and settled back in 1998 have been resuscitated, such as the suggestion that the Agreement was an appeasement of violence. Journalist Ian Jack outlined some of these interventions:

On 15 February [2018], the Irish historian Ruth Dudley Edwards wrote a Daily Telegraph article on the 13-month impasse at Stormont that concluded: 'Realists believe the [deal] has served its purpose and run its course, leaving behind the unintended consequence of enshrining sectarianism in the political process.'

The following day the Tory MP Owen Paterson, a former Northern Ireland secretary, tweeted a link to the piece with a comment:

'The collapse of power-sharing in Northern Ireland shows the Good Friday agreement has outlived its use'. Last Saturday the Tory MEP Daniel Hannan wrote, again in the Telegraph, that the agreement was 'often spoken about in quasi-religious terms ... but its flaws have become clearer over time'. Finally, two days later, the Labour MP Kate Hoey told the Huffington Post that she thought the agreement needed 'a cold, rational look', and that the power-sharing Northern Ireland executive it mandated was 'not sustainable in the long term'.[10]

As Ian Jack's comments illustrate, critics of the Brexiteer analysis of the Agreement are by no means confined to Ireland. The First Minister of Scotland Nicola Sturgeon referred to what she called 'the utterly despicable attitude and ignorance of the extreme Brexiteers towards Ireland and Northern Ireland'.[11] Former UUP official Alex Kane wrote in December 2017:

My view is that the Assembly should be closed and the last rites performed over Good Friday and St Andrews. It was worth exploring those particular avenues and opportunities; but it is time to switch off the life support. It's a brutal conclusion, I know: but sometimes it is easier to solve a problem by first acknowledging brutal realities; then abandoning all previous failed approaches; and, finally, beginning again from scratch. Unionism and republicanism can never be forced to reconcile. Let's stop pretending they can be.

Is there an alternative? Possibly. Leave it to the parties/people themselves. Let them organise their own negotiations and political vehicles (allow new parties to emerge, too) and produce their own deal – however long it takes. If they reach a deal then the two governments can provide the necessary legislation and funding. If not, then leave it to the governments to cut their own deal. The local parties have been pampered and indulged for far too long.[12]

He returned to the theme in a March 2018 article calling for Northern Ireland Secretary Karen Bradley to govern Northern Ireland until such time as the parties came up with an agreement themselves:

The official line from the British and Irish governments is that the Good Friday Agreement remains 'too big, too important, to fail'. The fact that the hopes it raised 20 years ago are now in history's hoover bag and that in political/electoral terms we're more polarised than ever, is neither here nor there. Better, it seems, to continue with the pretence that the rogue virus can be removed from the system and replaced with a spanky new Pollyanna download, than to face the fact that maybe, just maybe, the problems can't be fixed. Pretence, ambiguity and naked self-interest are the deadliest enemies of reality and political progress. Between 2004–2007 the DUP and Sinn Féin worked together to cut a deal that would cripple the UUP/ SDLP and secure their own roles as joint top dogs. They promised stability and consensus instead of the stop-start of 1998–2007. Well, in terms of politics and reconciliation, we're in a worse place than we were, with almost two-thirds of the electorate backing the DUP/SF. That's quite a mess.[13]

To avoid throwing out the proverbial baby with the bathwater, it is important to acknowledge, first, that the Agreement represents not only a unique collaboration across the political spectrum in Northern Ireland, but also a binding international agreement. Second, even a breakdown of the executive does not detract from the wide range of other commitments and agreements contained within the text. The whole cannot be jettisoned simply because one element is working imperfectly. Bearing those parameters in mind, can anything be done to deal with the inherent instability of the Agreement?

Economists would suggest that actors make decisions on the basis of incentives, and might suggest that to maximise the prospects of organised government in Northern Ireland there would have to be some form of disincentive for parties to bring down the institutions. While decisions on such matters are for the political system, one obvious starting point is the Work Plan agreed by the two governments in 2006 when this situation previously arose. The consequences of failure to form an executive by a date specified by the governments were to be as follows: 'Salaries and allowances for MLAs and financial assistance to parties stop. ... BIIGC [British Irish Intergovernmental Conference] at Prime Ministerial Summit level to launch new British Irish partnership arrangements.'[14]

There are of course other possible options – each has pros and cons depending on one's point of view, and any judgements must be left to the political process.

If agreement between the political parties in a breakdown situation cannot be reached, then perhaps the least controversial option, and an obligation in any event, would be to focus on those aspects of the Agreement that can be implemented independently of devolution. That was the response of the Irish government to the original suspension of the assembly in 2000. On that occasion, Taoiseach Bertie Ahern stated that: 'there is no reasonable alternative to the full implementation of the Good Friday Agreement and, pending the re-establishment of the institutions, we will continue to implement resolutely all the outstanding elements of it within our responsibility'.[15]

Rights and Identity Issues

The Vienna Convention on the Law of Treaties provides that: 'Every treaty in force is binding upon the parties to it and must be performed by them in good faith.'[16] This reflects customary international law in any event; indeed, 'There would be no international law without the principle.'[17] The relevant implication here is that even if one element of the Agreement cannot be implemented (due to, for example, a breakdown of devolution), the other remaining parts do not fall away, but require implementation insofar as that is within the power of the contracting states acting in good faith. In practical terms, insofar as concerns the rights and identity agenda, and insofar as the Agreement requires parity of esteem to be addressed, that is an obligation that must fall on the governments, and, in particular, the UK government, in the absence of devolution or even where devolved institutions are in place but fail to take the required steps. The Vienna Convention goes on to provide that 'A party may not invoke the provisions of its internal law as justification for its failure to perform a treaty.'[18] In short, if legislation to address rights issues is an obligation of a treaty, the fact that a devolved institution has failed to enact such legislation does not absolve the national parliament – in this case Westminster – of its duty to do so. Rights and identity issues are central to the difficulties that arose in 2017. But the Agreement is clear on the principle of parity of esteem and equal respect for the traditions. That commitment remains, whether or not the devolved institutions are functioning. Legacy inquests and measures for victims and survivors are also, in principle, capable of being progressed even in the absence of devolution.

The Agreement envisaged a possible Bill of Rights for Northern Ireland, which was to have been examined had the draft February 2018 agreement text been finalised. Indeed, the putting in place of strong rights protections, including a Bill of Rights for Northern Ireland, has been a feature of the political agenda before even the Good Friday Agreement.

Accommodating both identities also raises the question of day-to-day co-existence in Northern Ireland. That is a multi-sided question which includes everything from harassment and internet abuse (which affect both sides) to the ostentatious celebration of past paramilitarism (again affecting both sides). Some of the more egregious elements of sectarianism may be addressed by the Commission on Flags, Identity, Culture and Tradition. But any measures or dialogue that can reduce tensions in this regard are surely worth considering.

John Wilson Foster stressed the point of the need for unionism to accommodate the Irish identity:

> For its part, the UUP's constitutionalism should take the form of a sincere and inclusive recognition of non-unionist culture as far as compatibility with current unionism as a bedrock principle allows. That requires admitting, cheerfully, the legitimacy of the desire for a united Ireland while respectfully, but firmly, at this time, dissenting from its desirability. The UUP's constitutionalism of the actual could happily consort with the SDLP's constitutionalism of the possible. And between the actual and the possible is a vast potential for stability and development. What Alliance started can be given impetus by the UUP and SDLP.[19]

The point was made by a correspondent to the *News Letter*:

> the Union will only survive if the individuals and organisations that believe in it make this United Kingdom a truly inclusive place in which people from all backgrounds are able to achieve their full potential. In order for this to happen, compromise is essential, as the consequence of failing to truly represent the views of everyone in Northern Ireland will be the creation of an environment in which many people from traditionally nationalist communities, who may until recently have been willing to accept the status quo, are more likely to conclude that their goals can only be achieved in a united Ireland. Two obvious examples are Brexit and the Irish language.[20]

'Irish identity' can be a difficult thing to define – Christopher McGimpsey referred to the task of creating such a definition as being 'as simple as nailing jelly to a wall'.[21] The Agreement is based on an either/or, with nationalist vs. unionist playing across the weighted majority barricades, with those categorised as 'other' being located off to one side. But even since 1998, the blurring of identities has become even more pronounced. Considering the ways in which a Northern Irish, Irish or British identity could line up, at least seven options are possible, as shown below together with the percentages so affiliated according to the 2011 census.

Table 2. Possible Identities within Northern Ireland

	Northern Irish	British	Irish
Only	(1) Northern Irish only (20.9%)	(2) British only (39.9%)	(3) Irish only (25.3%)
+Northern Irish	N/a	(4) Northern Irish + British (6.2%)	(5) Northern Irish + Irish (1.1%)
+British	See 4	N/a	(6) British + Irish (0.7%)
+Irish	See 5	See 6	N/a
Northern Irish, British and Irish	(7) Northern Irish, British and Irish (1%)	See 7	See 7

Throw in 'other' (5 per cent), and more options could become available. Perhaps there are ways in which space can be found culturally for a more diverse range of options than those limited ones enumerated in 1998.

The Agreement presupposes that each tradition is entitled to pursue and express its own particular identity and culture on the basis of parity of esteem. Thus, measures to promote the Irish culture and language need to be balanced by measures acknowledging the British or Ulster Scots identity as appropriate. That was the principle behind the abortive February 2018 draft agreement.

The nationalist narrative of the background to the Irish language controversy, in the perhaps questionable version as told by journalist Siobhán Fenton, is that 'it was hardline unionists who first stoked tensions in the otherwise seldom discussed issue'. She cites the incident of Gregory Campbell MP, who upset delicate republican sensitivities in November 2014 by parodying mangled 'cúpla focal'-type pronunciations of 'go raibh maith agat, a Cheann Comhairle' as 'curry my yoghurt can coca coalyer'. Humour is, of course, somewhat subjective, and while some people will take offence, 'Campbell told RTÉ Raidió na Gaeltachta he couldn't see how what he said was offensive, adding that anyone who was insulted needed a "humour bypass" as it was just a joke. He said he was "not against those who use the language but those who abuse the language".'[22] (He later said that he would treat a proposed Irish Language Act 'as no more than toilet paper'.)[23]

Compounding the upset, according to Fenton, was a funding cut for an Irish language summer school and the renaming of a boat from Banríon Uladh, to 'Queen of Ulster'. Further nationalist offence was taken at Arlene Foster's comment that 'if you feed a crocodile it will keep coming back and looking for more'.[24] Fenton's response is that 'This comparison, which quite literally dehumanised

Irish language speakers and compared them to dangerous animals, only escalated tensions further.'[25]

Of course, the history of the matter goes back well before any such unionist interventions. The status of the Irish language has been a topic on the political agenda for many years. By contrast, the unionist narrative is one that sees the Irish language as having been used by Sinn Féin for political purposes. The DUP's Nelson McCausland sees the Irish language strategy in this way:

> [Republican activist] Feargal Mac Ionnrachtaigh has written about it in his book [Language, Resistance and Revival[26]] and Gerry Adams has also referred to it. It is a strategy based on the republican view that Northern Ireland is a colony that has to be decolonised and that this will be accomplished through culture. Gerry Adams made the same point when he said: 'The revival of the Irish language is a central aspect of the reconquest.' The strategy is to use the Irish language to Gaelicise Northern Ireland and thereby accomplish a 'cultural decolonisation'. For them that 'cultural reconquest' is the first step towards a 'political reconquest' and a united Ireland. If you don't believe me, you can read his book yourself.[27]

Other commentators consider, as it was put in a *Guardian* editorial, that 'The darker truth here is that Sinn Féin has chosen to weaponise the language question for political ends, less to protect a minority than to antagonise unionists.'[28] John Wilson Foster endorses that conclusion:

> Human rights and the Irish language are being used as Macbeth's enemies used Birnam Wood – to fulfil

prophecy by sophistry, advancing on the objective of a united Ireland behind the manipulation of social reality. Unionists are dismayed that the constitutional parties in the South seem to have fallen in behind Sinn Féin on these (with all due respect) fabricated issues.[29]

Unionist fears in relation to heightened status for Irish include, according to another *News Letter* correspondent, 'a gradual migration of Irish civil service staff to run positions in Northern Ireland and hollow out the Union ... and the discrimination and extreme division it would bring about. There would be language activists everywhere ... taking down English signs and putting up Irish ones instead illegally, as they do in the Republic.' Thus 'there can be little doubt as to the significance of forcing Irish down people's throats as a matter of social inclusion/exclusion'.[30]

John Wilson Foster describes the idea of Irish being 'co-equal with English in the courts, administration, commerce, education and place-naming of Northern Ireland' as 'a surreal demand'. He continues:

Talk of 'language rights of persons belonging to a national minority' has no sensible bearing on Northern Irish reality. The language activists try another tack. The Irish language 'is part of our shared heritage'. Of course our place-names and syntax are often Irish in origin and these are to be relished. The literature I study often has an Irish language dimension. But speaking Irish in daily life and in official transactions – no, that is not my heritage.

Again, the theme of Irish as a Trojan horse for the nationalist agenda is highlighted: 'since Irish is an all-Ireland affair, widespread official recognition on both sides of the border would surely encourage the questioning of the existence of that border'. [31]

Returning to the origins of the language controversy, an important background development was the ratification of the European Charter for Regional or Minority Languages by the UK in March 2001,[32] which specified Irish on the basis of an equivalent suite of rights similar to Scottish Gaelic and Welsh, and put Ulster Scots on a lower level equivalent to Scots, Cornish and Manx Gaelic. Measures taken under the Charter include administrative practices to recognise the right to use Irish in dealings with public bodies, although not the right to receive a reply in Irish. The St Andrews Agreement provides that:

> The British Government has also agreed to take forward a number of measures to build confidence in both communities and to pursue a shared future for Northern Ireland in which the culture, rights and aspirations of all are respected and valued, free from sectarianism, racism and intolerance. Details of all these issues are set out in Annex B.[33]

Annex B included the following commitments:

> The Government will introduce an Irish Language Act reflecting on the experience of Wales and Ireland and work with the incoming Executive to enhance and protect the development of the Irish language. The Government firmly believes in the need to enhance and develop the Ulster Scots language, heritage and culture and will support the incoming Executive in taking this forward.[34]

So, the governments agreed that there would be measures to develop both local languages, albeit in terms phrased to suggest that the Irish Language Act will be a stand-alone measure introduced in the Westminster parliament separate from any measures regarding Ulster Scots, which are not necessarily to be legislative. This suggested some degree of imbalance that might be thought not to be in keeping with the parity of esteem envisaged by the Good Friday Agreement, even bearing in mind the significantly greater use made of Irish in practice. What emerged was something less than what the St Andrews text envisaged – Westminster legislation providing for language strategies. The 2006 legislation implementing the St Andrews Agreement provided as follows in relation to the Northern Irish Executive (called the Executive Committee in the relevant UK legislation[35]):

> Strategies relating to Irish language and Ulster Scots language etc
>
> (1) The Executive Committee shall adopt a strategy setting out how it proposes to enhance and protect the development of the Irish language.
>
> (2) The Executive Committee shall adopt a strategy setting out how it proposes to enhance and develop the Ulster Scots language, heritage and culture.
>
> (3) The Executive Committee—
>
> (a) must keep under review each of the strategies; and
>
> (b) may from time to time adopt a new strategy or revise a strategy.[36]

Draft strategies were prepared but not adopted, leading to the Northern Irish High Court declaring there to have been a breach of this statutory obligation,[37] but without apparent effect. Furthermore, this has not been followed up with any specific language legislation, in the absence of agreement. The Irish Language Act originally envisaged was not necessarily guaranteed to replicate protections in the Irish and Welsh legislation, merely to reflect on the experiences of such legislation. What would that involve in practice? The main elements of the Official Languages Act 2003 in force in the South are as follows:

- a right for individuals to do business with the state in Irish;
- a duty on the state to use both languages on stationery and documents;
- a duty on the state to publish certain documents, such as reports, in both languages and furnish official information in Irish, including many publications, customer information and announcements, and signs;
- a requirement on public bodies to prepare schemes for services in Irish;
- provision for Irish only place names in the Gaeltacht and for orders specifying what the Irish version of specified place names is to be;
- provision for a Commissioner to enforce the Act.

In the Welsh context, 1993 UK legislation[38] provided for obligations to prepare schemes for the use of the Welsh language. This was developed by 2011 legislation passed by the Welsh National Assembly,[39] which summarises the position as follows:

1. (1) The Welsh language has official status in Wales.

(2) Without prejudice to the general principle of subsection (1), the official status of the Welsh language is given legal effect by the enactments about—

(a) duties on bodies to use the Welsh language, and the rights which arise from the enforceability of those duties, which enable Welsh speakers to use the language in dealings with those bodies (such as the provision of services by those bodies);

(b) the treatment of the Welsh language no less favourably than the English language;

(c) the validity of the use of the Welsh language;

(d) the promotion and facilitation of the use of the Welsh language;

(e) the freedom of persons wishing to use the Welsh language to do so with one another;

(f) the creation of the Welsh Language Commissioner; and

(g) other matters relating to the Welsh language.

(3) Those enactments include (but are not limited to) the enactments which—

(a) require the Welsh and English languages to be treated on the basis of equality in the conduct of the proceedings of the National Assembly for Wales;

(b) confer a right to speak the Welsh language in legal proceedings in Wales;

(c) give equal standing to the Welsh and English texts of—

(i) Measures and Acts of the National Assembly for Wales, and

(ii) subordinate legislation;

(d) impose a duty on the Welsh Ministers to adopt a strategy setting out how they propose to promote and facilitate the use of the Welsh language;

(e) create standards of conduct that relate to the use of the Welsh language, or the treatment of the Welsh language no less favourably than the English language, in connection with—

(i) delivering services,

(ii) making policy, and

(iii) exercising functions or conducting businesses and other undertakings;

(f) create standards of conduct in promoting and facilitating the use of the Welsh language;

(g) create standards of conduct for keeping records in connection with the Welsh language;

(h) impose a duty to comply with those standards of conduct that are created, and create remedies for failures to comply with them; and

(i) create the Welsh Language Commissioner with functions that include—

(i) promoting the use of the Welsh language,

(ii) facilitating the use of the Welsh language,

(iii) working towards ensuring that the Welsh language is treated no less favourably than the English language,

(iv) conducting inquiries into matters relating to the Commissioner's functions, and

(v) investigating interference with the freedom to use the Welsh language.

(4) This Measure does not affect the status of the English language in Wales.

Does the Agreement require such legislation in Northern Ireland? In the absence of agreement to the contrary, the spirit of parity of esteem would probably lean against a stand-alone Irish language Act and rather more in favour of an overarching language Act which provides for both traditions (or equivalently, an arrangement whereby two separate pieces of legislation were introduced simultaneously – as proposed in February 2018).

What should such legislation contain? Parity of esteem involves the right of the individual to interact with the state in a language of his or her choice. If one accepts that principle as flowing from the Agreement, one would also have to accept the knock-on effect of requiring public bodies to do business in each of the three languages, with a certain cost impact and with recruitment implications. One does not have to go the whole distance travelled by the Irish and Welsh systems in order to provide legal protection for the right to express one's culture, which must be equally valued by the Agreement.

One of the more egregious instances of legal compulsion to use English is in the legislation dating from 1737 that continues to require the use of English in courts in Northern Ireland.[40] A challenge to the Act as contrary to the Charter on Regional and Minority Languages and the ECHR was dismissed in 2010.[41] Reviewing this legislation seems a natural first port of call if one is to seek to acknowledge the equal legitimacy of the traditions.[42] Sinn Féin's Mairtín Ó Muilleoir was among those to publicly highlight the argument for repeal of the Act.[43] In February 2018, a draft agreement between Sinn Féin and the DUP, never finalised, would have involved a commitment to repeal the 1737 Act in the context of broader language legislation, subject to the rider that 'English will remain the working language of the courts. Irish and other languages will be facilitated when deemed necessary by the courts.'[44]

In terms of physical infrastructure, road signs, place names, street names and so forth, one could see the position as encompassing two broad options:

- A one-size-fits-all approach to public signage, with a single set of rules and exceptions across the six counties; or
- Allowing local variation in terms of what language will be used.

The one-size-fits-all approach could take a number of forms:

- English being used everywhere; public signage would be excluded from any language legislation. Even the ambitious 26-county legislation on official languages excludes traffic signage, no doubt for safety and comprehension reasons; because such signs need to be understood at speed. Theory presumably must take second place to safety in that context.
- English being used everywhere with some limited exceptions; thus, a default position of English public signage would exist, although some designated types of signage would be in all three languages throughout Northern Ireland without local variation.
- All three languages being used on public signage throughout Northern Ireland (apart from specified exceptions for safety and comprehension reasons, such as traffic signs) – no doubt the most tolerant and inclusive solution, but possibly complex in implementation.

The major disadvantage of allowing local variation is that it would provide a visible official symbol of community division on the ground. There could be two ways of doing this: either local authority area by local authority area or at some more micro level of individual communities. The more granular the local variation, the more acute would be the tribal signalling involved. On the other hand, wider areas that opted out of an English default would capture enclaves within such areas that might resent having additional languages 'imposed'. A hypothetical nationalist majority in Belfast, for example, that adopted a city-wide policy, would be thrusting it on a number of local areas that might take a different view. Ultimately, allowing variation in signage by local authorities could create something of an infrastructural re-partition of Northern Ireland, with visible Irish in the south-west, and English-only signs in the north-east. Whether this is a good thing or a bad thing is no doubt a question for political debate in terms of what the endgame of the language legislation is meant to be. The UUP's Robin Swann referred to this aspect, according to one report, as follows:

> Ulster Unionist leader Robin Swann says any new legislation on the Irish language would lead to further division in society in Northern Ireland.
>
> ...
>
> Mr Swann told his supporters that the party has no issue with those who cherish the Irish language.
>
> However, he insisted it is not scaremongering to be concerned about the impact of an Irish language act.
>
> He said that if one is passed, people would no longer be reliant on flags or painted kerbstones – instead they would know whose territory they were in by looking at the road signs.[45]

One way to limit the extent of community division involved would be to prohibit local authorities from requiring Irish-only signs (or, say, English and Ulster Scots only). If a local authority wished to opt out from a default of English only, the only other option available would be to use all three languages. An exclusion for traffic signs, where English would remain everywhere, might also limit the scope for divisiveness.

Deciding which of these options should apply is a matter for political judgement, but perhaps one might be allowed to venture one observation. Northern Ireland is already enough of a divided society and has enough physical and cultural barriers and place-markers not to make one immediately rush to seek more ghettoisation through official Gaeltachtaí, or indeed Ulster-Scots-signage-only areas (should that be demanded at some future point). An official Gaeltacht is not a threatening concept in the South – in the North it takes on a different dimension to some minds as a land grab and a territorial marker. As it was put by a *Guardian* editorial, 'Bilingual road signs, for instance, would take the issue into every street in Northern Ireland, with pointless provocative effect.'[46]

Finally, it should be remembered that the Constitution of Ireland does not itself afford linguistic equality – it provides not only that Irish is the first official language but that the Irish text of the Constitution takes precedence over the English text in cases of conflict (as does the Irish text of any statute enacted in both languages). If there is to be an attempt to introduce greater equality between languages in Northern Ireland perhaps it could usefully be co-ordinated with efforts to put English on an equal footing with Irish in the South, which was the recommendation of the Constitution Review Group.[47] It is perhaps only the disdain of unionism for making any comment as to affairs in the South (in order to reject the legitimacy of any reciprocal comment directed at itself) that would prevent a more joined-up approach being taken towards a greater equality of language status on an island-wide basis.

Chapter 6

Beyond Working the Institutions

Implementing the spirit and letter of the Agreement in all its aspects is not just a question of operating the devolved institutions. Apart from the specific commitments that are not dependent on there being a devolved government, the principle of respect for all of the sets of relationships has broader ramifications for the laws and practices across the islands of Britain and Ireland. This chapter considers areas where, in due course, the implementation of the Agreement could be pursued and broadened, especially after devolution is restarted.

Extending Devolution

The 1998 legislation providing for devolution sets out various areas on which Stormont is entitled to legislate ('transferred matters'), and other areas such as international relations which are confined to Westminster ('excepted matters'). There is an intermediate category called 'reserved matters'. These are 'issues where legislative authority generally rests with Westminster, but where the Northern Ireland Assembly can legislate with the consent of the Secretary of State'.[1]

Laws may be made in relation to reserved matters by the British government by way of Order in Council without primary legislation.[2] The Secretary of State may, by Order in Council, provide that a reserved matter shall become transferred so as to be within Stormont's competence (or vice versa).[3] While the arrangements for Stormont are situated within a wider set of arrangements for transferred matters to the other devolved legislatures in the UK, in Scotland and Wales, nonetheless there may be flexibilities to increase the scope of Stormont's powers assuming functioning devolution.

Into the longer term, the more that can be transferred to Stormont, the less significant would be any possible future transition of sovereignty in the event of a majority for a united Ireland, because the local devolved institutions could simply continue to deal with such matters without any major discontinuity and without new interference from Dublin.

A related question is the possibility of extending areas of North/South co-operation. In the Brexit context, there may be renewed practical arguments for extending such co-operation, and perhaps just as urgently there may be renewed arguments for a refocus on the practical benefits of intensified East/West co-operation, whether executive, legislative or even judicial, across a wide range of subjects, perhaps starting with the common travel area. In that context, Taoiseach Varadkar's April 2018 proposal for joint British-Irish cabinet meetings could have a valuable role.[4]

Developing the Agreement's Institutional Architecture

Another critical aspect to be considered is the widening and development of the Northern Ireland, North/South and East/West institutional architecture to strengthen all of the relevant relationships under the Agreement.

One might consider all of the sets of possible institutions in the form of a matrix with two axes: one being the different sets of relationships and the other consisting of the forms of institution required – legislative, executive, judicial, administrative and related to civic society. The matrix of relationships can be considered in tabular form.

Table 3. Institutional Architecture by Strand under the Good Friday Agreement and Subsequent Agreements

	Strand One Northern Ireland	Strand Two North/South	Strand Three East/West
Legislative	Assembly – statutory	North/South Inter-Parliamentary Association – non-treaty basis	British-Irish Parliamentary Assembly – non-treaty basis
Executive	Northern Ireland Executive – statutory	(1) North/South Ministerial Council – treaty basis (2) North/South Ministerial Meetings on Criminal Justice Co-operation – treaty basis (3) North/South Ministerial Meetings on Criminal Justice Co-operation – treaty basis	(1) British-Irish Inter-governmental Conference – treaty basis (2) British–Irish Council – treaty basis
Judicial	No new institutions, Pre-existing courts continue	None	None

	Strand One Northern Ireland	Strand Two North/South	Strand Three East/West
Administrative	Some new institutions relating to human rights, equality, victims, and identity – statutory	(1) North/South implementation bodies – treaty basis (2) Joint Committee bringing together North and South Human Rights Commissions – non-treaty basis (3) Joint Agency Task Force – non-treaty basis (4) Independent Reporting Commission – treaty basis (5) Independent Commission for the Location of Victims' Remains – treaty basis	None
Civic Society	Civic Forum – statutory but non-functioning Civic Advisory Panel – non-statutory	None	None

There is certainly scope to implement the full promise of the Agreement and, indeed, build on it towards new institutions. While pros and cons are a matter for the political system to evaluate, possibilities for consideration include the following:

- Developing the civic dimension of Northern Ireland beyond the minimal 6-member advisory panel currently proposed by reverting to a model closer to the more inclusive forum contained in the 1998 Agreement;
- Creating a civic forum in the South and a joint body bringing together civic society North and South, as envisaged by the Agreement;
- Building new East/West connections with a possible new East/West civic society forum;
- Developing an administrative arm to the British-Irish Council to allow the creation of East/West administrative bodies. Such a development could significantly change perceptions and would be a tangible acknowledgement of the wider British dimension within the British-Irish space;
- Strengthening executive co-operation between the two sovereign governments, with joint cabinet meetings and possible new shared executive agencies on key areas where joint action is to mutual benefit;
- To give further expression to the full set of relationships, including the East/West dimension, there would be the radical option of creating North/South and East/West judicial bodies to adjudicate (or provide opinions by way of preliminary reference) on the interpretation of the Strand Two and Three elements of the Agreement respectively;
- Consideration could be given to whether some of the non-statutory Strand One bodies could be strengthened by becoming statutory;
- Likewise, some of the non-treaty Strand Two or Three bodies could be strengthened by becoming treaty bodies;

- Possible further areas for North/South or East/West co-operation could be identified. For example, the 2003 Joint Declaration contemplated the possibility of a North/South justice-related implementation body.

Identifying these options is not to be taken as advocating them but, given the current deadlock, there may perhaps be benefits to widening the debate by teasing out future possibilities that have not yet been envisaged. One commentator indirectly highlighted the essentially reactive historical position of unionism in terms of its failure to make the case for extended East/West links:

The DUP and unionists are missing the opportunities to frame various narratives. I feel they should as a matter of urgency:

...

Seek more East–West institutions between the UK and Ireland and between Northern Ireland and Great Britain (i.e. a Scots language board between NI and Scotland).

[Seek a] paper on the current benefits of the Union specifically for Northern Ireland and a Westminster paper on the Union regarding the whole UK along with recommendations on how to enhance and strengthen the Union.[6]

As far as the courts are concerned, no additional structures were proposed by the Good Friday Agreement. An all-island court to deal with security matters had been a feature of previous proposals to deal with issues such as extradition,[7] but in the light of the changed security situation, and indeed developments in European law, the pressure for such a mechanism has reduced. However, the absence of North/South and East/West judicial bodies does pose some issues. Relevant legal questions relating to the agreements will be answered by the courts of two separate jurisdictions, with the possibility of different results. There may be an argument for a judicial mechanism to avoid this problem and as a visible expression of the broader sets of relationships that transcend state sovereignty in this area.[8] The establishment of such judicial bodies could, therefore, possibly be a matter for consideration, with East/West structures balancing for unionists the North/South structures that would express the all-island perspective for nationalists. However, much as the old Article 3 copper-fastened partition in its own way,[9] it would appear that the new Article 3 likewise could raise an issue about such cross-border judicial bodies. But it seems possible, at least, that, despite the issues involved, such a mechanism, if thought desirable, could be framed in a constitutional manner. The Independent Monitoring Commission, when it existed, had a role in determining whether there had been a breach of the pledge of office. However, it no longer exists to play this role.

There is also the question of extending the areas covered by the North/South bodies. To balance this exercise politically, there can be no absolute argument in principle against putting in place East/West administrative bodies where this would provide joint gains. Again, one could not rule out a constitutional issue in relation to such hypothetical bodies. Indeed, the All-Party Oireachtas Committee on the Constitution rejected a more general enabling clause for inter-state executive co-operation in 2003.[10] But some sense of realism must also be brought to bear; very many international treaties to which Ireland is a party allow for some measure of international administrative co-operation. Not all of these have an express constitutional basis. Again, it must, at least, be possible to devise a constitutional method to enhance any such co-operation, should the governments be able to identify areas where East/West bodies could provide benefits. Nor should constitutional adjustment to reflect the most inclusive possible approach to wider relationships be regarded as unthinkable should that ultimately fall for consideration.

Some flexibility must be allowed for. The Good Friday Agreement itself envisages possible amendment to the British-Irish Agreement in the event of 'difficulties ... which require remedial action across the range of institutions, or otherwise require amendment'.[11] While the Irish Constitution[12] allows the state to ratify the British-Irish Agreement, that does not automatically need to be read to preclude possible further bilateral development or amendment of that agreement within its objectives.

Developing Wider Sets of Relationships

Tánaiste and Minister for Foreign Affairs and Trade Simon Coveney said, in January 2018: 'The genius of the agreement is that it provides a framework for all of the relationships on our two islands – between communities in Northern Ireland, between north and south on the island of Ireland, and across the Irish Sea.'[13]

The strands of relationships identified by the Agreement are as follows:

- Strand One relates to relationships within Northern Ireland.
- Strand Two relates to the relationship between North and South and matters relating to the whole island.
- Strand Three relates to the overall relationships within the two islands and their individual jurisdictions.

But one can look more broadly to other strands of relationships within the islands not specifically enumerated in the Agreement, although covered by it to some extent. One could call these Strands Four to Seven:

- Strand Four would relate to matters within the twenty-six counties.
- Strand Five would relate to matters within the island of Great Britain.
- Strand Six would relate to matters within the UK as a whole and the relationship between Northern Ireland and Great Britain.
- Strand Seven could describe the relationship between the twenty-six counties and the island of Britain, separately from Northern Ireland.

Simplistically, one might suggest that Strand Four is a matter for Ireland alone and Five and Six for the UK alone, and Seven for the two governments. But that would possibly be to miss the point that the lesson of inclusion, pluralism and equal respect for the traditions has relevance even for these relationships. And, indeed, one can look to a wider set of strands of relationships involving the relationship within Europe, which was perhaps taken for granted up to the Brexit vote. Constitutional provisions and legislation within these various contexts, particularly the internal Irish context, are touched on by the Agreement, but one can make a case for broadening the debate further.

A Possible Constitution for Northern Ireland

Reflecting on making Northern Ireland work, which is meant to be a shared objective from all sides of the equation, one possibility for more medium-term consideration would be the adoption of a Constitution for Northern Ireland. In terms of UK constitutional practice, this would be done by ordinary legislation that either set out a formal constitution in a schedule (as was done in 1922 for the Free State constitution) or alternatively set out constitutional provisions in a series of substantive sections, in line with normal legislative drafting. The benefits of a constitutional statute could include the following:

- It would be a huge visible commitment to the stability of Northern Ireland.
- It could strengthen the sense of local identity, place and community in Northern Ireland and could be a small step away from the binary either/or of British or Irish identities that has contributed to conflict.
- It would create visibility as to the high level constitutional commitments of Northern Ireland to parity of esteem and protections for all.
- It could, depending on how it was managed, provide an opportunity for wider agreement on improving elements of the constitutional architecture and making them more inclusive.
- Simply in legal, educational and practical terms, it would be beneficial to have all of the principal

constitutional law of Northern Ireland brought together in a single document.

- Looking to the long term, such a constitution could provide significant stability in the event of a change in the constitutional status of Northern Ireland, because it could be continued in force as a regional constitution within the overall context of a new island-wide arrangement.

There are, presumably, downsides also – for example, the traditional British suspicion of overarching, supra-legal constitutions, and the difficulty of agreeing such a document. Legalistic objections would no doubt be made but there is nothing in British constitutional law that would stop the Westminster parliament from putting in place a Northern Ireland Constitution Act – indeed an Act with that title and objective was previously passed in 1973.[14]

That could raise the question of how such a constitution would be put in place. Here there are, perhaps, three possible broad options:

- A top-down approach – the UK government would take the lead and produce a technical text simply drawing together existing statute law of a constitutional nature, enacting this as a form of consolidation Act subject to any consensus change that arose through consultations.
- A bottom-up approach – a constitutional convention could prepare a document consistent with the Agreement and submit such a document to the UK government and parliament for enactment, subject to there being sufficient cross-community agreement.

- Or the Westminster parliament could enact the technical consolidation as an interim constitution to be followed by a constitutional convention to endeavour to produce a wider, agreed text.

A sense of local identity, place and community in Northern Ireland does not, in itself, have to in any way diminish either the British or Irish identities. Just to take one example, a Northern Irish regional flag on an agreed, inclusive basis, would not take away from the status of any national flag. Lord Kilclooney's view in the context of the Haass talks was: 'It should now be possible to design a regional flag, not to replace the Union Flag, which is acceptable to both communities in Northern Ireland and flown at all local authority buildings irrespective of which party controls these councils.'[15]

A final possibility worth mentioning is that either as an exercise worth doing in its own right for legal reasons, as a step towards modernising and promoting reconciliation, or as a prelude to more ambitious consolidation, Northern Ireland could consider putting in place a statute law revision programme to review the statute book, along the lines of that which has operated in the South, and which produced legislation reviewing all primary Acts prior to independence.[16] That might involve reactivating the Northern Ireland Law Commission or establishing an alternative structure. It would be an opportunity for Northern Ireland to come to terms with its legislative past and to mark a new and modern beginning.

Promoting Inclusiveness on the British Side

The lesson of the Agreement is the requirement for parity of esteem and accommodating all identities. In that regard, questions need to be posed about a number of blatantly anti-Catholic pieces of legislation still on the Westminster Statute Book. These occur within what this work has referred to as the Strands Five and Six contexts – issues that arise within Britain, or within the UK as a whole. The following are particularly notable.

The Coronation Oath Act 1688[17] embodies an oath to uphold Protestantism in the following form:

Arch Bishop or Bishop.

Will You to the utmost of Your power Maintaine the Laws of God the true Profession of the Gospell and the Protestant Reformed Religion Established by Law? And will You Preserve unto the Bishops and Clergy of this Realme and to the Churches committed to their Charge all such Rights and Priviledges as by Law doe or shall appertaine unto them or any of them.

King and Queene.

All this I Promise to doe.[18]

The Bill of Rights 1688[19] goes further in a specifically anti-Catholic direction. It lists among its complaints against King James that he had caused 'severall good Subjects being Protestants to be disarmed at the same time when Papists were both Armed and Imployed contrary to Law' and it goes on to enact 'That the Subjects which are Protestants may have Arms for their Defence suitable to their Conditions and as allowed by Law'. It sets out a specifically anti-Catholic oath of supremacy in the following terms:

Supremacy.

I A B doe sweare That I doe from my Heart Abhorr, Detest and Abjure as Impious and Hereticall this damnable Doctrine and Position That Princes Excommunicated or Deprived by the Pope or any Authority of the See of Rome may be deposed or murdered by their Subjects or any other whatsoever. And I doe declare That noe Forreigne Prince Person Prelate, State or Potentate hath or ought to have any Jurisdiction Power Superiority Preeminence or Authoritie Ecclesiasticall or Spirituall within this Realme Soe helpe me God.

The Act goes on to provide that:

all and every person and persons that is are or shall be reconciled to or shall hold Communion with the See or Church of Rome or shall professe the Popish Religion ... shall be excluded and be for ever uncapeable to inherit possesse or enjoy the Crowne and Government of this Realme and Ireland and the Dominions thereunto belonging or any part of the same or to have use or exercise any Regall Power Authoritie or Jurisdiction within the same And in all and every such Case or Cases the People of these Realmes shall be and are hereby absolved of their Allegiance And the said Crowne and Government shall from time to time descend to and be enjoyed by such person or persons being Protestants as should have inherited and enjoyed the same in case the said person or persons soe reconciled holding Communion or Professing ... as aforesaid were naturally dead And that every King and Queene of this Realme who at any time hereafter shall come to and succeede in the Imperiall Crowne of this Kingdome shall on the first day of the meeting of the first Parlyament next after his or her comeing to the Crowne sitting in his or her Throne in the House of Peeres in the presence of the Lords and Commons therein assembled or at his or her Coronation before such person or persons who shall administer the Coronation Oath to him or her at the time of his or her takeing the said Oath (which shall first happen) make subscribe and audibly repeate the Declaration mentioned in the Statute made in the thirtyeth yeare of the Raigne of King Charles the Second Entituled An Act for the more effectuall Preserveing the Kings Person and Government by disableing Papists from sitting in either House of Parlyament.

The 1688 Act was amended in 2013 to remove the disqualification for 'marrying a papist'[20] but the disqualification for *being* a 'papist' remains. As it is put in the official Explanatory Notes to the Act, 'There is no comparable statutory provision about any other religion. The prohibition on the Sovereign being a Roman Catholic is not changed by the Act.'[21]

Similar and more forceful legislation was passed in Scotland as the Claim of Right Act 1689 (what we are calling here a Strand Five issue, operating within Britain only rather than the wider UK), which begins inauspiciously that:

Wheras King James the Seventh Being a profest papist did assume the Regall power and acted as King without ever takeing the oath required by law wherby the King at his access to the government is obliged to swear To maintain the protestant religion and to rule the people according to the laudable lawes.

It goes on to complain:

By takeing the children of Protestant Noblemen and gentlemen sending and keeping them abroad to be bred papists makeing great fonds and dotationes to popish schooles and Colledges abroad bestowing pensiones upon preists and perverting protestants from ther Religion by offers of places preferments and pensiones

...

By Dissarmeing protestants while at the same tyme he Imployed papists in the places of greatest trust civil and military such as Chancellor Secretaries Privie Counsellors and Lords of Sessione thrusting out protestants to make roome for papists and Intrusting the forts and magazins of the Kingdome in ther hands

...

By Subverting the right of the Royal Burghs The third Estate of Parliament imposeing upon them not only magistrats But also the wholl toune Councill and Clerks contrary to their liberties and express chartours without the pretence either of sentence surrender or consent so that the Commissioners to Parliaments being chosen by the magistrats and Councill The King might in effect alswell nominat that entire Estate of Parliament and many of the saids magistrats put in by him were avowed papists and the Burghes were forced to pay money for the letters Imposeing these illegall magistrats and Councils upon them.

The Act legislates accordingly, although the following rather wide-ranging provision still appears not to have been repealed: 'That by the law of this Kingdome no papist can be King or Queen of this realme nor bear any office whatsomever therin nor can any protestant successor exercise the regall power untill he or she swear the Coronation Oath.'

It seems remarkable that legislation providing that Catholics may 'not bear any office whatsoever' in the Kingdom remains unrepealed on the statute book. The Confession of Faith Ratification Act 1690,[22] another Act of the Scottish parliament, recites:

> by ane Article of the Claime of Right It is declared that prelacie and the superiority of any office in the Church above presbyters Is and hath been a great and insupportable greivance and trouble to this Nation and contrary to the inclination of the generality of the people ever since the reformation they haveing reformed from popery by Presbiters and therefore ought to be abolished Lykeas by ane Act of the last Session of this Parliament Prelacie is abolished Therefore Their Majesties with advyce and consent of the saids three Estates Doe hereby revive ratifie and perpetually confirme all lawes statutes and acts of Parliament made against popery and papists and for the maintenance and preservation of the true reformed protestant religion and for the true Church of Christ within this kingdom In swa far as they confirme the same or are made in favours thereof.

Chapter XXIV, 'Of Marriage and Divorce', para. 3, goes on to enact:

IT is lawfull for all sorts of people to marry who are able with judgement to give their consent yet it is the duty of Christians to marry only in the Lord and therefore such as profess the true reformed religion should not marry with infidels papists or other idolaters neither should such as are godly be unequally yoked by marrying with such as are notoriously wicked in their life or maintain damnable heresies.

The Crown Recognition Act (Ireland) 1692[23] includes the following preambular text:

whereas our soveraign liege lord and lady, and delivered by K. William and Q. Mary at great expence of blood and treasure, and hazard of the King s person from miseries of civil war and rebellion raised by Irish papists, and abetted by the French King, King William and Queen Mary, since their happy accession to the crown of England, with great expence of blood and treasure, and the extream hazard of his Majesties royal person, have delivered this their kingdom from the miseries and calamities of an intestine war, and most horrid rebellion, raised up amongst us by the Irish papists, and instigated, abetted and supported by the power of the French King; thereby securing us against the danger of popery and arbitrary power, with which we were threatned in a most eminent manner, and have most happily reduced this their kingdom to a state of peace and order, and restored to us our laws and liberties, and the free and impartial administration of justice.

The Act of Settlement 1700[24] recites the text of the anti-Catholic provisions of the Bill of Rights 1688. It confines the throne to Protestants but also makes a specifically anti-Catholic provision:

> Provided always and it is hereby enacted That all and every Person and Persons who shall or may take or inherit the said Crown by vertue of the Limitation of this present Act and is are or shall be reconciled to or shall hold Communion with the See or Church of Rome or shall profess the Popish Religion ... shall be subject to such Incapacities as in such Case or Cases are by the said recited Act provided enacted and established.[25]

The Treason Act (Ireland) 1703,[26] an Act of the Irish parliament, provides in its preambular paragraph:

> Forasmuchas the future security of your Majesty's protestant subjects of this kingdom doth (next under God) depend upon the safety of your Majesty's royal person (whom God long preserve to reign over us) and upon the succession in the protestant line, as the same is limited by an act of Parliament passed in England, intituled, 'The Bill of Rights'; and by one other act made in England in the twelfth year of the reign of his late Majesty King William the third of blessed memory, intituled, 'The Act of Settlement'; by which it is enacted, 'That the imperial crown and government of the kingdoms of England, France, and Ireland, and of the dominions thereunto belonging, with the royal state and dignity of the said realms, and all honours, styles, titles, regalities, prerogatives, powers, jurisdictions and authorities to the same belonging and appertaining, should, after the deceases of his said Majesty, and of her then royal highness the princess Anne of Denmark

(our now most gracious sovereign lady Queen Anne) without issue of her body, and for default of issue of her said Majesty and of his said Majesty respectively, be, remain, and continue to the most excellent princess Sophia electoress and dutchess dowager of Hanover, daughter of the most excellent princess Elizabeth, late Queen of Bohemia, daughter of our late sovereign lord King James the first of happy memory, and the heirs of her body, being protestants:' and forasmuch as it most manifestly appears that the papists of this kingdom, and other disaffected persons, do still entertain hopes of disappointing the said succession, as the same stands limited.

The Union with Scotland Act 1706 (an Act of the English parliament)[27] provides:

that all Papists and persons marrying Papists [note that the marriage clause is inoperative although not formally repealed] shall be excluded from and for ever incapable to inherit possess or enjoy the Imperial Crown of Great Britain and the Dominions thereunto belonging or any part thereof and in every such Case the Crown and Government shall from time to time descend to and be enjoyed by such person being a Protestant as should have inherited and enjoyed the same in case such Papist or person marrying a Papist was naturally dead.[28]

The Union with England Act 1707[29] (in force in Scotland) makes identical provision.[30]

The Scottish Episcopalians Act 1711[31] (in force in Great Britain), provides:

Provided likewise That neither this Act nor any Clause Article or Thing herein contained shall extend or be construed to extend to give any Ease Benefit or Advantage to any Papist or Popish Recusant whatsoever or to any Person that shall deny in his preaching or writing the Doctrine of the blessed Trinity.[32]

The Roman Catholic Relief Act 1829[33] provided for abolition of much discrimination against Catholics, but the following provision remains in force:

Offices witheld from Roman Catholics.

Provided also, that nothing herein contained shall extend, or be construed to extend to enable any person or persons professing the Roman Catholic religion to hold or exercise the office of guardians and justices of the United Kingdom, or of regent of the United Kingdom, under whatever name, style, or title such office may be constituted; nor to enable any person, otherwise than as he is now by law enabled, to hold or enjoy the office of lord high chancellor, lord keeper or lord commissioner of the great seal of Great Britain ... ; or his Majesty's high commissioner to the general assembly of the Church of Scotland.[34]

While this probably has little relevance, it remains on the statue book. Other exceptions are:

Not to extend to offices, &c. in the established church, or ecclesiastical courts, universities, colleges, or schools; nor to presentations to benefices.

Provided also, that nothing in this Act contained shall be construed to enable any persons, otherwise than as they are now by law enabled, to hold, enjoy, or exercise any office, place, or dignity, of, in, or belonging to the Church of England, or the Church of Scotland, or any place or office whatever of, in, or belonging to any of the ecclesiastical courts of judicature of England and Ireland respectively, or any court of appeal from or review of the sentences of such courts, or of, in, or belonging to the commissary court of Edinburgh, or of, in, or belonging to any cathedral or collegiate or ecclesiastical establishment or foundation: ... ; or to repeal, abrogate, or in manner to interfere with any local statute, ordinance, or rule, which is or shall be established by competent authority within any university, college, hall, or school, by which Roman Catholics shall be prevented from being admitted thereto, or from residing or taking degrees therein: Provided also, that nothing herein contained shall extend or be construed to extend to enable any person, otherwise than as he is now by law enabled, to exercise any right of presentation to any ecclesiastical benefice whatsoever; or to repeal, vary, or alter in any manner the laws now in force in respect to the right of presentation to any ecclesiastical benefice.[35]

...

No Roman Catholic to advise the Crown in the appointment to offices in the established church.

It shall not be lawful for any person professing the Roman Catholic religion directly or indirectly to advise his Majesty, or any person or persons holding or exercising the office of guardians of the United Kingdom, or of regent of the United Kingdom, under whatever name, style, or title such office may be constituted, or the lord lieutenant of Ireland, touching or concerning the appointment to or disposal of any office or preferment in the Church of England, or in the Church of Scotland; and if any such person shall offend in the premises he shall, being thereof convicted by due course of law, be deemed guilty of a high misdemeanor, and disabled for ever from holding any office, civil or military, under the Crown.[36]

A modest start to reviewing discriminatory legislation was the 2011 agreement between the UK and its fifteen relevant Commonwealth partners to scrap the ban on royal marriage to Catholics. That agreement paved the way for the 2013 UK legislation. The background is outlined in the Explanatory Notes to that legislation:

The Prime Minster announced at the Commonwealth Heads of Government Meeting in Perth on 28 October 2011 that, with the agreement of the fifteen other Commonwealth Realms of which Her Majesty is also Head of State, the United Kingdom would change the rules of royal succession to end the system of male preference primogeniture and the bar on those who marry Roman Catholics from succeeding to the Throne.[37]

The repeal of the ban on royals marrying Catholics and the draft agreement of February 2018 to repeal the 1737 language legislation are perhaps small, encouraging signs that some of the discriminatory legislation of the past that remains on the statue book can be revisited. However, in the case of the anti-Catholic legislation discussed above, this would have to be addressed by the UK parliament (or possibly the Scottish parliament in the case of the two regional Acts) rather than Stormont. It is certainly open to the nationalist parties or the Irish government or both to seek from the British government the introduction of legislation at an early stage for the repeal of these measures. Such a step would build confidence in the process and ensure that momentum was maintained in pursuing the right to equality of treatment. The repeal of discriminatory legislation would also put down a marker that equality of treatment is of benefit to all and would also reinforce the message that, likewise, the unionist minority would not be discriminated against in the event of a hypothetical united Ireland. Many countries have a state religion or give a head of state a role in that regard, so even leaving to one side the question of changing the position of the Crown as head of the Church of England, or the status of the Church of England as the established church, further progress could still be made in removing the more egregious elements of discrimination at this stage. And keeping a state religion or having the crown as the head of that religion does not require such provisions to be phrased in a specifically anti-Catholic way. A positive expression of Protestantism does not have to be expressly negative about Catholicism any more than the opposite. Admittedly, even this sort of modest rephrasing might have to require the agreement of all countries that have the Crown as head of state (as was the case for the 2013 repeal), but that in itself is not a reason not to tackle the issue.

If at a future point, the requirement that the monarch him or herself no longer had to be a protestant, the precedent of the Lord Chancellor (Tenure of Office and Discharge of Ecclesiastical Functions) Act 1974[38] could be followed, which declares that the Lord Chancellor may be a Catholic, and if so his or her ecclesiastical functions are to be performed by the Prime Minister or another minister.[39]

In addition, some other provisions of UK law are contrary to either the letter or spirit of the Agreement. For example, the Acts of Union of 1800 are out of step with the Agreement insofar as they recite that the UK and [Northern] Ireland are united 'for ever'.[40] Clearly this should be amended to reflect the fact that the union lasts only so long as the self-determination of the Irish people North and South so decides.

Representation of Northern Ireland in Irish Political Institutions

Colum Eastwood has made the point that the Southern state has not yet fully taken on board its role of engagement with the six counties:

> The second step on this journey involves civic and political life in the 26 counties. In the South, an evolution of thought and action must take hold. The bedding down of the institutions at Stormont should not have been the beginning of a leave of absence for the South's civic and political involvement in the North. This betrays the spirit and logic of 1998. The historic reconciliation of the Anglo-Irish conflict, through the signings of our political agreements, marked perhaps the greatest political change to the 1937 constitution. In building a post-crash Ireland, the South should understand and re-engage with its responsibilities and

its attachment to the North of the country. The South is a fundamental part of who we are but, equally, we are a fundamental part of who they are too. That spirit can't just express itself on All-Ireland Sunday in Croke Park. It needs to be broader and more extensive than that. That cultural and community attachment cannot be allowed to drift as we build for political unity across the island.[41]

Enhancing the all-island political identity, within the confines of the Agreement, has focused on a number of major areas:

(a) votes for Irish citizens in Northern Ireland in presidential elections;
(b) votes for Irish citizens in Northern Ireland in reformed Seanad elections;
(c) speaking rights for Northern Irish public representatives in the Oireachtas; and
(d) representation of Northern Ireland in the Dáil.

We can consider each of these in turn. But, first of all, there is a threshold question as to whether such political representation accords with and enhances the Agreement or contradicts it.

Sinn Féin has been open about their agenda to extend political representation to Northern Ireland. Matt Carthy MEP said in 2018:

Sinn Féin is campaigning for the Oireachtas to introduce automatic Dáil membership for MPs from the North and, pending this, to immediately introduce speaking and consultative rights for Northern MPs and Assembly members in the Dáil and Seanad. We have also demanded that the Government initiate the promised referendum on Presidential voting rights for citizens in the North and the Irish diaspora.[42]

Many countries, the UK included, afford their own citizens voting rights, even where such voters live outside the jurisdiction. Sometimes these rights are limited to persons who were previously registered to vote from a home constituency and have emigrated within a specified period of time. Sometimes they are more liberally granted – for example, in the UK, emigrants can vote in parliamentary and (for the time being) European elections for up to fifteen years after leaving the UK as long as they are otherwise eligible to vote and were registered to vote in a UK constituency within the previous fifteen years.[43] So, in principle, it is not unthinkable for the state to offer such rights to Irish citizens, whether in Northern Ireland or more generally – although one can certainly see an argument that a more liberal voting entitlement in Northern Ireland as compared with Irish citizens elsewhere could raise questions as to equality between citizens.

Speaking rights in committees appear to be a relatively uncontroversial measure, although of limited effectiveness since, at present, the only MPs or MEPs from a nationalist or 'other' perspective are from Sinn Féin, which is represented anyway in both Houses. Speaking rights in the Dáil chamber for Northern Irish representatives (at least when dealing with Northern Irish matters) could potentially change the character of proceedings, although there are clearly pros and cons depending, for example, on which representatives are to be included in such rights. Rights for MPs would not significantly enhance the biodiversity of debate. Rights for MLAs would, however, open up a wider suite of views, which could enhance the quality of debate and understanding and could contribute to a greater sense of reality in engagement with Northern Ireland. Speaking rights as such are not an assertion of sovereignty in contradiction to the Agreement's clear position that Northern Ireland is part of the UK. Such rights could possibly be less threatening if some form of reciprocity could be worked out to give a wider suite of nationalist opinion speaking entitlements in Westminster also. For example, the Northern Ireland Affairs Committee of the House of Commons, which consists of thirteen MPs,[44] could consider measures to allow a hearing to other parties, even those not represented at Westminster.

Actual representation of Northern Irish constituencies in the Dáil, as has been mooted by Sinn Féin, is contrary to UK sovereignty over Northern Ireland as copper-fastened (for the time being and subject to possible future consent to the contrary) by the Agreement. To advance such an arrangement in advance of consent to Irish unity is not in accordance with the Agreement.

Votes in Presidential Elections

The concept of allowing Irish citizens outside the twenty-six counties to vote in presidential elections was a Sinn Féin agenda item for some time and received a considerable boost with a positive recommendation from the report of the Constitutional Convention in November 2013, proposing that citizens outside the State, including in Northern Ireland, should be allowed to vote in elections for President.[45] The government announced its acceptance of this idea on St Patrick's Day, 2017.[46] As of June 2017, the format envisaged was leaning towards allowing such a vote to Irish passport holders as opposed to emigrants only.[47] The government has announced an indicative date of June 2019 for the proposed referendum.[48]

Votes in Seanad Elections

Another demand has been for an election system for the Seanad that would include representation for Northern Ireland. In October 1922, the leader of the Labour Party Tom Johnson proposed that when the Senate was being established, steps should be taken to provide that organisations representing 'the northern parts of Ireland' would be included. He suggested, for example, the Trades Councils of Belfast or Derry.[49] And indeed the Seanad, as originally operated, did seek to include significant representation of the unionist community, at least from the South. However, that positive tradition of diversity has long since been superseded although, intermittently, individual nominated Senators are chosen from the Northern Ireland milieu in a personal rather than a representative capacity. This has been operated on a cross-community basis whereby individuals such as Gordon Wilson, Maurice Hayes, Edward Haughey, Sam McAughtry, Bríd Rodgers and Seamus Mallon have been nominated for membership of the Upper House.

In view of the flexibility of the constitutional provisions in the Seanad, it may be possible to arrange Seanad representation of Irish citizens outside the state without further constitutional amendment.[50] The government established a working group on Seanad reform in December 2014.[51] The group reported in 2015 and recommended that the Seanad be elected on a one person,

180 Beyond the Border

one vote system, which would extend the franchise to Irish passport holders abroad and to Irish citizens in Northern Ireland. If this proposal involves a differentiation between the franchise for citizens in Northern Ireland and those elsewhere, it certainly could raise questions about equality before the law as between citizens, and by enfranchising citizens in Northern Ireland on a more generous basis than citizens abroad more generally, possibly raises sensitivities and issues that could be seen as less than accepting of the clear position under the Agreement that Northern Ireland is currently part of the UK.

Taoiseach Leo Varadkar accepted the thrust of this element of the proposal when speaking to the Seanad in February 2018, saying: 'I believe we should look to elect senators from Northern Ireland – from both nationalist and unionist communities – so that the Seanad has an all-island dimension and provides different voices on issues which concern us all.'[52] He proposed a new committee to examine the matter further and report within eight months.

Speaking Rights in the Oireachtas

The question of representation of politicians from the Northern Irish political parties in the Oireachtas has been considered by the All-Party Oireachtas Committee on the Constitution which, in 2002, recommended a cautious approach to the subject.[53] A number of options were discussed in their report, including both the possibility of an unlimited right of audience for Northern representatives, as well as a more limited option for a right of audience for particular debates.

The issue of giving Northern MPs speaking rights in the Dáil emerged again in August 2005 when Gerry Adams,

President of Sinn Féin, claimed that the Taoiseach Bertie Ahern had already 'given a commitment that MPs elected in the six counties will be able to speak in the Dáil'.[54] The Taoiseach's position in reply was that all that was involved was a 'proposal', which was 'ultimately a matter for the Oireachtas', and which 'would not involve speaking rights or privileges in the Dáil, but rather facilitate committee discussions with Northern MPs on matters relating to Northern Ireland and the Good Friday Agreement'.[55] Sinn Féin subsequently sought to square the circle by suggesting that what had been envisaged was that the Dáil Committee would meet in plenary session in the Dáil Chamber, with speaking arrangements for Northern MPs in that setting.[56] However, to date such arrangements have not found favour on a cross-party basis and have not been progressed.

Under current Dáil standing orders,[57] MEPs elected from Northern Irish constituencies may be given attendance and speaking rights at meetings of departmental select and joint committees. MPs elected to Westminster from Northern Irish constituencies are now invited to attend the Joint Oireachtas Committee on Implementation of the Good Friday Agreement.[58]

Thus far, more radical measures have not been put in place. Sinn Féin has called for a range of further steps to involve the six counties electorally in the structures of the state, including speaking rights for Northern Irish MPs on the floor of the Dáil, rather than simply in the Good Friday Agreement committee.

The All-Party Committee on the Constitution reported in 2002 as follows on this issue:

The committee acknowledges that the immediate emphasis of the Sinn Féin submission, in particular, is on the possibility that Northern Ireland Westminster MPs might have a limited right of audience within the Dáil. This would not require a constitutional amendment, and might technically be effected through the Dáil periodically forming itself into a Committee of the Whole House for the purposes of selected debates, most obviously for instance on Northern Ireland matters and on the operation of the Good Friday Agreement. The frequency and organisation of such debates could easily be altered – as no constitutional amendment is required – over time, in the light of experience.

We accept that any addition to the Dáil of participants, even if temporary and non-voting, other than those elected from constituencies within this state, could be held to be inconsistent with the thrust of our approach. We also accept that any participation in the Dáil by Northern representatives might potentially run the risk of opening up basic constitutional issues settled in the Good Friday Agreement. However, we think that in this case those risks are relatively mild and should be kept in perspective. The expertise and experience upon which Northern MPs could draw could certainly enhance the quality of certain important Dáil debates. Such an initiative would be strongly welcomed by certain Northern representatives and their supporters, and would address the continuing desire of many nationalists for further concrete expression of their Irish identity and their membership of the wider national family. The Dáil could consider taking the necessary procedural steps to allow MPs elected for Northern Ireland constituencies to speak in periodic debates on Northern Ireland matters and on the operation of the Good Friday Agreement. The committee is of the view that any such participation should take place on a cross-community basis with parity of esteem for the different communities in Northern Ireland.

An alternative which is worth considering is that ministers in the Northern Ireland Executive, and perhaps also members of the Assembly, might be invited instead of or as well as Westminster MPs. However, on reflection this is a more problematic option. The numbers involved might be much greater, which would cause practical difficulties. More particularly, drawing upon those serving in institutions established by the Agreement, and especially ministers, might be held more directly to cut across the balance within the Agreement, and lines of accountability and reporting, above all in relation to the North/South institutions. For that reason we would prefer the involvement of MPs from Westminster, which is also a sister sovereign legislature.[59]

In the aftermath of the 2017 Westminster election, Sinn Féin MPs attended Leinster House requesting such representation. According to one report:

Cavan-Monaghan TD Caoimhghín Ó Caoláin said the provision of speaking rights on the floor of the Dáil was recommended by an Oireachtas committee as far back as 2003 [*sic* – in fact it was 2002]. However, despite extensive discussions with the Taoiseach of the day, Bertie Ahern, MPs were only given access to the Oireachtas Committee on the Good Friday Agreement ... He insisted that allowing MPs access in relevant debates on the floor of the Dáil 'would be a critical first step'.[60]

One might of course ask, a first step to what? The obvious answer is to actual representation of Northern Ireland in the Dáil. But that objective would have to wait until after Irish unity, if that happens. There certainly would be a vivid argument that an arrangement whereby the parliamentary institutions of the state are extended to Northern Ireland could be seen as cutting across the architecture of the Good Friday Agreement. On the other hand, that must be balanced against the need to recognise all sets of relationships, and particularly give recognition to the Irishness of Northern nationalists.

One option which has not as yet been considered is the question of extending the speaking arrangements to also include the East/West dimension, to include mutual attendance rights between a relevant committee of the two sovereign parliaments. Even the Northern Irish speaking rights are limited to MPs and not MLAs or members of the House of Lords, so there is perhaps room for a more inclusive form of arrangement to allow a wider diversity of voices to be heard.

On the other hand, there must be few parliaments in the world that would open their doors on an open-ended basis to persons who are not members of the parliament. The Ulster Unionist Party strongly rejected the proposal for speaking rights in the Dáil, describing it as 'an embryonic all-Ireland Parliament' and said that 'if it is pursued by Dublin we will no longer be obligated to our support for North/South institutions'.[61] The British Conservative Party also warned against the creation of 'a thirty-two county Dáil in shadow form' which would 'undermine the principle of consent'. Such a move 'is very unhelpful in terms of fostering genuinely good relations within Northern Ireland'.[62]

Writing in 2005, commentator Jim Duffy summarised the advantages for Sinn Féin of speaking rights for Northern MPs:

Having Sinn Féin MPs in Leinster House would achieve the key symbolism of turning Dáil Éireann from what they used to call 'the Free State Parliament' into a *de facto*, even if not actually *de jure*, all-Ireland Dáil. It would also benefit Sinn Féin electorally.[63]

He suggested that the existing Sinn Féin TDs were under-performing as the public face of the party, but 'send the big guns of Gerry Adams MP, Martin McGuinness MP and others into Leinster House and their Oireachtas Parliamentary Party would jump from division three to premier division overnight'. That particular point may have less force now. It is no reflection on the energy of Northern MPs but they are not necessarily all household names in the Southern part of the island.

Ongoing speaking rights were to be distinguished from existing arrangements for guest speakers, which are 'once-off occasions, not the continuous right to participate that Sinn Féin is seeking'. Likewise, the proposed arrangements were to be distinguished from the longstanding practice of nominating Northern figures to the Seanad, because 'nominees have an explicit constitutional status'. This echoes a point floated (rather than developed) in the Report of the All-Party Oireachtas Committee on the Constitution, namely that an open-ended right to attend the Oireachtas might be in conflict with the Constitution. Duffy also pointed out that Sinn Féin MPs would take up time that would no longer be available to elected TDs, would absorb office and secretarial facilities, would be involved in advocating the spending of resources of the state to which they did not contribute, and would not have to vacate their 'seat' at a Dáil general election. Insofar as they occupied safe seats under the Westminster system, they would effectively be there for life. In Duffy's analysis, the proposal was in breach not only of the constitutional parameters but also the spirit of the Agreement.

On balance, it is hard to conclude that a standing right of audience in a special committee of the Dáil for a class of individuals who are not members of the Dáil would be unconstitutional. Standing Orders of each House at present give a continuing right of audience to Ministers of State who are members of the other House[64] and, perhaps more significantly, the Government, by executive decision, has made arrangements for Ministers of State, including the Chief Whip and super-juniors, to have a right of audience at cabinet meetings despite not being members of the Government. Even the Attorney General's right to attend cabinet is not of constitutional origin.[65] Unless such arrangements are also unconstitutional, it is hard to see how the 'thicker end of the wedge' that would be represented by a right of audience for 6-county parliamentarians would be unconstitutional. Rather, such rights would appear to be a legitimate decision of the body concerned to organise its own affairs as it sees fit and benefiting from a presumption of constitutionality, especially as it refers to the indoor management of the body itself and does not infringe the rights of any third party.[66] Whether such an arrangement would be politically appropriate – even acknowledging that it is probably constitutional – is, of course, a matter for political rather than legal decision.

Dáil Representation

Affirmative representation of Northern Ireland in the Dáil has been mooted by Sinn Féin on occasion but that argument has been rejected by the All-Party Oireachtas Committee on the Constitution in 2002 for a number of reasons, which remain, to some extent, valid insofar at least as the constitutional point is concerned:

> The committee does not favour the direct election of Northern Ireland representatives to the Dáil, or the participation as full members of those elected for Westminster constituencies. It believes, first, that this would be at odds with the function of the Dáil as the primary gathering-place of the representatives of the people of this state, who are bound by the laws enacted by the Oireachtas and who are served by a government drawn primarily from the Dáil and accountable to it. Those citizens resident in Northern Ireland are not affected to anything like the same degree by the actions of the Dáil as are those within the state: and indeed would continue to operate under laws enacted at Westminster or in the Assembly.

> Secondly, the committee fears that the inclusion on equal terms of Northern representatives in the Dáil could be interpreted as a refusal on our part to accept the implications of the careful balance on constitutional issues achieved in the Good Friday Agreement. This would damage the prospect of durable cross-community support for the Agreement, and put at risk the enormous gains made in the Agreement. If the highest current national priority in relation to Northern

Ireland remains the successful implementation and operation of the Agreement, as we believe it should, then it would be imprudent to contemplate such a step.

Thirdly, the committee believes that a constitutional amendment would be required to confer an unlimited right of audience on any person who is not elected to Dáil Éireann.[67]

An alternative approach would be to allow votes for Irish citizens abroad but only if they previously lived in a particular constituency in the twenty-six counties, by analogy with the UK legislation. But a wider approach involving 'reserved constituencies' for citizens abroad was envisaged by an Oireachtas committee report in November 2014.[68]

Also related is the question of whether Irish citizens in Northern Ireland should be entitled to vote in, for example, referenda. Before his appointment to the Supreme Court, Donal O'Donnell SC suggested that it is 'difficult … to explain in a satisfactory and constitutional way' why such persons should be omitted from political participation.[69] On the other hand, the objections to Northern Irish representation in the Dáil seem equally valid as against extension of voting rights in referenda, if not more so. The All-Party Committee on the Constitution rejected the Sinn Féin submission to allow extended voting rights in referenda in its 2002 report.[70]

Chapter 7

Removing the Obstacles to Uniting the Peoples of the Island

John Hume frequently commented that the task of the peace process was to unite people rather than territory.[1] And it is true that the new Article 3.1 of the Irish Constitution speaks literally of seeking 'to unite all the people who share the territory of the island of Ireland'. However, it must be said that the people are, in turn, defined by reference to the territory, and the application of law in Article 3.1 by reference to 'area and extent' makes it clear that unity involves a territorial extension of the state as well as uniting hearts and minds. It might, therefore, be more precise to say that the new Articles 2 and 3 seek to unite both the peoples of these islands and, ultimately, the territory of the island of Ireland itself. In this chapter, we will examine legal aspects of the efforts to build confidence between the two communities and unite the peoples who share these islands, as well as preparing for unity in ways compatible with, albeit not strictly required by, the Good Friday Agreement.

Article 3.1 of the Irish Constitution, as envisaged by the Agreement itself, specifies the will 'in harmony and friendship, to unite all the people who share the territory of the island of Ireland, in all the diversity of their identities and traditions'. It is not a question of unity at any cost and in any circumstances, but rather by promoting harmony and friendship and recognising diversity. So, what are the obstacles to such harmony and friendship, and in what way are the equal diversities of traditions not being accommodated?

Parity of Esteem South of the Border

If Northern Ireland and the wider UK are falling short, to some extent, of the Agreement's aspiration for parity of esteem between the traditions, that is considerably more true of the twenty-six counties. Having been allowed to develop in isolation from the six counties and having, for a long period, presented a relatively mono-cultural and stiflingly Catholic/nationalist front, with a history of seeking to shake off British rule, the twenty-six counties have seen little need to redefine their presuppositions to take on board the British identity. Despite the aspiration to inclusiveness, the Good Friday Agreement seems to have done little in practice to change that mindset. There are several possible schools of thought regarding the failure of the Irish state to seriously afford recognition to the British identity.

- First there are 'comfortable Southerners' – those at home with the insular traditional narrative of the twenty-six counties who see no reason for cultural change, whether by way of a united Ireland or otherwise.

- A second category are the 'pluralistic sceptics' – those who perhaps see the need for a more inclusive recognition of the British identity in the South but see no need for, or benefit in, a united Ireland, at least at the moment.
- Then there are 'unreconstructed republicans' – those equally comfortable with Southern culture, who expect a united Ireland on essentially nationalist terms without any seismic change in cultural orientations, at least in the Southern part of the island. This sort of 'four green fields' Irish unity is certainly incompatible with the Agreement.
- Then we have the 'accommodation but not yet' school of thought – those who recognise the need for a greater recognition of the British identity but see that as being something to be traded and negotiated at the time when unity is up for discussion, much as Articles 2 and 3 of the Constitution, though widely seen as problematic, were left in their original form until the Good Friday Agreement.
- Finally, there are those who support 'accommodation now' – who recognise that the Irish state falls well short of acknowledging both identities and who would seek to rectify that well in advance of any concrete discussion about Irish unity.

The first two categories are basically opposed to a united Ireland. The third category seeks a green version of unity that is simply ruled out by the Agreement's commitment to parity of esteem.

That leaves two possible options, depending on one's view of the balance between principle, politics and pragmatism – to put the South's house in order now, or to wait until one is around the hypothetical negotiating table. The major problem with the 'wait and see' approach is that the Agreement specifically commits the Irish side to taking further steps to accommodate the British identity.

A number of points can perhaps be made without wishing to comment on matters for political judgement. The first is that practice in the South has been that a fairly detailed set of implementing proposals is prepared to accompany a referendum, in order to ensure that the people know what they will be getting. This began in earnest with the publication of a draft Divorce Bill accompanying the 15th amendment in 1995 and has continued on a number of occasions since. With a situation as fraught, complex and uncertain as Irish unity, some clear form of 'offering' for any border poll is essential. That offering would need to be as inclusive as possible and involve as much consensus as possible. So, the clarification of what constitutional, legal, policy and cultural changes would be put in place could not meaningfully be postponed until after the border poll. Fairly detailed work would have to be done, at least by the proponents of a yes vote in such a poll, on what unity would look like. In a 2016 academic article, Conor Donohue comments:

> the changes to the constitution necessary to enable the continuation of the Northern Ireland government will need to be made either at the time of the self-determination referendum, or beforehand. To do so beforehand is preferable, as it means the terms on which the Northern Irish people would be accepted into a united Ireland would be made fully known to them. This is in keeping with the state's obligation to

ensure that voters are fully informed of the implication of the referendum results.[2]

Journalist Pat McArt poses the critical question:

So how can we begin a process of creating the conditions that would assuage unionism's fears about unity on the island of Ireland? How far are we willing to reach out to the 900,000 people who would regard themselves as both unionist and British? And, perhaps, most importantly of all, the question has to be asked, are modern day republicans up to the task of making major concessions in the pursuit of real unity?[3]

SDLP leader Colum Eastwood also stressed the need for clarification of what would be involved:

Most importantly, building a New Ireland means putting flesh on the bones of the idea. Rhetoric will not tear down the border. It won't even put a dent in it. Our people, unionist, nationalist and the many who now don't subscribe to either of these categorisations, have to be given a much fuller and firmer idea of what is meant and imagined within the context of a New Ireland. Unionism needs to understand how it will be welcomed into it. How their identity, their culture, their political representation will be respected and retained in a reunified state. They need to feel reassurance that they'll feel, and be made to feel, a sense of belonging. But what is too often forgotten is that Northern Nationalism also needs reassurance as to what the structures of a New Ireland will look like.[4]

The need for an 'offering' in relation to Irish unity to be set out was stressed by Raymond McCartney, Sinn Féin MLA:

> Republicans believe that Irish unity, on the basis of equality, offers the best future for all the people of this island. Therefore it is our responsibility to spell out to unionists what sort of agreed Ireland we seek and to reassure the unionist people of their place in an Ireland of equals. Whilst we demand the entitlement to promote and to persuade for our vision of a United Ireland, we are also open to engage with unionism on their vision for the future. We're willing to listen to unionism about why they believe the union is the best option.[5]

Matt Carthy, Sinn Féin MEP, went further to contend that the responsibility for setting out such an offering was broader than one upon republicanism: 'those of us who advocate for reunification need to come together to discuss the practical issue of how we win such a referendum'.[6] That follows if one accepts as a starting point the proposition that there should be an offering which sets out precisely what would happen in the event of a yes vote. Delivering on such an offering is a broad responsibility and not that of just one player; hence the broadest agreement would have to be achieved.

The alternative case, that it seems premature to discuss the detail of unity now, was adverted to by Micheál Martin in February 2018.[7] From that perspective, it is too early to start talking about 'winning' a border poll before one has removed the obstacles to both reconciliation and to Irish unity more broadly.

The first and primary obstacle, as we saw in previous sections, relates to the difficulties in ensuring that Northern Ireland works as a functioning political entity. Any road to a united Ireland in harmony and friendship runs through a fully functioning Northern Ireland at peace with itself. The politics of grievance and the idea of the North as a failed political entity that can be allowed to fester to advance ulterior ends are simply not compatible with the approach mandated by the Agreement.

Secondly and relatedly, any route to Irish unity also runs through the full implementation of the Agreement, both for the benefits of that Agreement in itself and in the service of the principle of parity of esteem, which benefits both sides of the equation.

A further major obstacle relates to the failure of the South to take on board the British identity and to orient itself towards a genuinely all-island mindset. The political process on the island is meant to be about uniting peoples rather than territory. One has to create a state, a culture and a milieu worth uniting with. One also has to bear in mind that promises are cheap and that actions speak louder. The sincerity of seeking to accommodate the British identity for its own sake now speaks a lot louder than loose, if not, to some, chilling promises about 'cherishing' unionists someday down the road after the tricolour is raised over Stormont. In this sense, only if and when one has removed those obstacles can one seriously start talking about detailed planning for what happens next.

Making Northern Ireland work is worth doing in itself, whatever one's persuasion. And, of course, all the changes in the world to the laws and customs of the South will not remove the unionist objection. But such changes could remove a great deal of the force and angst surrounding that objection and could significantly reduce the temperature of the debate going forward.

In 2018, Matt Carthy, MEP of Sinn Féin, acknowledged the need to protect the British identity in a new Ireland, commenting:

> The type of united Ireland that we put forward must be one that is agreed, inclusive, pluralist and which is constructed by all our citizens, from all backgrounds and traditions ... In any referendum campaign, those advocating a united Ireland must demonstrate an understanding that we have different traditions on this island. That there are people on this island who consider themselves British. We must emphasize that the British identity can and will be accommodated in an agreed, united Ireland. This may involve constitutional and political safeguards and we must be open, flexible and imaginative in that discussion.

The emphasis in this approach is on the 'accommodation but not yet' approach. Republicans will 'emphasise' the accommodation of the British identity, but that seems to mean from a position of strength once a nationalist majority is in sight – there is no suggestion of any practical steps that might be taken to accommodate that identity above and beyond the verbal. He went on to say:

> We are also seeking the establishment by the Oireachtas of a national forum to bring together all parties and key sectors representative of civic society on the island

to consult together on the constitutional and political future, including the issue of Irish unity and national reconciliation. It is time now for the Irish Government to encourage and lead an informed, reasoned and respectful public dialogue on the issue of Irish unity. It is also time that the Government prepared a realistic plan for Irish reunification, including the establishment of an Oireachtas all-party group to bring forward a Green Paper for Irish reunification.[8]

Again, one has to raise the question of how the details of Irish unity can be considered before one has first addressed the removal of the obstacles to such a discussion in the first place.

The Oireachtas Committee on the Implementation of the Good Friday Agreement made a number of recommendations on this issue in August 2017, principally:

- The establishment of a New Ireland Forum 2 is recommended, to set a pathway to achieve the peaceful reunification of Ireland;
- [To e]stablish an international task force with experts in security so that plans to meet any risks may be devised and implemented;
- [That the f]ears and concerns of the Unionist community need to be examined, understood and addressed comprehensively by all stakeholders in advance of any referendum.[9]

The context of the discussion about pathways to unity has changed significantly over the past decade. From one point of view, the focus should be, in the first instance, on removing obstacles to reconciliation and removing the obstacles to uniting the peoples of the island. From that perspective, the question of whether the South should examine its own arrangements to see to what extent the British identity is accommodated is timely and very much in accord with the spirit of the parity of esteem envisaged by the Agreement, and could, perhaps, be legitimately progressed by a New Ireland Forum type body to take up the uncompleted work of the previous New Ireland Forum.

As must be recognised, however, there can be little hope that the unionist objection can be 'addressed comprehensively'. Just as nationalists have the right to be nationalists, unionists can and will be unionists, and are entitled to their scepticism. John Wilson Foster comments:

> On the constitutional issue, Sinn Féin does not 'do' dialogue, or conversation. That might, after all, expose the cracks through which the light gets in, to borrow Leonard Cohen. Better dogma than debate. Instead, the inevitability of Irish unity is magical thinking, like poor Hamlet's belief that thinking doth make it so ... But the predestined nature of a sovereign, 32-county Irish republic was born with the party. The Easter 1916 proclamation was intended to short-circuit the tedium of reform, persuasion, compromise and consent and cut to history's chase.[10]

When Taoiseach Garret FitzGerald proposed his 'constitutional crusade' in September 1981, a major factor in Fianna Fáil's rejection of this idea was the concept that changes such as those proposed by FitzGerald should not be considered until the unionists were 'around the negotiating table'.[11] One recalls the long debate about the form of

Articles 2 and 3 of the Constitution, where some voices argued for unilateral change; others for pausing change until such time as there was a prospect of comprehensive political and constitutional agreement between the two governments and the Northern Irish parties. Possibly the 1998 outcome could provide support for the latter approach, but who knows how the counterfactual former approach might have softened tensions during the Troubles period. Also, the theory that the amendment of Articles 2 and 3 was, in the end, balanced by important corresponding measures from the British government does not hold very much water because the corresponding measure, the repeal of the Westminster jurisdiction clause in the Government of Ireland Act 1920, was legally meaningless as the clause was immediately replicated in new language in the Agreement itself and in the 1998 implementing legislation. UK sovereignty in Ireland derives not from the Government of Ireland Act but from the Acts of Union of 1800, which remain in force in Northern Ireland as they have done for two centuries.

As against that, it is arguable that in order to marshal a majority in favour of unity, there must be clarity about what unity would involve – and therefore a case for legislating for inclusion in advance to make clear that only the most inclusive form of unity will be proposed. One approach in the unity context might be to leave over any reforms that would need to be revisited following a decision to change the constitutional status of Northern Ireland, such as a new national flag or anthem (in that respect, Sinn Féin leader Mary Lou McDonald suggested in March 2018 'that nothing was off the table when discussing what a new Ireland would look like, even the flag'[12]), but to consider addressing legal or constitutional change at this stage where a case for improvement on the merits in any event presented itself.

Creating Additional Protections for Unionism Post-Unity

Going beyond the letter of the Agreement, the SDLP proposed corresponding protections for unionism to those currently in existence for nationalism:

> East/West cooperation would continue. In particular, just as the Irish Government has a say in the North now, the British Government would have a say in the North in a United Ireland.

> Just as there is northern representation in the Seanad at present, those in the North who want it should have representation in the House of Lords in a united Ireland.[13]

The arguments in favour of such protections were trenchantly made: 'unity must not be about the entrapment of a new minority ... in a united Ireland we will still need to find a way of sharing our society as equals every bit as much as we do today'. Such additional provisions for British involvement might well require specific constitutional amendment.

Constitutional Change to Accommodate a Devolved Executive

It is clear that the form of united Ireland envisaged by the Good Friday Agreement is one that would involve the continued existence of the Northern Ireland executive. The absence of any provision for a devolved executive in the Constitution would need to be rectified to provide for such an eventuality. This would involve the extension of the existing terms of Article 15, which provides for devolved legislatures, to also cover devolved executive authority.

The 1937 Constitution as drafted had no difficulty in envisaging the future reunification of the island, making appropriate provision for that eventuality – in particular by allowing recognition of subordinate parliaments and by allowing membership of the Commonwealth. Given the change in circumstances brought about by the Good Friday Agreement, this provision could, at an appropriate time, be updated so as to be capable of operating in the event of the Good Friday Agreement's provision for reunification being put into effect.

Constitutional Rights for Those with a British Identity

An issue with the existing text of the Irish Constitution is that, in general, it expressly gives rights only to citizens of Ireland. The courts have bridged the gap by implying certain rights for non-citizens, but this generally does not cover political rights.

During the history of partition, there has been a persistent misconception – the now deprecated assumption on which the 1937 Constitution was originally framed – that all of the people living on the island of Ireland, including unionists, are fundamentally Irish. This view has even included the proposition that unionists would only be entitled to remain in a united Ireland if they opted for Irish citizenship,[14] the alternative to which would be 'returning' to the UK. Such a view cannot now survive the recognition of the two traditions enshrined in the Good Friday Agreement. Aside from the Northern Irish context, there may also be a wider human rights case for expressly recognising the inherent rights of non-Irish citizens within the state.[15]

The Good Friday Agreement envisages that the right of all of the people of Northern Ireland to Irish or British citizenship or both would be preserved even after a united Ireland.[16] In essence, there is a central contradiction in the Constitution as it now stands. Having been initially adopted on the now discredited theory that the island consists of one nation, it must now serve an island that after the 1998 amendment expressly contains at least two. The absolute equivalence in the Constitution between the people it serves and the Irish nation can no longer hold, but the contradictory concepts continue to sit uneasily side by side in the current text.

If Irish unity were to be achieved under the text as it currently stands, there would be a very substantial number of people who reside within the new state (the hypothetical 32-county united Ireland) who would not, in fact, be citizens of that state but would rather be British citizens, maintaining their right to assert their British identity as guaranteed by the Good Friday Agreement itself. It would be ludicrous in that situation if the right to engage in important aspects of state activity would be confined only to Irish citizens – for example, the right to vote in referenda or presidential elections. Similarly, it would be unacceptable to maintain the position that the human rights guaranteed by the Constitution itself are expressly conferred only on Irish citizens, as are almost all of the rights set out in Articles 40, 44 and 45.

Indeed, more broadly, the language of restriction of human rights guaranteed by the Constitution to Irish citizens is dubious from the point of view of Ireland's compliance with international human rights norms, given that the international human rights instruments to which Ireland is a party require the state to secure rights to 'everyone' within its jurisdiction,[17] not simply to citizens. This has been redressed to some extent by some decisions of the courts,[18] although these have not been entirely consistent, and at statutory level by legislation to incorporate the European Convention on Human Rights.[19]

Before the 2004 referendum on citizenship, Prof. William Binchy pointed out[20] what he saw as the negative consequences of depriving persons born in Ireland of citizenship in terms of the knock-on effect of depriving them of express constitutional rights. This contention gave rise to an amendment proposed to the Bill[21] so as to guarantee the extension of constitutional rights to other persons in the state, not just to Irish citizens. This amendment was ruled out of order by Rory O'Hanlon TD, the Ceann Comhairle, and consequently could not be discussed.

It is hard to avoid the conclusion that the failure of the Constitution to confer virtually any express rights on any non-Irish citizens is simply incompatible with the Agreement's provisions giving an entitlement to any member of the people of Northern Ireland to regard themselves as British. Such a person, when in Ireland, enjoys no express constitutional rights – although, of course, the courts have stepped in with implied rights in some but by no means all areas. The basic problem is, of course, that the theory on which the Constitution was drafted is contradicted by the 1998 Agreement, but that contradiction has not been resolved and the two sets of language lie side by side in the one text.

However, the problem becomes more acute when one turns to the question of political rights. Can it be said that preventing those in the twenty-six counties who have a British identity from voting in presidential elections or referenda is consistent with the principles of parity of esteem and equal respect for the traditions?

One attempt in this regard was the Bill[22] to confer voting rights on British citizens, which was introduced by Garret FitzGerald's government in the mid-1980s and subsequently held to be unconstitutional.[23] Significant progress towards recognising the rights of British citizens in the state was made with the inclusion of a new Article 16.1.2° of the Constitution,[24] which permitted not only all citizens but, in addition, 'such other persons in the state as may be determined by law' to have the right to vote at an election for members of Dáil Éireann. Pursuant to this provision, legislation[25] was enacted permitting British citizens to vote in Dáil elections.[26] Under the constitutional amendment, this is confined to Dáil elections and does not apply to referenda or presidential elections, even though the original Bill had been more ambitious.

There is a case for revisiting this aspect as an initial means of giving recognition to the British identity within Ireland. Certainly, following a united Ireland, a provision preventing the best part of a million British citizens on the island of Ireland from voting in referenda or presidential elections would be untenable, so it is at least reasonable to consider whether to make provision for such an entitlement at this stage, as well as extending the category of persons entitled to sit in parliament. Given the role of the President as first citizen and representative of the state internationally, one can see a counter argument to the concept that the President of Ireland could be a non-Irish citizen, but even that difficulty would no longer apply after unity since the commitment to rigorous impartiality would preclude any prohibition on participation in any political office by British citizens. Even in advance of any hypothetical unity, the same objection carries less force in the context of membership of the Houses of the Oireachtas.

Based on that view, the existing constitutional restriction on voting rights seems hard to reconcile with the provisions of the Agreement. And, in any event, a case can be made in the interests of promoting reconciliation and allowing recognition for the British dimension of the Irish community and cultural experience for making provision, by way of an enabling provision, for the extension of the franchise. Any constitutional amendment to extend the franchise for presidential elections and referenda could be modelled on the provision which enables British citizens to vote for the Dáil. The constitutional right would be conferred on Irish citizens, with provisions being made for such other persons in the state as may be prescribed by law to exercise the franchise.[27]

Having regard to the Agreement's recognition of the equivalence of both traditions, one can make a case that the current arrangement does not comply with the spirit or language of 1998. For example, it means that a unionist could not take up a seat in the Seanad at the moment without asserting Irish citizenship in the process. That seems impossible to reconcile with the notion of parity of esteem between the traditions.

One minor feature of the constitutional landscape is the provision for Seanad representation for third-level institutions, at present confined to the NUI and Dublin University. It has been pointed out that this would have to cover Northern universities in the event of unity, but the matter has been superseded now by the power given to adjust Seanad representation by legislation.[28]

A New Constitution for Ireland

While the 1937 Constitution is capable, with some amendment, of dealing with the thirty-two counties, the unionist minority on the island of Ireland feels no attachment to that document. Indeed, even the nationalist community of Northern Ireland had no part in the formulation of the Constitution, notwithstanding that it purports to have been adopted by the 'people of Éire'.

There would, therefore, be a strong case for a revision of the Constitution – if not a new text altogether – on an agreed and cross-community basis in the context of a united Ireland. However, it is hard to envisage that the negotiations on such a new constitutional text could take place until such time as reunification was actually in prospect, as there would be no particular incentive for the unionist minority to engage with the issue prior to that point.

However, there would appear to be a tangible value in making clear that the Constitution in its entirety would be on the table for renegotiation in the event of a united Ireland. This is not to say that, for example, major human rights provisions would be scheduled for omission from a new Constitution, but rather that, subject to Ireland's international obligations, the negotiations on a new

Constitution could effectively start with a blank piece of paper and with full openness to the views and proposals to be put forward from the unionist side.

Nor does it mean that the Constitution is immune from review prior to hypothetical Irish unity. As stated in the rights section of the Agreement: 'the Irish Government will: ... continue to take further active steps to demonstrate its respect for the different traditions in the island of Ireland.'[29]

It is hard to see how such respect could be sincere and meaningful if it excludes examination of constitutional provisions. It is to that matter that we now turn.

Denominationalism and Symbolism in the Constitution of Ireland

Prefiguring the 1998 Agreement, the 1993 Downing Street Declaration includes the commitment that:

> In recognition of the fears of the unionist community ... the Taoiseach will examine with his colleagues any elements in the democratic life and organisation of the Irish State that can be represented to the Irish Government in the course of political dialogue as a real and substantial threat to their way of life and ethos, or that can be represented as not being fully consistent with a modern democratic and pluralist society, and undertakes to examine any possible ways of removing such obstacles. Such an examination would of course have due regard to the desire to preserve those inherited values that are largely shared throughout the island or that belong to the cultural and historical roots of the people of the island in all their diversity.[30]

The original form of this commitment is less than absolute in that it allows for the expression of majoritarian values – either for that reason alone or because unionism fails to engage in the 'course of political dialogue' that is a precondition for change. However, these qualifications were dropped in the 1998 Agreement, which simply commits the Irish government to demonstrate its respect for the different traditions on the island.

But if one asks what precisely has been done to implement this commitment in the Downing Street Declaration, it is difficult to identify much in the way of tangible progress, beyond perhaps the inclusive nature of some of the centenary commemorations. This may perhaps be justified on the very basis that the Declaration is phrased in terms of matters brought to the attention of the Irish government 'in the course of political dialogue', a dialogue which has not been engaged in by unionism in any organised way, perhaps for understandable reasons from their particular point of view.

This topic was considered by the Forum for Peace and Reconciliation, which established a sub-committee on obstacles to reconciliation but never produced a final report.[31] A draft report was, however, prepared[32] but never formally published. The draft Forum report dealt with a number of topics including constitutional change, symbolism, education, health, anti-discrimination and the acknowledgment of the British-Irish dimension. A clear division of opinion emerged in the Forum draft report. The minutes of a plenary debate on 24 February 1995 indicate, for example, the view of one protagonist regarding changes in symbolism: 'Bertie Ahern (FF) ... saw no great public demand for change ... while ready to discuss different symbols for a new Ireland, he saw no need to launch a major debate until unionists came to negotiate.'[33]

Changes which involve negotiation with unionism, and those areas fundamental to the Irish Constitution, such as whether it should be replaced in its entirety, are ones likely to be put off until future negotiations, rather than being dealt with in the short term. But that does not rule out dealing with some aspects of denominationalism or symbolism in the nearer term.

The most egregious feature of the 1937 Constitution as enacted, namely the special position of the Catholic Church,[34] was deleted in 1973.[35] The former prohibition on divorce previously figured in debate regarding pluralism, although during the 1995 campaign to modify the absolute prohibition, the question of the impact on the Northern situation did not loom large.[36]

The draft Forum report considered a number of provisions, in particular the Preamble,[37] which expresses an altogether nationalist perspective on history and is worded in a manner that can hardly be accused of inclusiveness. Its religious references seem expressly denominational in character. John Rogers SC has pointed out shortcomings in the Preamble and Article 1 of the Constitution, in particular on the ground that: 'the difficulty with the Constitution is that it fails to acknowledge our current and historic problem: that the Irish people are divided. The Constitution recognises the territorial division of the island but not the divisions between the people of the island.'[38]

The solution proposed by Rogers was that attention be given to the flaw that the Constitution, on its face, claims to have been enacted by 'the people of Éire', whereas equating 'Éire' with the state led to the problem that the Constitution claimed a national territory which is greater in extent than Éire. Rogers went on to propose that the Preamble and Article 1 be amended to recognise the plural origins of our people and 'the absence of an acknowledged history and common allegiance'. The provisions should 'acknowledge the division of our people and should make it a common purpose and interest of the people to respect the heritage and allegiance of all people on the island'.

The Preamble gives the impression that Ireland is primarily established to cater for the requirements of nationalists and republicans and pander to their version of historical narrative, rather than, as the concept of a republic implies, for all members of the community on a basis of equality and respect. To that extent, the terms of the Preamble both contradict the principle of parity of esteem that permeates the Agreement, and indeed tend to undermine the case for Irish unity.

The Constitution Review Group suggested that the Preamble be ditched in its entirety and only the formal words of enactment retained.[39] The reason for this proposal was stated to be because 'the substantive elements in a Preamble tend to be expressly provided for in the various Articles'.[40] Perhaps that is too pessimistic about the possibilities of creating an inclusive text. The fall-back position of the Group was to insert a reference to unity in the preamble, phrased by reference to the view that 'the aspiration to unity of many in Ireland will be sought peacefully and through reconciliation and consent'.[41] It is notable that the group suggests rather weakly that unity is aspired to by 'many', as opposed to, for example, 'the majority' on the island overall, or is the 'firm will of the Irish nation', as it is now put in Article 3.1 of the Constitution.

Moving on to other constitutional provisions, the Forum draft report suggested that the references to God be toned down, by removing the specifically Christian and Trinitarian references, but that the political aspects be left aside pending overall developments.[42]

Another possible change would be to amend the text of the Constitution which refers to the name of the state as Éire, or, in the English language, Ireland. A clearer formula would be that the name of the state is Ireland. The Irish version could provide simply that 'Éire is ainm don Stát'. Indeed, one of the benefits of the Agreement was to bring consistency to the use of the term 'Ireland' by the UK, so why retain a constitutional provision that muddies the waters, one might ask. On the other hand, the government has been using both names in international organisations since 2006, for whatever reason.[43]

Another area where attention might be given to reform and updating as part of the respect for both traditions as committed to in the Agreement is the reference to religion in other parts of the Constitution. One instance of this is the religious formula for the declarations of office for the President and members of the Council of State and Judiciary.[44] The United Nations Human Rights Committee has drawn attention to the undesirable nature of such provision, although their concern might possibly be described as selective in that their first report refers only to the President and judiciary, and not Councillors of State, and in their second report the concerns regarding the President are not referred to and the only proposal made is limited to a declaration for the judiciary.[45] The Constitution Review Group also addressed the issue, producing what might be considered an unnecessarily complicated and unsatisfactory formula. They recommended that the

President and Councillors of State be given the option of either making a declaration (presumably in the existing formula) or alternatively making a (presumably secular) affirmation, but judges should take a secular declaration only by reason of the need to ensure that the judge's impartiality is not cast into doubt by a public declaration of his or her values.[46] But one might pose the question as to whether it can be said that public confidence in the judiciary would be undermined by a public declaration of whether the judge believes in God or in taking declarations to God, but public confidence in the President would not. The value of a uniform declaration is that it applies neutrally to all, and insofar as a religious declaration may oppress the conscience of a minority, a standard secular declaration would achieve both objectives – that is neutral application to all and accommodation of conscience. From this viewpoint, there would be no reason not to apply these benefits to all offices where a declaration is required, and, in fairness to the Review Group, no real reasons are offered for the recommendation they assert, other than that the case for a neutral declaration is stronger in the case of the judiciary.

The extent to which some of the rights provisions of the Constitution[47] are influenced by Catholic thought may also be a matter for discussion and consideration. Other provisions also appear to be influenced by Catholic doctrine, such as the vocationalist principle underlying the make-up of the Seanad and of possible vocational bodies.[48]

It may be that some form of consultative process could be put in place involving the churches and elements of civic unionism that might enable a more broadly acceptable wording to be hammered out. A close examination of such issues and of the possible consultative processes that could be put in place to progress such issues could be a tangible form of implementing the commitment in the Agreement, if not of making the case for an inclusive Ireland. Ultimately, of course, drawing attention to any such areas for possible change is not intended to provide recommendations but is simply identifying matters for possible consideration; but decisions are a political matter and, if referenda are proposed, they are a matter for the people.

The unionist attitude to change in the 26-county state has been described by Prof. Arthur Aughey as follows:

> While Unionists might applaud the emergence of a more pluralist society in the Republic, they do not see any *necessary* connection between such developments and better relationships on the island of Ireland. Certainly, they see no connection at all between such changes and the claims of Irish political unity. Unionist politicians have made and continue to make unfavourable comment about the Catholic and Gaelic ethos of the south and it is possible to examine the nature of their criticisms. However, this does not mean that they or those whom they represent are prepared to discuss the conditions for the removal of these elements in the life of the southern State. To do so, as they see it, would implicate themselves in negotiating their place in a united Ireland. That is the reason why no official representatives of traditional unionism have involved themselves so far in the work of the Forum for Peace and Reconciliation.[49]

Of course, unionism is certainly no longer monolithic. There is a middle ground there that has some interested in the extent to which the South is prepared to look at its own laws, constitutional provisions, and practices, in the interests of pluralism. And there is also an obligation in that regard under the Agreement itself.

It might be said that Ireland can make all the amendments to its law and Constitution that it wishes, but at the end of the day the unionist objection will still be there. That is undeniably the case as a generalisation, but only because of the nature of the clash of identities in Northern Ireland. It is a precise mirror-image of the situation under the current dispensation, whereby the United Kingdom can make all of the changes to its own law, and that of Northern Ireland, that it sees fit, including human rights for all and sundry, and any other items on the nationalist/republican wish list, but at the end of the day the nationalist and republican objection to the United Kingdom will still be there. But, as mentioned earlier, such changes can open up new possibilities and vistas, erase red lines and create new perspectives and, above all, can reduce the temperature and the angst attaching to the constitutional issue. In 1996, Aughey commented in relation to the possibility of a united Ireland:

A united Ireland would still not be multi-cultural in the North American sense. But everything that is solid in the Republic would have to melt into air and a new, more ethically neutral order be established. There could be no apology then for the State behaving in a conservative and a Catholic manner. To describe Irish unity in this way reveals the unlikelihood of its attainment. The achievement of unity and its consequences would most likely introduce a general instability into one of the most stable regions in the European Union.[50]

Over twenty years on from that view, what seems to have
melted into the air is, instead, the glum certainty about the
permanent solidity of institutional and cultural certainties
south of the border. Ireland has changed in many ways,
both towards multi-culturalism and ethical neutrality in
laws and constitutional provisions. That which seemed
inconceivable twenty years ago is now taken for granted.

In an analysis commissioned by the Forum for Peace
and Reconciliation, Prof. Brice Dickson identified a
number of features of the Irish constitutional order which
are uncomfortable for unionists.[51] The first of these is
the very idea of a constitution itself. Dickson says that
'unionists are naturally wary of condensing complex
constitutional principles to numbered paragraphs in one
written document, as this would risk compromising the
position they have gradually won for themselves since the
Plantations'.[52] It is hard to reconcile this objection with
the concept of a constitution at all, although perhaps it
is an objection that may have declined in force since the
Good Friday Agreement, which is of a constitutional
character and looks to the drawing up of a bill of rights.
In a tentative reaction to this view, one comment included
(in square brackets) in the draft Forum report was that
Dickson's view represented 'a level of instinctive reaction
to the Constitution ... rather than considered thought'.[53]
Dickson's second objection is that unionists: 'do not wish
to live in a State where parliament's pronouncements
can be negated by the edict of unelected judges, however
eminent or erudite those judges may be. Nor do they want
their parliament to be subservient to any other Parliament
(i.e. the Dáil).'[54]

In respect of this objection, it is hard to imagine that
nowadays the concept of judicial review of legislation

would be a fundamental unionist stumbling block to the Irish Constitution. Judicial review of legislation for compatibility with the separation and hierarchy of powers in the Northern Ireland Act 1998 is entrenched in that Act, and, since the Human Rights Act 1998,[55] all parts of the United Kingdom have become familiar with judicial review of legislation, on top of the reviewability of the validity of legislation since 1973 by reference to European Union Law. The objection that a Northern Irish parliament should not be subservient to any other parliament is hard to reconcile with existing constitutional arrangements in the United Kingdom.

A further unionist objection to the human rights provisions of the Irish Constitution is 'either because those provisions are not balanced by a set of fundamental duties or because the rights conferred are not those to which unionists would themselves accord priority within society'.[56] It might be that these are not insuperable difficulties in the context of a renegotiated constitution following a united Ireland. Dickson goes on to refer to unionist suspicion of the Office of President,[57] a consequence of their loyalty to the Crown. He goes on to say that 'the Preamble to the Constitution is perhaps one of the most offensive parts in this regard, even though it does not have any substantive content'.[58] As regards the national flag, he says that precluding any reference to the Union Jack is 'virtually unthinkable for unionists'.[59] Furthermore, unionists do not see the necessity for the language provisions of the Constitution, especially combined with the subsection giving priority to the Irish language text of laws.[60] However, the survey is not all negative. For example, Dickson states that: 'In that part of the Irish Constitution ranging from Articles 9 to 39 there is precious little which any Northern unionist could reasonably find objectionable and much that he or she might well applaud.'[61]

Dickson criticises the provision of the Constitution that precludes citizens (Dickson incorrectly says 'any person')[62] from accepting membership of the Privy Council or a knighthood or other honours (although this is hardly a major bar because such honours can be received with government approval, which post the Agreement could presumably not be unreasonably refused).[63] And, indeed, Irish society has yet to completely accommodate itself to the entirely legitimate position that its citizens may allow themselves a recognition of British identity by accepting such honours with such executive approval. For example, the April 2018 award of a damehood to that giant of Irish literature, Edna O'Brien, provoked some painfully hectoring and dispiritingly ill-informed reactions. The commitments of the Agreement to equality of identity mean that no one should have to apologise for or explain their acceptance of any British honour.

Dickson goes on to comment that the treatment of the family and religion is antipathetic to unionist sensibilities.[64] Other legal provisions may also come under scrutiny as being unduly influenced by Catholic thinking – the Forum received a number of comments about aspects of 'Rome rule' in, for example, education, health and censorship, but no recommendations for legal change in these areas appeared in the draft report.[65] It is the educational issue that was focused on by John Wilson Foster in an October 2017 article:

Unionists are assured by Senator [Mark] Daly that their British identity would be 'protected' and 'cherished' in a unified Ireland. If you need protecting, why go there (memo to nationalist authors of manifestos of persuasion/coercion: lose the word 'cherish', which began its Orwellian career in the 1916 proclamation)?

...

May I cut to the chase myself? From my quiver of reasons why I don't wish to live in an independent, unified Ireland, let me pluck merely one. Ninety-six per cent of primary schools over the border are owned by and under the patronage of religious denominations, 90 per cent of them owned and run by the Catholic Church. End of.

...

Those who campaign for a united Ireland should think twice. They seem to have no idea that the current Republic would have to reinvent itself so extensively to resemble secular and Protestant-shaped Britain that a united Ireland would be virtually pointless.

Neither the current nor envisaged public-policy Republic could possibly accommodate my British identity. It simply doesn't have the cultural storage space.[66]

Acknowledging the British Identity

A significant aspect of the situation lies in the question of national identity, which is at the core of the clash between the two versions of the constitutional future for Northern Ireland. The unionist case is one of attachment to the British identity, an identity which, it is perceived, cannot be celebrated and achieved within a united Ireland, but of course that is not the case any more than that it is not possible to celebrate Irishness within the UK. The challenge for nationalism, therefore, is to identify legal measures which would recognise the legitimacy of the British identity and the British dimension to Irish life.

There is a significant British dimension to the Irish experience. The primary language in which Ireland speaks to itself is English. The broad outline of Irish public institutions is drawn from the British experience. British culture permeates Irish society. The two islands are very much linked in destiny and by closely knit relationships at an individual level. The British experience is very much a part of life for significant numbers of people in the state, whether through family relationships, travel, work, emigration or media. Indeed, the average person in the twenty-six counties is probably significantly closer culturally to London than to Belfast, particularly given the exciting, metropolitan, outgoing, modern and culturally open face that London presents to the world, by contrast with the somewhat more monochrome images and legacies that come to mind in contemplating the Belfast experience.

The relationship between Ireland and Britain is by no means a straightforward one of neighbourly solidarity, as has been identified in a British Council survey of attitudes to Britain in Ireland.[67] However, under the Agreement, Ireland is required to 'demonstrate its respect for the different traditions'. Properly interpreted, this surely includes legal measures, if appropriate, to recognise and cherish the British identity within the 26-county state.

To date, the Irish and nationalist side have only taken limited steps towards acknowledging the British dimension, such as including commemorations of the Great War within the decade of centenaries.[68] Recognition of the British dimension within Ireland, both North and South, is the counterpoint of the necessity to recognise the Irish dimension of Northern Ireland.

That the question of accommodating the British dimension is still an issue was illustrated by the passing of a motion in Derry City and Strabane District Council on 29 March 2018, with Sinn Féin support and SDLP abstention, which stated, in language that could have come from a couple of centuries ago: 'Given the history of British imperialism in Ireland, this Council calls on local educational facilities for children and young people to refuse British Armed Forces access to children/pupils as part of their attempt to glamourise/recruit for their imperialist ventures.'[69]

Of course, given that the Agreement itself recognised UK sovereignty over Northern Ireland, it is hard to see how one could mount an objection at the level of principle to the UK armed forces offering a recruitment role there to those who are interested in it. UUP MLA Doug Beattie responded:

> Yet again the Sinn Féin respect, equality and integrity agenda is in tatters.
>
> It is perfectly clear that their call for 'equality' is as warped as their commitment to 'human rights'. Both are only to be delivered on their terms, viewed through a prism of a rabid and pathological bias against anything or anyone who links themselves to the British state or British military. For Sinn Féin to back a motion – no matter how ludicrous – to prevent

anyone considering a career in the British military receiving career advice while at school sets a clear sectarian agenda.

...

Does Sinn Féin want equality? Do they promote respect? Are they truly advocates of integrity? The actio[n] of their councillors in backing this motion sends a clear message to what they ironically call their 'unionist brothers and sisters.' That is – 'you are not welcome now and you are not welcome in the future and you will never be welcome in any United Ireland in which we have any influence'.[70]

From one viewpoint, before any question of considering Irish unity in the terms of fraternity envisaged by the Agreement could have any meaning, there would first of all have to be a searching examination of the extent to which nationalism is prepared to combat sectarianism and fossilised attitudes within its ranks and to take concrete steps towards accommodating the British identity. Otherwise, talk of parity of esteem is something of a sham.

Reactivating Commonwealth Membership

One issue which has been put on the agenda by a number of commentators is the question of rejoining the Commonwealth or, to be more precise, reactivating Commonwealth membership. De Valera's official biographers point out that the Costello government never, in fact, withdrew from the Commonwealth – they merely 'took certain steps which ... led the British and the rest of the Commonwealth to conclude that Ireland was not a member',[71] so perhaps it may be contended that the state has been a member all along, in law. All that is needed would be to reactivate Irish membership. In March 2018, journalist Pat McArt wrote:

> One gesture that would almost certainly send out positive signals would be for Ireland to rejoin the Commonwealth. The possibility of increasing the links with Scotland by means of a tunnel running from the Co. Antrim coast, should also be explored. Strengthening where possible and practicable the 'East–West' relationship would give considerable comfort to people who see Scotland, more than England, as the motherland.

> The construction of a new Irish Constitution would be another massive step in creating the right mood music.[72]

It is clear that the original reasons for parting company with the Commonwealth no longer apply. Ireland disengaged because it was thought necessary to declare a republic and also thought that republics could not be Commonwealth members. But almost immediately upon Ireland leaving, it was agreed that republics can be members. Simultaneously, the 'British' Commonwealth title ceased to exist, and it became 'the Commonwealth of Nations'. The Crown now has no automatic legal status in any particular member country, and a member country has no necessary legal relationship with the UK. Since 1973, the Commonwealth has had its own, neutral, flag, not associated with the UK flag.

Membership of the Commonwealth would not now have major ramifications for Irish foreign policy and practice. The only practical implications would appear to be in terms of exchanging High Commissioners rather than Ambassadors and in mutual diplomatic representation in territories where one's own representation was not available. In the grand scheme of things, these changes are relatively minor compared to what would have been seen, prior to 1949, as the more major issue of recognising the crown for legal purposes. That is no longer a requirement. At this stage in the evolution of the Commonwealth, the positive implications for Irish membership would tend to be on the cultural side and would involve a more tangible sense of affinity with the Anglosphere as well as with the United Kingdom itself. Participation in cultural and sporting events such as the Commonwealth games would, for some, be reason enough to put the issue back on the agenda.

The argument against rejoining the Commonwealth would primarily be that it would be seen as involving a recognition of the Crown. However, first of all, the link with the Crown is not what it was. The Queen happens to be head of the Commonwealth at present but this is not automatic into the future and does not involve the Crown being head of state in any member countries unless they so decide. The role of head involves no executive or other powers in the countries themselves, so the recognition is only external in the capacity of being head of the organisation, not any internal recognition. The very minimal link involved is now a very modest quid pro quo for de Valera's view that the Commonwealth was a bridge between the traditions.[73] Imbued perhaps by that spirit, de Valera's grandson, Minister Eamon Ó Cuiv, floated the concept of rejoining the Commonwealth.[74] A final point, perhaps worth making, is that a renewed Commonwealth context would open up a range of institutional points of contact in East/West relations, including parliamentary and civic links across the Anglosphere. In a post-Brexit environment, an intensification of the East/West dimension may bring benefits to all. It would also provide a common point of cultural contact North and South.

The radical nature of renewed Irish membership of the Commonwealth would be an attraction from the point of view of charting a new course as an inclusive state that recognised the validity of the British dimension. Insofar as that decision involves political judgement, for some, the move would be too much of a change to contemplate in advance of reunification; whereas for others such a move would, all the more so because of its striking nature, send a strong signal of inclusiveness and reconciliation. Such decisions can be left to the political process. What can be said from a legal point of view, however, is that it is clear that rejoining the Commonwealth would not involve any legal implications that would be in conflict with the Irish constitutional order.[75]

Symbolism in the South

In an interesting discussion on national symbols, Prof. Arthur Aughey summarises the unionist attitude to the national flag as being that 'the fate of the Irish tricolour was the fate of a hypothetically inclusive nationality falling victim to an actually exclusive nationalism'.[76] He draws a distinction between symbols of the Irish state, on the one hand, and those of 'Irish nationality', on the other hand, which 'are the expressions of a non-political sense of Irishness and value precisely because they are part of the affective identity of everyone who lives on the island of Ireland'.[77] In the latter category, he refers to the many all-Ireland (or as he puts it 'island-wide')[78] institutions such as the Church of Ireland, the Irish Association, the Baptist Union and the Irish Rugby Football Union, and symbols such as the harp, shamrock and the colour green, as well as the Irish language.[79] Aughey's version of nationality is one that includes unionists living on the island of Ireland, who thus enjoy an affinity by nationality with Ireland while retaining their British citizenship. His conclusion is that the Irish state ought not to agonise about its own symbols 'from green letter boxes to the Angelus',[80] and that the reasonable approach might be to extend recognition to other symbols and events, as had been done with Remembrance Day.[81] The other side of this coin, in Aughey's analysis, was to ensure that things symbolic of Irish nationality ought not to be corrupted by their appropriation for nationalist ends. He commends the fact that Amhrán na bhFiann is not played before rugby matches and, indeed, the comment by the former Taoiseach John Bruton that the national anthem itself may be reviewed. In that regard he says:

> If the anthem were to be changed it would not of itself change unionist attitudes towards Irish unity but it would be an interesting symbolic statement about how the Republic seeks to represent itself today. It might contribute to a more positive 'mood music' which might in turn contribute to a more relaxed political atmosphere throughout the island.[82]

That is basically the argument made by the present study. There are many changes that could be envisaged within all sets of relationships which, in themselves, will not resolve the ultimate constitutional objections of the two traditions, but one can seek to reduce the temperature, the tensions and the angst attaching to the constitutional issue by means of such changes, even if the eventual constitutional question still remains to be answered in different ways.

In the context of any future overall revision of the Constitution in the setting of a United Ireland, it is hard to envisage that the existing national symbols could remain unaltered. In South Africa, for example, the new national flag combined elements of both the apartheid era state and the ANC flag, a new set of national languages was adopted on an inclusive basis, covering the languages of the different South African communities, and a new multilingual anthem was adopted. Likewise, while the current Irish national flag embodies the noble republican aspiration of uniting orange and green with the white of peace, the original message has not made itself clear to the unionist community, and it is hard to see how this flag would not be a matter for negotiation in the context of a united Ireland. Similarly, the national anthem, which is not a constitutional phenomenon, and which contains the same problematic, exclusively nationalist, narrative as the Preamble, would also need to be reviewed. However, one reason why there might be no question of changing the flag or other such national symbols in advance of unity is that to do so would make a gift of the existing flag or other symbols to elements of republicanism, which might be happy to take possession of the vacuum created by a withdrawal of state recognition.

The constitutional priority for the Irish language might also fall for reconsideration. Apart from the question of recognising Ulster Scots, and apart from the issue of whether priority for one of the official languages over the other or others would be a sustainable proposition, the need to protect individuals in the state against discrimination on the grounds of lack of facility in Irish would also arise. In that context, the question of compulsory Irish for students and others, and compulsory Irish courses for lawyers, would be a matter for consideration.

An alternative might be the 'two flags' approach, where the symbols of both communities would be adopted for various public purposes. This would not, presumably, remove the need for the state to have a single national flag and anthem for international purposes. Different countries have come up with different solutions in times of constitutional change. For instance, on the unification of Germany, the Federal Republic of Germany retained its name and other markers of identity. However, German reunification involved the joining of two sections of a nation, each of which was culturally compatible with the other. The German example did not present the kind of radical constitutional disconnect which one can see in Northern Ireland and, to that extent, the South African precedent is a much closer one.

Other proposals to recognise the British identity included overcoming the resistance to displaying the Union flag in the twenty-six counties,[83] and a proposal by the ICTU to make 12 July a public holiday in the twenty-six counties.[84] Again, such gestures would be a matter for political judgement. Certainly, any proposal to commemorate 12 July might need to be balanced with a nationalist holiday, such as recognising the birth of modern independence with the treaty of 6 December 1921, Ireland's legislative independence day on 6 December

1922, or executive independence on April Fool's Day – 1 April 1922. The contested histories on the republican side, however, would suggest that no date for independence could be passed by unanimous vote. Even though it may not suit a revolutionary narrative, those dates are, however, historical facts.

Providing Reassurance

The question also might be asked about how evolved public opinion is in relation to the need to recognise and reassure the British identity. Opinions in some quarters, including elements of Irish-America, seem to lag somewhat behind more recent pluralistic developments. For example, the idea that a St Patrick's Day banner 'England get out of Ireland' is one that 'always gets the loudest cheer'[85] shows a certain failure to take on board the right of people of Northern Ireland to regard themselves as British, approved by overwhelming majorities twenty years ago. Mark Lindsay of the Police Federation for Northern Ireland said 'Parading under such a banner shows a complete lack of understanding of the political landscape in Northern Ireland in 2018'. Presumably it is for the Irish government and nationalist parties to show leadership on such issues.

Unionist fears and concerns were stressed to the Oireachtas Committee on the Implementation of the Good Friday Agreement by unionist commentator Dr James Wilson, that much of the opposition of northern Protestants to Irish unity has been based on fear – 'Fear of dispossession, fear of retribution, and fear of assimilation into an alien Gaelic culture that eliminates their ethno-cultural diversity as British/Ulster Scots'.[86] Raymond McCartney, Sinn Féin MLA, made a similar point:

> Political unionism over the years has suffered from a leadership that has fluctuated between supremacist arrogance and a fearful, inarticulate uncertainty. This instilled a fear in many Unionists that, if respective roles were ever reversed, nationalists would imitate the sectarian excesses of Unionism. Republicans must deal with these fears by redoubling our efforts to communicate with the unionist constituency not just through their political representatives but also directly, with a reassuring message that under no circumstances will we visit upon any section of society the exclusion, domination and discrimination from which we are emerging.[87]

How or whether such anxieties can be assuaged may need to be the subject of a difficult national discussion; what Gerry Adams and Declan Kearney call 'uncomfortable conversations' to dispel the idea that 'the boot would be on the other foot'.[88] But, of course, the legal context is now different given the Agreement's context of permanent and overarching rights protection. One viewpoint is that before any such reassurances can be meaningful, nationalism/republicanism needs to have a lengthy conversation with itself about what sort of Ireland it wants to create. While republicanism has spoken every so often of 'cherishing' unionists, it is also, as we have seen, capable of sending different messages. One example of many is the question of how accommodating is its surrogate language and narrative regarding conflict elsewhere in the world.[89] In an accumulation of such ways are words about accommodating unionist identity undermined. To that extent, and from such a perspective, the broader nationalist position needs to have its own searching and very lengthy conversation first before it can credibly talk about planning in detail for altered constitutional futures.

Conclusions

In a situation as complex and multi-faceted as Northern Ireland's political, constitutional and cultural dilemma, the Good Friday Agreement provides a way forward across a terrain bereft of any other or better agreed solutions. While many voices have been raised about the flaws and difficulties with the Agreement, no one has yet come up with a better Mark II solution that stands a chance of attracting equal or greater consensus support. If conclusions from the present study can be offered, it is suggested that an analysis of the Agreement shows that there are a number of fundamental principles relevant to this issue that can be derived from the Agreement, which are of relevance to the future debate.

1. **The Agreement cannot be changed without consent.** The British-Irish Agreement is a legally binding international treaty. It cannot be changed by either government without the consent of the other. It cannot be cast aside because it is seen by some as inconvenient in the Brexit context, for example. On the contrary, the Agreement potentially provides scope for solutions and mechanisms for co-operation after Brexit, along both a North/South axis but also an East/West one. More generally, the Agreement rules out unilateral alteration, by changing the ground rules once a

nationalist majority starts emerging. Any suggestion that UK legislation could require, to take a fanciful example, a supermajority as a prerequisite for unity is ruled out by the Agreement.

2. **The obligation to implement the Agreement in good faith precludes undermining Northern Ireland as a functioning jurisdiction or refusing on political grounds to operate the institutions.** The Agreement calls time on the days of regarding the North as a failed political entity and commits all sides to supporting the institutions of the six counties. Indeed, any stable context for a debate on Irish unity depends on there being a functioning Northern Ireland within which such change could be discussed and managed. Furthermore, the Agreement requires the parties to work the institutions in good faith. Participation in the institutions is not dependent on political agreement with partners in governmental institutions and, therefore, cannot be legitimately withheld on the basis of political disagreement or for political grounds or party advantage.

3. **Whether devolution operates fully or breaks down, the other provisions of the Agreement remain binding.** This must include addressing all commitments regarding internal Northern Irish matters that can be progressed at the level of Westminster legislation, in the absence of devolved institutions. It also includes co-operation between the two governments across all sets of relationships (apart from the North/South Ministerial Council, which does not function in the absence of a devolved executive). All remaining obligations of the Agreement are binding and need to be upheld – for example, the equality and rights commitments, legislation required to give effect to parity of esteem,

and maintaining existing commitments such as the entrenched status of the European Convention on Human Rights in Northern Ireland. It would not be open to the UK to unilaterally de-entrench the Convention, at least in the absence of Irish consent.

4. **If devolution breaks down, it is for the two governments to review the situation through the British-Irish Intergovernmental Conference, including the right of the Irish government to make proposals on internal Northern Irish issues.** The Agreement makes clear the legitimacy of the Irish government's role, if devolution has collapsed, in reviewing the overall political agreement (including the internal Northern Irish aspects) within the British-Irish Intergovernmental Conference. Contrary to some suggestions, the Conference has every right to function during a breakdown of devolution; its role to review arrangements in that context is specifically provided for in the Agreement itself. The right of the Irish government to put forward views and proposals regarding non-devolved matters covers the full range of internal Northern Ireland-related matters where devolution is not operating. Another consequence is that it would not be open to either government to neglect to operate the Conference if requested to do so by the other government.

5. **The fall-back to devolution is not joint authority but UK sovereignty, subject to the provisions of the Agreement and subject to the right of the Irish government to put forward views and proposals.** UK sovereignty arises from the Acts of Union, which remain in force. The right of Westminster to legislate for Northern Ireland is acknowledged in the Agreement

and its implementing legislation. The British-Irish Intergovernmental Conference is not a mechanism for joint rule but only for the Irish side to put forward views and proposals. Westminster is legally entitled, and indeed where necessary is required, to legislate for Northern Ireland if the parties will not work the Agreement, albeit with Irish views as an input. Apart from that, the other provisions of the Agreement, such as East/West co-operation, continue in force even if devolution is not operating. The general legislative competence of Westminster is expressly preserved by the Agreement, which provides that that power 'would remain unaffected'.[1] The repeal of the provision in the Government of Ireland Act 1920 that provided that 'the supreme authority of the Parliament of the United Kingdom shall remain unaffected and undiminished over all persons, matters, and things in Ireland and every part thereof'[2] made no difference, because the Agreement itself provides for exactly the same principle of Westminster jurisdiction as regards Northern Ireland. The 1998 Act implementing the Agreement provides that legislative power for the assembly 'does not affect the power of the Parliament of the United Kingdom to make laws for Northern Ireland'.[3]

6. **Equality of cultural rights and parity of esteem involves legislative protection for equality and diversity, which inevitably includes recognition of language rights.** The equality of cultural rights, expressly acknowledged in the strongest terms by the Agreement, makes it inevitable that the right of the people of Northern Ireland to do business with the state in the Irish language on the basis of equality must be protected. The effective exercise of such a right requires statutory procedures, not least to

repeal the legal prohibition on using any language in court other than English. Any such legislation should presumptively afford equal protections to Ulster Scots. The Agreement's commitment to 'rigorous impartiality' is binding on all elements of 'the power of sovereign government'; meaning that legislation to protect equality and diversity must be introduced by Westminster, if the devolved legislature fails to do so. The precise content of the language legislation is a matter for consideration; the principle of parity of esteem does not commit the British or unionist sides to supporting the most extensive version of such legislation.

7. **Parity of esteem also requires the UK to review any laws or practices that fail to achieve rigorous impartiality.** As well as reviewing practices in Northern Ireland that fail to recognise the Irish identity, the very strong commitments of the Agreement to rigorous impartiality and to the achievement of parity of esteem between the traditions imply that laws in force across the wider UK that involve anti-Catholic language or discrimination require review.

8. **The obligation on the Irish government to take further active steps to demonstrate its respect for the different traditions requires a review of constitutional provisions, laws and practices in Ireland.** This obligation requires, in the first instance, the identification of laws and practices that fail to afford such respect and consideration of possibilities for change. In this regard, a searching examination of the obligation to accommodate the British identity has yet to take place – indeed, it has yet even to be seriously considered, seeing as the New Ireland Forum examination of the

issue never managed to produce a report. Completing the work of the original New Ireland Forum in this respect could, from one viewpoint, be a meaningful first step. In particular, it can be noted that the question of reactivating Commonwealth membership, if a political decision was taken to do so, poses no adverse implications for the Irish constitutional order.

9. **The articulation and pursuit of either the constitutional aspiration to unity or continued union with Britain is legitimate.** The Agreement allows unionists to be unionist and nationalists to be nationalist, so the aspiration to unity is as valid as that to continued union. Whether it makes sense for nationalists to make detailed plans now for eventual Irish unity, or whether this is premature and agitates an already difficult situation, or whether some in-between position is appropriate, is a matter for political judgement. But one cannot dispute the entitlement to argue for Irish unity, as that right is enshrined in the Agreement itself.

10. **The test for Irish unity is a simple majority of those present and validly voting in polls North and South.** The principle of equality between the traditions also means that the test for unity cannot be asymmetrical with the test for a United Kingdom – which does not depend on nationalist consent or on anything other than 50 per cent + 1 support for the union with Britain as expressed by those present and validly voting in a particular border poll. Thus the 50 per cent + 1 rule is also the legal test for a united Ireland (subject to similar simple majority consent of those present and validly voting in a poll in the South). The Agreement clearly contemplates that a simple majority of those who vote in referenda North and South will suffice for

unity. There is no rigged threshold required, such as a supermajority or a majority of those on the electoral register. There is no principle of unionist consent. That does not diminish the desirability of maximum support for any change in constitutional arrangements. Nor is such a threshold a 'sectarian headcount', any more than the continuance of a United Kingdom on the basis of 50 per cent + 1 for the union is a sectarian headcount. The use of a simple majority as the constitutional tie-breaker on the ultimate issue is not 'crude tribal majoritarianism' because it is balanced by extensive counter-majoritarian measures on all issues other than the question of ultimate status, in order to involve all sides in government and administration and to protect the rights of all. The challenge is to make Northern Ireland work in such a way that a transition of constitutional status, if it ever happens, will make little difference in practice and will be as unthreatening as possible.

11. **Repartition, independence or any other solutions apart from a United Kingdom or a united Ireland are ruled out by the Agreement.** The Agreement rules out all other exotic solutions. Thus, there can, for example, be no question of repartition, absent the presumably unlikely scenario of consent by the Irish government to an amendment of the Agreement to that effect. However, it might be more realistic to consider that a future offering on unity could (subject to agreement with the UK and approval in the constitutional amendment required for unity in the South) include enhanced UK involvement in a way that is not legally required by the Agreement, in both the medium term (for example, a lengthy period of transitional joint management akin

to joint authority) and long term (for example, a permanent consultative role corresponding to the role that the Irish government now has in Northern Irish affairs under the Agreement).[4] But unionism does not have the luxury of drawing a new line along the River Bann as a backstop.

12. **If unity comes about, the Good Friday Agreement will remain an obligation, including a devolved power-sharing government, an internal border within Ireland for the six counties as a separate jurisdiction, and a British identity and dimension in perpetuity.** The pinch points of the Agreement for nationalism include the permanent nature of the 6-county entity within either a united Ireland or the United Kingdom, and the permanent nature of the Northern Irish Assembly and executive. These are not 'transitional' arrangements – under the Agreement they are there in perpetuity, unless the UK government were hypothetically to agree otherwise in an amending treaty. Likewise, there is the correspondingly permanent nature of the border as an internal legal frontier on the island of Ireland. Even if it ceases to be an international boundary, the border will mark a distinct political and legal jurisdiction in perpetuity (again absent such hypothetical UK agreement). The permanent nature of the link to Britain is also embodied in the Good Friday Agreement, both through the East–West institutions and also through the ongoing entitlement to UK citizenship and British identity.

The Joint Oireachtas Committee on the Implementation of the Good Friday Agreement reported in 2017,[5] recommending the desirability of a further New Ireland

Forum to consider the implications of constitutional change. Whether such a forum is timely or not, or what its terms of reference might be, or whether there are other ways to de-escalate the potential for conflict and to promote reconciliation, are matters for political judgement. But if opinion could be coalesced around the foregoing principles one could look to a position where Northern Ireland, as a functioning entity under the Agreement, can bed down, when nationalist Ireland can reconcile itself to recognising the British identity in practical terms, and vice versa, and when the relevant parties can internalise and accept the full implications of the Agreement. After such steps had been taken, one view might be that there could be conditions under which the nationalist side of the equation could advance a credible argument for its aspirations in the sort of terms of fraternity and tolerance envisaged by the Agreement.

If such a context of mutual cohabitation were to become firmly established, any change from a United Kingdom to a united Ireland would make little practical difference, other than having MPs moving from Westminster to Dublin. The vast bulk of legislation and governance would continue to be determined in permanent institutions of government in Northern Ireland under the Agreement; both traditions would continue to be afforded equality of rights and expression; and strong East/West links would buttress the British identity irrespective of the formal constitutional position. On such an approach, any ultimate realignment of sovereignty within an all-island framework would happen slowly, naturally and almost imperceptibly over a long period of time within a stable constitutional context and through a communitarian approach where the rights and identities of all were protected. There would be no jagged or unnatural discontinuities. There would be no sudden, triumphalistic hoisting of a tricolour at Parliament Buildings in Stormont at 12 noon on some wet Tuesday following a border poll.

There is nothing automatically inevitable about Irish unity or any other outcome. Such hypotheticals may or may not happen. But whether one aspires to unity or continued union, the agenda of teasing out the implications of the Agreement, ensuring its full implementation, and respecting all identities, is one that should have the capacity to gather support across communities as it serves the common interest, irrespective of one's ultimate constitutional aspirations.

W.C. Sellar and R.J. Yeatman suggested that Gladstone 'spent his declining years trying to guess the answer to the Irish Question; unfortunately, whenever he was getting warm, the Irish secretly changed the Question'.[6] But perhaps there could be an argument for changing the question at least a little. The broader issues beyond making devolution work may need to be looked at. How can systems and legally effective backstops be designed to ensure that such impasses do not constantly repeat in the future? What are the obstacles to reconciliation and to respecting the different traditions equally? What principles of the Agreement can be progressed even without universal agreement?

A broader look at all of the various strands of opinion and sets of relationships may also contribute. One of the possible weaknesses of the Agreement is that it renders many parties less relevant in crisis situations, playing the role of 'slipping notes under a locked door' as suggested by the Alliance Leader Naomi Long.[7] How can the political and civic protagonists, beyond the largest parties, be brought constructively into the solution? The downgrading of the

Civic Forum possibly does not assist in this regard. The Agreement addresses relationships within Northern Ireland and on the Island, and between the two states, but what are the challenges for the other strands of relationships not focused on by the Agreement – relationships and attitudes within the twenty-six counties, within the island of Britain, within the UK as a whole, and directly between the twenty-six counties and Britain, outside a specifically Northern Ireland context? More broadly, how can relationships with Europe be developed? Here there is possibly neglected scope for broadening the debate and pursuing pluralism in language, approaches and legislation.

More broadly, in an age of fluidity of previously fixed categories, how can space be found for cultural fluidity – beyond the monochrome either/or, nationalist/unionist/other that is cemented into the Agreement? How much space is there in nationalism to be comfortable with British aspects of one's own identity, and vice versa? And overall, perhaps, how can the greatest happiness for the greatest number in Northern Ireland be advanced?

The opportunity of implementing and building on the Agreement and respecting both identities awaits full realisation. Space may need to be found for new initiatives, whether by parties willing to progress those objectives, or civic society, or by the governments in their respective and co-operating spheres, to offer equal accommodation, move the previously immovable, break logjams, erase red lines and open new vistas in which future change and more broadly agreed progress might become possible, and where the ultimate constitutional disagreement may not matter so much.

Endnotes

CHAPTER 1

1   British-Irish Agreement, art. 2.
2   John F. Larkin QC, '*Miller* and Northern Ireland: The Northern Ireland Constitution before the UK Supreme Court', Part II: Firing the Brexit Bullet – Who Pulls the Article 50 Trigger? (symposium), in Daniel Clarry (ed.), *The UK Supreme Court Yearbook*, vol. 8, *2016–2017 Legal Year* (Appellate Press, 2018), 285, p. 287.
3   Northern Ireland Act 1998, ss. 23(1) and (2).
4   Police (Northern Ireland) Act 2000 (c. 32), s. 38(1).
5   Agreement, Strand One, para. 5(a) to (c) and (e).
6   *Ibid.*, para. 5(d).
7   *Ibid.*, paras 14 and 15.
8   *Ibid.*, para. 33.
9   Memorandum of Understanding and Supplementary Agreement between the United Kingdom Government, the Scottish Ministers, the Welsh Ministers, and the Northern Ireland Executive Committee (October 2013), para. 14, as discussed in Christopher McCrudden and Daniel Halberstam, '*Miller* and Northern Ireland: A Critical Constitutional Response', pp. 314–15, n. 69.
10 Agreement, Strand One, para. 34.
11 Stormont House Agreement, 23 December 2014, para. 67.
12 Agreement, Strand Two, para. 1.
13 *Ibid.*, para. 10.
14 *Ibid.*, para. 18.
15 *Ibid.*, para. 19.
16 See http://www.oireachtas.ie/parliament/tdssenators/northsouthinter-parliamentaryassociation/ (accessed 17 April 2018).

17   All-Party Oireachtas Committee on the Constitution: Seventh Progress Report (Stationery Office, 2002), https://www.taoiseach. gov.ie/eng/Publications/Publications_Archive/Publications_ for_2002/All-Party_Oireachtas_Commitee_on_the_Constitution_ Seventh_Progress_Report_-_Parliament.html (accessed 17 April 2018).

18   Agreement, Strand Three, para. 11.

19   *Ibid*., British-Irish Intergovernmental Conference, para. 5.

20   'Taoiseach proposes recall of intergovernmental body', 21 November 2017, rte.ie, https://www.rte.ie/news/ulster/2017/1121/ 921633-may-meeting-sinn-fein-dup/ (accessed 17 April 2018).

21   Pat Leahy, 'Dublin will seek "meaningful role" in North if powersharing efforts fail', *The Irish Times*, 22 December 2017, https://www.irishtimes.com/news/politics/dublin-will-seek-meaningful-role-in-north-if-powersharing-efforts-fail-1.3335525 (accessed 17 April 2018).

22   Dáil debates, Tuesday, 20 March 2018, https://www.kildarestreet. com/debates/?id=2018-03-20a.43 (accessed 17 April 2018).

23   Newton Emerson, 'Coveney blunders in on the British-Irish Conference', *The Irish Times*, 22 March 2018, https://www. irishtimes.com/opinion/coveney-blunders-in-on-the-british-irish-conference-1.3435333 (accessed 17 April 2018).

24   Newton Emerson, 'What kind of joint authority is Dublin smoking?', *The Irish Times*, 21 December 2017, https://www. irishtimes.com/opinion/newton-emerson-what-kind-of-joint-authority-is-dublin-smoking-1.3333874 (accessed 17 April 2018).

25   Agreement, Strand Two, para. 13.

26   See http://www.cain.ulst.ac.uk/issues/politics/conference/biic221002. htm (accessed 17 April 2018).

27   See http://www.cain.ulst.ac.uk/issues/politics/conference/biic181202. htm (accessed 17 April 2018).

28   See http://www.cain.ulst.ac.uk/issues/politics/conference/biic200503. htm (accessed 17 April 2018).

29   See http://www.cain.ulst.ac.uk/issues/politics/conference/biic020703. htm (accessed 17 April 2018).

30   See http://www.cain.ulst.ac.uk/issues/politics/conference/biic180903. htm (accessed 17 April 2018).

31   See http://www.cain.ulst.ac.uk/issues/politics/conference/biic220104. htm (accessed 17 April 2018).

32   See http://www.cain.ulst.ac.uk/issues/politics/conference/biic210404.
     htm (accessed 17 April 2018).

33   See http://www.cain.ulst.ac.uk/issues/politics/conference/biic070704.
     htm (accessed 17 April 2018).

34   See http://www.cain.ulst.ac.uk/issues/politics/conference/biic151204.
     htm (accessed 17 April 2018).

35   See http://www.cain.ulst.ac.uk/issues/politics/conference/biic020305.
     htm (accessed 17 April 2018).

36   See http://www.cain.ulst.ac.uk/issues/politics/conference/biic270605.
     htm (accessed 17 April 2018).

37   See http://www.cain.ulst.ac.uk/issues/politics/conference/biic191005.
     htm (accessed 17 April 2018).

38   See http://www.cain.ulst.ac.uk/issues/politics/conference/biic010206.
     htm (accessed 17 April 2018).

39   See http://www.cain.ulst.ac.uk/issues/politics/conference/biic020506.
     htm (accessed 17 April 2018).

40   See http://www.cain.ulst.ac.uk/issues/politics/conference/biic250706.
     htm (accessed 17 April 2018).

41   See http://www.cain.ulst.ac.uk/issues/politics/conference/biic241006.
     htm (accessed 17 April 2018).

42   See http://www.cain.ulst.ac.uk/issues/politics/conference/biic260207.
     htm (accessed 17 April 2018).

43   Agreement, Declaration of Support, para. 5.

44   '"Not appropriate" – Arlene Foster criticises Leo Varadkar's
     suggestion to break Stormont deadlock', *Irish Independent,* 25
     March 2018, https://www.independent.ie/irish-news/politics/not-
     appropriate-arlene-foster-criticises-leo-varadkars-suggestion-to-
     break-stormont-deadlock-36705491.html (accessed 18 April 2018).

45   Agreement, Strand Three, British-Irish Intergovernmental
     Conference, para. 9.

46   *Ibid.*, Rights, Safeguards and Equality of Opportunity, para. 1.

47   *Ibid.*, New Institutions in Northern Ireland, para. 5.

48   *Ibid.*, para. 6.

49   *Ibid.*, Comparable Steps by the Irish Government, para. 9.

50   *Ibid.*, A Joint Committee, para. 10.

51   *Ibid.*, Rights, Safeguards and Equality of Opportunity, Economic,
     Social and Cultural Issues, para. 4.

52   *Ibid.*, Decommissioning, para. 4.

53   *Ibid.*, Policing and Justice, para. 3.

54   *Ibid.*, Validation and Implementation, para. 1.

CHAPTER 2

1. 11 February–30 May 2000, 10 August 2001 (24-hour suspension), 22 September 2001 (24-hour suspension) and 14 October 2002– 7 May 2007.

2. John F. Larkin QC, 'Miller and Northern Ireland: The Northern Ireland Constitution before the UK Supreme Court', Part II: Firing the Brexit Bullet – Who Pulls the Article 50 Trigger? (symposium), in Daniel Clarry (ed.), *The UK Supreme Court Yearbook,* vol. 8, *2016–2017 Legal Year* (Appellate Press, 2018), 285, p. 287.

3. Northern Ireland Act 1998, Schedule 1.

4. See First Minister and Deputy First Minister, Statements, set out in 'Trimble/Mallon Statement of What was Agreed', *The Irish Times,* 19 December 1998.

5. Department of Foreign Affairs, Press Release, 'Minister for Foreign Affairs and Secretary of State for Northern Ireland to sign international agreements supplementing the British Irish Agreement, Dublin Castle, 8 March 1999', 7 March 1999.

6. *Ibid.*, p. 2.

7. *Ibid.*

8. *Ibid.*

9. Exchange of Letters Constituting a Supplementary Agreement Between the Government of Ireland and the Government of the United Kingdom of Great Britain and Northern Ireland concerning the Interpretation of Certain Terms in the Implementation Bodies Agreement signed at Dublin on 8 March 1999, ITS No. 29 of 2000, https://www.dfa.ie/media/dfa/alldfawebsitemedia/treatyseries/ uploads/documents/treaties/docs/200029.pdf (accessed 18 April 2018).

10. Agreement between the Government of Ireland and the Government of the United Kingdom of Great Britain and Northern Ireland Establishing the Independent Commission for the Location of Victims' Remains, ITS No. 31 of 2000, https:// www.dfa.ie/media/dfa/alldfawebsitemedia/treatyseries/uploads/ documents/treaties/docs/200031.pdf (accessed 18 April 2018).

11. 'The Report of the Independent Commission on Policing for Northern Ireland', September 1999, http://cain.ulst.ac.uk/issues/ police/patten/patten99.pdf (accessed 18 April 2018).

12. See Government Information Services, 'Statement by the Taoiseach Mr Bertie Ahern T.D. to Mark the Entry into Force of the British-Irish Agreement, Dáil Éireann, Wednesday, 1 December 1999 at

   10.45 a.m. approx.' (Dublin, 1999), http://oireachtasdebates. oireachtas.ie/debates%20authoring/debateswebpack.nsf/takes/ dail1999120100008 (accessed 18 April 2018).

13   *Ibid.*

14   Anglo-Irish Treaty 1921, art. 12.

15   *Ibid.*, art. 15.

16   See Government Information Services, 'North/South Ministerial Council Inaugural Plenary Meeting, Armagh, 13 December 1999 remarks by Taoiseach'. North/South Ministerial Council, 'Joint Communiqué, North/South Ministerial Council Inaugural Plenary Meeting Armagh, 13 December 1999' (Armagh 1999).

17   Government Information Services, Press Release, British-Irish Council Inaugural Summit Meeting, London, 17 December 1999, Introductory Statement by the Taoiseach.

18   Government Information Services, 'Inaugural Meeting of the British/Irish Inter Governmental Conference Opening Statement by the Taoiseach', Dublin, 17 December 1999.

19   Police (Northern Ireland) Act 2000 (c. 32) s. 1.

20   See 'Full text of governments' peace plan', *The Irish Times*, 1 August 2001, https://www.irishtimes.com/news/full-text-of-governments-peace-plan-1.391951 (accessed 18 April 2018); http://cain.ulst.ac.uk/events/peace/docs/bi010801.htm (accessed 18 April 2018).

21   Agreement between the Government of Ireland and the Government of the United Kingdom of Great Britain and Northern Ireland on Police Co-operation, ITS No. 2 of 2002, https://www.dfa.ie/media/dfa/alldfawebsitemedia/treatyseries/ uploads/documents/treaties/docs/200202.pdf (accessed 18 April 2018).

22   Justice (Northern Ireland) Act 2002 (c. 26).

23   *Ibid.*, s. 22.

24   *Ibid.*, s. 30(1).

25   *Ibid.*, s. 66.

26   *Ibid.*, s. 67 amending Flags (Northern Ireland) Order 2000 (S.I. No. 1347 (N.I. 3)) art. 3(1).

27   ITS No. 5 of 2002, Exchange of Notes dated 19 November 2002 Between the Government of Ireland and the Government of the United Kingdom of Great Britain and Northern Ireland concerning certain Decisions of the North/South Ministerial Council and related matters, https://www.dfa.ie/media/dfa/ alldfawebsitemedia/treatyseries/uploads/documents/treaties/

docs/200205.pdf (accessed 28 April 2018), set out in the Schedule to the implementing legislation, British–Irish Agreement (Amendment) Act 2002.

28   Agreement between Government of Ireland and Government of the United Kingdom by means of exchange of letters dated 19 November 2002, Letter of Minister for Foreign Affairs, Brian Cowen TD, para. 1, https://www.dfa.ie/media/dfa/alldfawebsitemedia/treatyseries/uploads/documents/treaties/docs/200205.pdf (accessed 18 April 2018).

29   *Ibid.*, para. 2.

30   Northern Ireland Assembly Elections Act 2003 (c. 3).

31   British and Irish Governments, Joint Declaration, dated April 2003 ('2003 Declaration') but published on 1 May 2003, http://cain.ulst.ac.uk/events/peace/docs/bijoint010503.pdf (accessed 18 April 2018).

32   Draft Agreement between the British and Irish Governments, April 2003.

33   British Government, Proposals in Relation to On The Runs (OTRs), April 2003, http://cain.ulst.ac.uk/events/peace/docs/biotrs010503.pdf (accessed 18 April 2018).

34   2003 Declaration, para. 9.

35   Good Friday Agreement, Strand Two, para. 18.

36   2003 Declaration, para. 11.

37   *Ibid.*, Annex 2.

38   *Ibid.*, Annex 2, para. 24.

39   *Ibid.*, Annex 1, paras 12 to 19. See Agreement between the British and Irish Governments, April 2003, para. 2.

40   Northern Ireland Assembly (Elections and Periods of Suspension) Act 2003 (c. 12).

41   Northern Ireland (Monitoring Commission etc.) Act 2003 (c. 25).

42   ITS No. 1 of 2004. Given effect to in Ireland by the Independent Monitoring Commission Act 2003. Agreement between the Government of Ireland and the Government of the United Kingdom of Great Britain and Northern Ireland establishing the Independent Monitoring Commission, done at Dublin on 25 November 2003, https://www.dfa.ie/media/dfa/alldfawebsitemedia/treatyseries/uploads/documents/treaties/docs/200401.pdf (accessed 18 April 2018).

43   Independent Monitoring Commission Act 2003, art. 6.

44   ITS No. 12 of 2012. Exchange of Notes terminating the Agreement between the Government of Ireland and the Government of

the United Kingdom of Great Britain and Northern Ireland establishing the Independent Monitoring Commission ('IMC Agreement') done at Dublin on 25 November 2003.

45 ITS No. 11 of 2012. Exchange of Notes terminating the Agreement between the Government of Ireland and the Government of the United Kingdom of Great Britain and Northern Ireland establishing the Independent International Commission on Decommissioning ('Decommissioning Agreement').

46 The Assembly had been formally dissolved on 28 April 2003 in anticipation of an election in May 2003 which was ultimately postponed until 26 November 2003; see Northern Ireland (Date of Next Assembly Poll) Order 2003 (S.I. 2003 No. 2697).

47 The DUP won 33 seats including 3 members elected as Ulster Unionists who subsequently joined the DUP, compared with 24 seats for the UUP. Sinn Féin won 24 seats compared with 18 for the SDLP.

48 Department of Foreign Affairs, Press Release, 'Opening Remarks by the Minister for Foreign Affairs, Mr Brian Cowen T.D., Plenary Meeting – Review of the Operation of the Good Friday Agreement, Parliament Buildings, Stormont, 3 February 2004'.

49 'Durkan raises concerns with Taoiseach on citizenship poll', *The Irish Times*, 17 April 2004. See also Mark Hennessy, 'S.D.L.P. tells Ahern of "profound concern" on referendum', *The Irish Times*, 17 April 2004.

50 Declaration of the parties to the Agreement between the Government of Ireland and the Government of the United Kingdom of Great Britain and Northern Ireland, published 19 April 2004.

51 Article 1(vi) and Annex 2.

52 See Mark Brennock, 'British back Irish Referendum', *The Irish Times*, 20 April 2004; Mark Brennock, 'Tánaiste staunchly defends citizenship poll plan', *The Irish Times*, 20 April 2004; Una McCaffrey, 'Ahern rejects S.D.L.P. concern at vote', *The Irish Times*, 20 April 2004.

53 Irish Nationality and Citizenship Act 2004.

54 Northern Ireland Office, Press Release 'Date Confirmed for Intensive Talks', 30 July 2004.

55 See http://webarchive.nationalarchives.gov.uk/20091013050118/ http://www.nio.gov.uk/proposals_by_the_british_and_irish_ governments_for_a_comprehensive_agreement.pdf (accessed 18 April 2018).

56 See Gerry Moriarty, Mark Brennock and Dan Keenan, 'Ahern and Blair to press on despite failure to agree N.I. deal', *The Irish Times*, 9 December 2004; British and Irish Governments, 'Proposals by the British and Irish Governments for a comprehensive agreement' *The Irish Times*, 9 December 2004, http://cain.ulst.ac.uk/issues/politics/docs/nio/bi081204proposals. pdf ('2004 Proposals') (accessed 18 April 2018).

57 2004 Proposals, para. 5.

58 *Ibid.*, para. 7.

59 *Ibid.*, Annex A.

60 *Ibid.*

61 *Ibid.*, Annex B.

62 *Ibid.*

63 *Ibid.*, para. 5.

64 *Ibid.*, para. 8.

65 *Ibid.*

66 *Ibid.*, Annex D.

67 Offences Against the State Act 1939, ss. 2 and 10.

68 2004 Proposals, Annex C. A later published version even omitted the word '[IRA]', http://cain.ulst.ac.uk/issues/politics/docs/nio/ bi081204proposals.pdf (accessed 18 April 2018).

69 Mark Durkan, 'Fundamentals of Agreement have been undermined', *The Irish Times*, 14 December 2004.

70 See SDLP's detailed document rejecting the deal, *Standing by the Will of the People: Why the S.D.L.P. Rejects the 'Comprehensive Agreement'* (Belfast, 2006).

71 'Belfast Accord not for renegotiation', *The Irish Times*, 21 May 2005.

72 See 'Editorial', *An Phoblacht (new series)*, 28(29), Thursday, 28 July 2005, p. 8.

73 See Taoiseach and Prime Minister, Joint Statement, 6 April 2006: 'Joint Statement Taoiseach and Prime Minister', *The Irish Times*, 7 April 2006, https://www.irishtimes.com/news/joint-statement-by-taoiseach-bertie-ahern-and-british-prime-minister-tony-blair-1.778379 (accessed 18 April 2018); Noel McAdam, 'This time around there is a Plan B', *Belfast Telegraph*, 7 April 2006.

74 See 'SDLP backs Dublin on joint authority for NI', *News Letter*, 6 September 2017, https://www.newsletter.co.uk/news/sdlp-backs-dublin-on-joint-authority-for-ni-1-8137178 (accessed 18 April 2018); Newton Emerson, 'Notion of "joint authority" in North is all smoke and mirrors', *The Irish Times*, https://www.irishtimes.

com/opinion/notion-of-joint-authority-in-north-is-all-smoke-and-mirrors-1.3002653 (accessed 18 April 2018).

75   'Joint Statement Taoiseach and Prime Minister', *The Irish Times*, 7 April 2006.

76   See Dan Keenan and Mark Hennessy, 'Ahern calls on SF to clarify position on policing: NI Assembly meets today for first time since 2002', *The Irish Times*, 15 May 2006, p. 1.

77   Northern Ireland Act 2006 (c. 17), sch. 2 para. 3.

78   Joint Statement by Bertie Ahern, then Taoiseach (Irish Prime Minister), and Tony Blair, then British Prime Minister, Stormont, Belfast (29 June 2006), http://cain.ulst.ac.uk/issues/politics/docs/pmo/tbba290606.htm (accessed 18 April 2018).

79   'Northern Ireland Political Process: Work Plan', http://cain.ulst.ac.uk/issues/politics/docs/pmo/tbba290606wp.pdf (accessed 18 April 2018).

80   Joint Statement by Bertie Ahern, then Taoiseach (Irish Prime Minister), and Tony Blair, then British Prime Minister, Stormont, Belfast (29 June 2006).

81   Northern Ireland (Miscellaneous Provisions) Act 2006 (c. 33).

82   *Ibid*., s. 21.

83   Implemented in Ireland by the British-Irish Agreement (Amendment) Act 2006.

84   St Andrews Agreement, para. 4 and Appendix A.

85   *Ibid*., para. 8 and Annex B.

86   *Ibid*., para. 12.

87   This also repealed the Northern Ireland Act 2000 (c. 32) (s. 2(5) and sch. 4. para. 1) and the Northern Ireland Act 2006 (c. 17) (s. 22).

88   Northern Ireland (St Andrews Agreement) Act 2006 (c. 53) s. 1.

89   Some commentators regard Ulster Scots as a dialect rather than a language but it is treated as a language in UK legislation, which will be the approach followed in this work.

90   2006 Act, s. 15, inserting a new s. 28D in the Northern Ireland Act 1998.

91   'I expected Irish Language Act after devolution was restored – Dermot Ahern', *Independent*, 8 October 2018, https://www.independent.ie/breaking-news/irish-news/i-expected-irish-language-act-after-devolution-was-restored-dermot-ahern-36207360.html (accessed 18 April 2018).

92   Agreement between the Government of Ireland and the Government of the United Kingdom of Great Britain and

Northern Ireland (*annexing the St Andrews Agreement*), 22 March 2007.

93 Agreement between the Government of Ireland and the Government of the United Kingdom of Great Britain and Northern Ireland, ITS No. 1 of 2008.

94 Northern Ireland (St Andrews Agreement) Act 2007 (c. 4) s. 1.

95 Justice and Security (Northern Ireland) Act 2007 (c. 6) s. 44.

96 Northern Ireland Act 2009 (c. 3).

97 ITS No. 35 of 2011. Agreement between the Government of Ireland and the Government of the United Kingdom of Great Britain and Northern Ireland on Co-operation on Criminal Justice Matters, https://www.dfa.ie/media/dfa/alldfawebsitemedia/treatyseries/uploads/documents/legaldivisiondocuments/treatyseries2011/no.-35-of-2011.pdf (accessed 18 April 2018).

98 *Ibid.*, art. 1.

99 *Ibid.*, art. 2.

100 ITS No. 26 of 2010. Agreement between the Government of Ireland and the Government of the United Kingdom of Great Britain and Northern Ireland on Co-operation on Criminal Justice Matters, https://www.dfa.ie/media/dfa/alldfawebsitemedia/treatyseries/uploads/documents/legaldivisiondocuments/treatyseries2010/no.-26-of-2010.pdf (accessed 18 April 2018).

101 ITS No. 226 of 2012. Exchange of Notes amending the Agreement between the Government of Ireland and the Government of the United Kingdom of Great Britain and Northern Ireland Establishing Implementation Bodies, https://www.dfa.ie/media/dfa/alldfawebsitemedia/treatyseries/uploads/documents/legaldivisiondocuments/treatyseries2012/no22-of-2012.pdf (accessed 18 April 2018).

102 Brian Rowan, 'Richard Haass talks: Inside the draft document they couldn't agree', *Belfast Telegraph*, 1 January 2014, https://www.belfasttelegraph.co.uk/opinion/columnists/brian-rowan/richard-haass-talks-inside-the-draft-document-they-couldnt-agree-29879701.html (accessed 18 April 2018).

103 Sinéad O'Shea, 'Why the Haass talks matter and why they could not succeed', *The Irish Times*, 10 January 2014, https://www.irishtimes.com/news/politics/why-the-haass-talks-matter-and-why-they-could-not-succeed-1.1650835 (accessed 18 April 2018).

104 Northern Ireland (Miscellaneous Provisions) Act 2014 (c. 13).

105 *Ibid.*, s. 7.

106 See https://www.fictcommission.org/en (accessed 18 April 2018).

107 'Claim flags on bonfires could be banned under new government proposals', *Belfast Telegraph*, 22 March 2018, https://www.belfasttelegraph.co.uk/news/northern-ireland/claim-flags-on-bonfires-could-be-banned-under-new-government-proposals-36731947.html (accessed 18 April 2018).

108 Stormont House Agreement, paras 16–20.

109 *Ibid.*, para. 30.

110 'Agreement establishing the Independent Commission on Information Retrieval (ICIR)', http://opac.oireachtas.ie/AWData/Library3/FATRdoclaid210116_100026.pdf (accessed 18 April 2018).

111 *Ibid.*, art. 13.

112 *Ibid.*

113 'Why the delay in giving pensions to the forgotten survivors of the Troubles brings shame on us all', *Belfast Telegraph*, 21 March 2018, https://www.belfasttelegraph.co.uk/opinion/news-analysis/why-the-delay-in-giving-pensions-to-the-forgotten-survivors-of-the-troubles-brings-shame-on-us-all-36725184.html (accessed 18 April 2018); 'Thousands take to Belfast streets calling for "truth and justice" over Troubles killings', *Belfast Telegraph*, 25 February 2018, https://www.belfasttelegraph.co.uk/news/northern-ireland/thousands-take-to-belfast-streets-calling-for-truth-and-justice-over-troubles-killings-36641585.html (accessed 18 April 2018).

114 'Victims Forum Meets with Tánaiste to Call for Progress on Legacy Mechanisms', Commission for Victims and Survivors, 21 March 2018, https://www.cvsni.org/news/2018/march/victims-forum-meets-with-t%C3%A1naiste-to-call-for-progress-on-legacy-mechanisms/ (accessed 18 April 2018).

115 Stormont House Agreement, para. 67.

116 *Ibid.*, para. 68.

117 *Ibid.*, para. 69.

118 'A Fresh Start', para. 3.2.

119 'North–South Cooperation – Cross Border Seminar on Organised Crime', 28 September 2016, https://merrionstreet.ie/en/News-Room/Releases/North-South_Cooperation_%E2%80%93_Cross_Border_Seminar_on_Organised_Crime.html (accessed 18 April 2018).

120 'A Fresh Start', para. 5.1.

121 Northern Ireland (Stormont Agreement and Implementation Plan) Act 2016, http://www.legislation.gov.uk/ukpga/2016/13/crossheading/the-independent-reporting-commission/enacted (accessed 18 April 2018).

122 Independent Reporting Commission Act 2017, http://www.irishstatutebook.ie/eli/2017/act/25/enacted/en/html (accessed 18 April 2018).

123 'A Fresh Start', Section F, Appendix F7.

124 'Civic leaders could offer an alternative NI voice at Brexit talks', *News Letter*, 14 February 2018, https://www.newsletter.co.uk/news/civic-leaders-could-offer-an-alternative-ni-voice-at-brexit-talks-1-8377816 (accessed 18 April 2018). Support was voiced for the work of the All-Island Civic Dialogue on Brexit initiated by the Irish Government.

125 Northern Ireland (Stormont Agreement and Implementation Plan) Act 2016 (c. 13).

126 Newton Emerson, 'Stormont's problem is vetoes, not powersharing', *The Irish Times*, 5 October 2017, https://www.irishtimes.com/opinion/newton-emerson-for-powersharing-to-work-the-veto-must-go-1.3244241 (accessed 18 April 2018).

127 'Michelle O'Neill says "legacy deal" still stands', BBC News, 25 February 2018, http://www.bbc.com/news/uk-northern-ireland-politics-43191710 (accessed 18 April 2018).

128 Amending the provisions of the Northern Ireland Act 1998.

129 Northern Ireland (Ministerial Appointments and Regional Rates) Act 2017 (c. 24).

130 *R (McClean) v. First Secretary of State* [2017] EWHC 3174 (Admin).

131 Northern Ireland Budget Act 2017 (c. 34).

132 Henry McDonald and Jessica Elgot, 'Talks to restore power-sharing government in Northern Ireland collapse', *The Guardian*, 14 February 2018, https://www.theguardian.com/uk-news/2018/feb/14/arlene-foster-no-prospect-restored-government-northern-ireland (accessed 18 April 2018). See also Eamonn Mallie, 'Why the Sinn Féin DUP deal crashed', 15 February 2018, http://eamonnmallie.com/2018/02/sinn-fein-dup-deal-crashed-eamonn-mallie/ (accessed 18 April 2018).

133 'Full "Draft Agreement Text"', 20 February 2018, http://eamonnmallie.com/2018/02/full-draft-agreement-text/ (accessed 18 April 2018).

134 Para. 3.3. of the draft agreement.

135 The suggestion was that they would be dealt with in a separate process. Brian Rowan, 'Stormont Chronology: to the cusp of compromise and then collapse', 1 March 2018, http://eamonnmallie. com/2018/03/stormont-chronology-cusp-compromise-collapse-brian-rowan/ (accessed 18 April 2018).

136 At least for the moment: *ibid.*

137 'Stormont talks collapse: May and Varadkar's visit on Monday a "distraction", says DUP negotiator', *Independent*, 25 March 2018, https://www.independent.ie/irish-news/politics/stormont-talks-collapse-may-and-varadkars-visit-on-monday-a-distraction-says-dup-negotiator-36604245.html (accessed 18 April 2018).

138 Suzanne Breen, 'DUP moving ahead with a shadow Assembly, Arlene Foster to say', *Belfast Telegraph*, 24 March 2018, https://www.belfasttelegraph.co.uk/news/politics/dup-moving-ahead-with-a-shadow-assembly-arlene-foster-to-say-36738006.html (accessed 18 April 2018).

139 Naomi Long MLA, Leader's Address, Alliance Conference, Saturday, 24 March 2018, https://allianceparty.org/document/naomi-long-mla-s-speech-to-alliance-conference-2018.docx (accessed 18 April 2018).

140 Mary Lou McDonald, 'Shadow Assembly represents retreat from power sharing - McDonald', 23 March 2018, http://www.sinnfein. ie/contents/48769 (accessed 28 May 2018). See also 'Sinn Féin delivering "absolutely nothing" for Northern Ireland – Foster', *The Irish Times*, 24 March 2018, https://www.irishtimes.com/news/politics/sinn-f%C3%A9in-delivering-absolutely-nothing-for-northern-ireland-foster-1.3439439 (accessed 18 April 2018).

141 Colum Eastwood, 'SDLP Leader's address to TDs, Senators and Civic leaders on political impasse' 22 February 2018, http://www.sdlp.ie/news/2018/sdlp-leaders-address-to-tds-senators-and-civic-leaders-on-political-impasse/ (accessed 28 May 2018); see also Colum Eastwood, 'I call on Ireland and Britain to break the Stormont deadlock', *The Guardian*, 22 February 2018, https://www.theguardian.com/commentisfree/2018/feb/22/ireland-britain-stormont-deadlock-dup-sinn-fein-sdlp (accessed 18 April 2018).

142 'Coveney inter-governmental conference call a red herring – Aiken', *Unionist*, 20 March 2018, https://uup.org/news/5455/Coveney-inter-governmental-conference-call-a-red-herring-Aiken#.WrvlUy7waUk (accessed 18 April 2018).

143 'Swann calls on Secretary of State to act now over political impasse', *Unionist,* 13 March 2018, https://uup.org/news/5444/ Swann-calls-on-Secretary-of-State-to-act-now-over-political-impasse#.Wrvlfi7waUk (accessed 18 April 2018).

CHAPTER 3

1   *Re McCord* [2016] NIQB 85.
2   *R (Miller) v. Secretary of State for Exiting the European Union* [2017] UKSC 5.
3   Jonathan Tonge, 'The Impact and Consequences of Brexit for Northern Ireland', Brussels: European Parliament, Briefing PE 583 116, March 2017, http://www.europarl.europa.eu/RegData/ etudes/BRIE/2017/583116/IPOL_BRI(2017)583116_EN.pdf (accessed 18 April 2018).
4   See http://www.consilium.europa.eu/media/24079/070329_uk_ letter_tusk_art50.pdf (accessed 18 April 2018).
5   'Guidelines Following The United Kingdom's Notification Under Article 50 TEU', Brussels, 29 April 2017 (OR.en) EUCO XT 20004/17, para. 11, http://www.consilium.europa.eu/media/21763/29-euco-art50-guidelinesen.pdf (accessed 18 April 2018).
6   'European Commission Draft Withdrawal Agreement on the withdrawal of the United Kingdom of Great Britain and Northern Ireland from the European Union and the European Atomic Energy Community', Position Paper – Commission to EU, 27, 28 February 2018, https://ec.europa.eu/commission/publications/ draft-withdrawal-agreement-withdrawal-united-kingdom-great-britain-and-northern-ireland-european-union-and-european-atomic-energy-community_en (accessed 18 April 2018).
7   'Backstop agreement on post-Brexit border is "legally firm"', rte.ie, 20 March 2018, https://www.rte.ie/news/politics/2018/ 0319/948513-coveney-brexit-brussels/ (accessed 18 April 2018).
8   'Brexit timeline: key dates in UK's divorce with EU', *Financial Times*, 14 June 2017, https://www.ft.com/content/64e7f218-4ad4-11e7-919a-1e14ce4af89b (accessed 18 April 2018).
9   Minutes of Special meeting of the European Council (Art. 50), held on 29 April 2017, Brussels, 23 June 2017, http://data. consilium.europa.eu/doc/document/XT-20010-2017-INIT/en/pdf (accessed 18 April 2018).

10   '"Entire territory" of Ireland would be part of EU if unity referendum passed', rte.ie, 28 April 2017, https://www.rte.ie/news/2017/0428/871185-brexit-northern-ireland-eu/ (accessed 18 April 2018).

11   See https://merrionstreet.ie/MerrionStreet/en/EU-UK/FAQs/Your_questions_answered.html (accessed 18 April 2018).

12   'Joint Committee on the Implementation of the Good Friday Agreement, The Implications of Brexit for the Good Friday Agreement: Key Findings', June 2017, 32/JCIGFA/01, http://www.oireachtas.ie/parliament/media/committees/implementationofthegoodfridayagreement/jcigfa2016/The-Implications-of-Brexit-for-the-Good-Friday-Agreement-Key-Findings.pdf (accessed 18 April 2018).

13   Tony Connelly, 'Brexit Deal: Lost Irish leverage, or the UK "getting real"?', rte.ie, 24 March 2018, https://www.rte.ie/news/analysis-and-comment/2018/0324/949780-brexit-blog/ (accessed 18 April 2018).

14   'Draft Agreement on the withdrawal of the United Kingdom of Great Britain and Northern Ireland from the European Union and the European Atomic Energy Community', 19 March 2018, TF50 (2018) 35 – Commission to EU27, https://ec.europa.eu/commission/sites/beta-political/files/draft_agreement_coloured.pdf (accessed 18 April 2018).

15   *Ibid.*

16   *Ibid.*, chapter I, art. 1.

17   On this issue, see Bernard Ryan, 'The implications of UK withdrawal for immigration policy and nationality law: Irish aspects', Immigration Law Practitioners' Association (ILPA), EU Referendum Position Paper, 18 May 2016.

18   *Ibid.*, chapter III, art. 3.

19   *Ibid.*

20   Chapter III, art. 8.1.

21   Chapter IV, art. 11.

22   Chapter V, art. 15.

23   Centre for Cross Border Studies, 'Brexit and the UK-Ireland Border: A New Briefing Paper Series', November 2017, http://crossborder.ie/site2015/wp-content/uploads/2017/11/Brexit-and-the-Border-BP1-with-Exec-Summary.pdf (accessed 18 April 2018).

24   'Brexit: Ireland's Priorities', Irish Government Publication, p. 6, https://dbei.gov.ie/en/What-We-Do/EU-Internal-Market/Brexit/

Government-Brexit-Priorities/Brexit-Irelands-Priorities.pdf (accessed 18 April 2018).

25 Simon Coveney, 'Brexit must not endanger the Good Friday agreement', *The Guardian*, 31 January 2018, https://www.theguardian.com/commentisfree/2018/jan/31/brexit-good-friday-agreement-britain-eu-ireland (accessed 18 April 2018).

26 See also 'The land border between Northern Ireland and Ireland', Northern Ireland Affairs Committee, Second Report of Session 2017–19, HC 329, 16 March 2018, https://publications.parliament.uk/pa/cm201719/cmselect/cmniaf/329/32902.htm (accessed 18 April 2018).

27 [2018] AC 61.

28 Chris McCrudden, 'The Good Friday Agreement, Brexit, and Rights', Royal Irish Academy, British Academy Brexit Briefing, October 2017, https://www.ria.ie/sites/default/files/thegoodfridayagreementbrexitandrights_0-1.pdf (accessed 18 April 2018).

29 Christopher McCrudden and Daniel Halberstam, '*Miller* and Northern Ireland: A Critical Constitutional Response', Part II: Firing the Brexit Bullet – Who Pulls the Article 50 Trigger? (symposium), in Daniel Clarry (ed.), *The UK Supreme Court Yearbook,* vol. 8, *2016–2017 Legal Year* (Appellate Press, 2018), 299, 300.

30 *Ibid.*, p. 327.

31 *Ibid.*, p. 328.

32 *Ibid.*

33 *Ibid.*

34 *Ibid.*, p. 329.

35 *Ibid.*, p. 334.

36 *Ibid.*, p. 343.

37 Michael Farrell, 'Brexit, Human Rights and the Good Friday Agreement', *Law Society Gazette*, Jan./Feb. 2018, p. 34.

38 Belfast (Good Friday) Agreement Joint Committee Warns of Brexit Human Rights and Equality Concerns, 13 March 2018, Joint Committee of the Irish Human Rights and Equality Commission and the Northern Ireland Human Rights Commission, 'Policy statement on the United Kingdom withdrawal from the European Union', March 2018, http://www.nihrc.org/news/detail/belfast-good-friday-agreement-joint-committee-warns-of-brexit-human-rights (accessed 18 April 2018); https://www.ihrec.ie/app/uploads/2018/03/Joint-Committee-IHREC-NIHRC-Brexit-Policy-Statement_March-2018.pdf (accessed 18 April 2018).

39   The Centre for Cross Border Studies, 'Brexit and the UK-Ireland Border, Briefing Paper series, Briefing Paper 2: Citizens' Rights and the UK-Ireland Border' (January 2018), http://crossborder.ie/ site2015/wp-content/uploads/2018/01/Briefing-Paper-2-Final.pdf (accessed 18 April 2018).

40   Paul Daly, Kirsty Hughes and Kenneth Armstrong, 'Brexit and EU Nationals: Options for Implementation in UK Law' (24 November 2017), University of Cambridge Faculty of Law Research Paper No. 1/2018, https://ssrn.com/abstract=3077036 (accessed 18 April 2018).

41   Paul Faith, 'Brexiteers launch broadside at Northern Ireland peace deal', *Politico*, 22 February 2018, https://www.politico.eu/article/ brexiteers-broadside-northern-ireland-peace-deal-good-friday-agreement/ (accessed 18 April 2018).

42   Dennis Kennedy, 'Growing gap between Irishness and Britishness is most dangerous', *The Irish Times*, 20 December 2017, https:// www.irishtimes.com/opinion/growing-gap-between-irishness-and-britishness-is-most-dangerous-1.3332807 (accessed 18 April 2018).

43   Christopher McCrudden and Daniel Halberstam, *'Miller* and Northern Ireland', p. 306.

44   *Ibid.*, p. 307.

45   *Ibid.* House of Lords, European Union Committee, Brexit: Devolution Inquiry (Tuesday, 21 February 2017), http:// data.parliament.uk/writtenevidence/committeeevidence.svc/ evidencedocument/european-union-committee/brexit-devolution/ oral/48137.html (accessed 7 April 2018), response to Q 92 (Jonathan Tonge).

46   David Trimble, 'The Irish government is dragging Brexit into dangerous territory', *Spectator,* 2 December 2017, https://www. spectator.co.uk/2017/12/david-trimble-the-irish-government-is-dragging-brexit-into-dangerous-territory/ (accessed 18 April 2018).

47   Tonge, 'The Impact and Consequences of Brexit for Northern Ireland'.

48   See House of Lords, European Union Committee, The UK, the EU and a British Bill of Rights, HL Paper 130, 9 May 2016, https://publications.parliament.uk/pa/ld201516/ldselect/ ldeucom/139/13911.htm, cited in 'Brexit, the Good Friday Agreement and the European Convention on Human Rights', 9 January 2017, Institute of International and European Affairs,

https://www.iiea.com/brexit/brexit-the-good-friday-agreement-and-the-european-convention-on-human-rights/ (accessed 18 April 2018). See also European Union Committee, 'The UK, the EU and a British Bill of Rights', 12th Report of Session 2015–16, 9 May 2016 – HL Paper 139, chapter 8.

49 'Leaving the EU: Human Rights', HC Debates, 8 December 2016, vol. 618.

50 David Smith, 'Brexit threatens Good Friday agreement, Irish PM warns', *The Guardian*, 14 March 2018, https://www.theguardian.com/world/2018/mar/14/brexit-threatens-good-friday-agreement-irish-pm-warns (accessed 18 April 2018).

51 Tracker Poll Questions and Results – Base Report, 8 December 2017 – Version 1, https://lucidtalk.co.uk/images/News/LTDec17 TrackerPoll-GUENGLProjectReportF.pdf (accessed 18 April 2018). See comment by Peter Leary, 'There are three ways out of the Irish border impasse. All are closed to Theresa May', *The Guardian*, 1 March 2018, https://www.theguardian.com/commentisfree/2018/mar/01/irish-border-hard-theresa-may-brussels (accessed 18 April 2018).

52 Bill White, 'Unionists need to turn on the charm with Alliance voters to ensure border poll goes their way', *Belfast Telegraph,* 8 January 2018, https://www.belfasttelegraph.co.uk/opinion/columnists/bill-white/bill-white-unionists-need-to-turn-on-the-charm-with-alliance-voters-to-ensure-border-poll-goes-their-way-36470662.html (accessed 18 April 2018).

53 Paul Gosling, 'Unionists facing a perfect storm of Brexit and demographic shift', *Belfast Telegraph*, 22 February 2018, https://www.belfasttelegraph.co.uk/opinion/news-analysis/unionists-facing-a-perfect-storm-of-brexit-and-demographic-shift-36628756.html (accessed 18 April 2018).

54 Matt Carthy, 'Turn desire for united Ireland into unstoppable momentum', 24 February 2018, http://www.sinnfein.ie/contents/48386 (accessed 18 April 2018).

55 Gerry Moriarty, 'SDLP calls for Border poll on united Ireland after Brexit negotiations', *The Irish Times*, 30 May 2017, https://www.irishtimes.com/news/politics/sdlp-calls-for-border-poll-on-united-ireland-after-brexit-negotiations-1.3101566 (accessed 18 April 2018).

56 'EU knows the border is weak point for the UK and is upping the ante', *News Letter*, 28 February 2018, https://www.newsletter.

co.uk/news/opinion/eu-knows-the-border-is-weak-point-for-uk-and-is-upping-the-ante-1-8396205 (accessed 18 April 2018).

CHAPTER 4

1   Agreement, Strand Three, Rights, Safeguards and Equality of Opportunity, para. 1.

2   Art. 3.1.

3   Deaglán de Bréadún, 'A curiosity or a practical roadmap to the long-sought goal of a united Ireland?' *The Irish Times*, 24 December 2008, https://www.irishtimes.com/opinion/a-curiosity-or-a-practical-roadmap-to-the-long-sought-goal-of-a-united-ireland-1.1275745 (accessed 18 April 2018).

4   'Varadkar hopes to see United Ireland "with cross-community support"', *The Irish Independent*, 24 March 2018, https://www.independent.ie/breaking-news/irish-news/varadkar-hopes-to-see-united-ireland-with-crosscommunity-support-36450647.html (accessed 18 April 2018).

5   Gibson cited in 'Minister Brands Attempts to Persuade Unionists about a United Ireland "Offensive"', *Irish News*, 11 September 2017.

6   Graham Gudgin, 'Why the Burning Question is not Whether a United Ireland is Desirable, but if it is Affordable', *Belfast Telegraph*, 24 April 2017; Graham Gudgin, 'Stop harassing unionists about a united Ireland', *The Irish Times*, 25 August 2017, https://www.irishtimes.com/opinion/stop-harassing-unionists-about-a-united-ireland-1.3196980?mode=sample&auth-failed=1&pw-origin=https%3A%2F%2Fwww.irishtimes.com%2Fopinion%2Fstop-harassing-unionists-about-a-united-ireland-1.3196980 (accessed 18 April 2018).

7   Mike Burke, 'Deepening the Unionist Veto', *The Pensive Quill*, 1 November 2017, http://thepensivequill.am/2017/11/deepening-unionist-veto.html (accessed 18 April 2018).

8   John Wilson Foster, 'United Ireland campaign is based on a delusion', *The Irish Times*, 19 March 2018, https://www.irishtimes.com/opinion/united-ireland-campaign-is-based-on-a-delusion-1.3431695 (accessed 18 April 2018).

9   'Varadkar united Ireland comments "lack judgment": Hamilton', *News Letter*, 2 January 2018, https://www.newsletter.co.uk/

news/varadkar-united-ireland-comments-lack-judgment-hamilton-1-8313417 (accessed 18 April 2018).

10 Dennis Staunton, 'Tony Blair: Government could oppose final Brexit deal', *The Irish Times*, 4 January 2018, https://www.irishtimes.com/news/world/uk/tony-blair-government-could-oppose-final-brexit-deal-1.3344253 (accessed 18 April 2018).

11 British-Irish Agreement, art. 1(ii), Good Friday Agreement, Constitutional Issues Section, para. 1(ii).

12 *Ibid.*, para. 1(iv).

13 British Response to Sinn Féin Request for Clarification of the Joint Declaration on Peace: The Downing Street Declaration (19 May 1994), http://cain.ulst.ac.uk/issues/politics/docs/nio/nio190594.htm (accessed 18 April 2018).

14 *J. M. Kelly: The Irish Constitution*, 4th edn (Bloomsbury, 2003), p. 76.

15 Agreement, Constitutional Issues, Annex A.

16 *Ibid.*, para. 1(i).

17 Suzanne Breen, 'Varadkar wants a united Ireland through consensus, not Border poll', *Independent*, 18 October 2017, https://www.independent.ie/irish-news/politics/varadkar-wants-a-united-ireland-through-consensus-not-border-poll-36238375.html (accessed 18 April 2018).

18 Newton Emerson, 'Varadkar Tears up the Good Friday Agreement', *The Irish Times*, 19 October 2017, p. 14. The online version has the softer headline 'Leo Varadkar courting trouble over Border poll', https://www.irishtimes.com/opinion/leo-varadkar-courting-trouble-over-border-poll-1.3260759 (accessed 18 April 2018).

19 'Do not return to the status quo without protection for Union', *News Letter*, 7 March 2017, https://www.newsletter.co.uk/news/opinion/do-not-return-to-the-status-quo-without-protection-for-union-1-8404868 (accessed 18 April 2018).

20 Fintan O'Toole, 'United Ireland will not be based on "50 per cent plus one"', *The Irish Times*, 15 August 2017, https://www.irishtimes.com/opinion/fintan-o-toole-united-ireland-will-not-be-based-on-50-per-cent-plus-one-1.3186234 (accessed 18 April 2018).

21 *Ibid.*

22 Burke, 'Deepening the Unionist Veto', citing Andy Pollak's blog, 'Are There Really 150,00 Unionists who are Persuadable for a United Ireland?', 25 April 2017, https://2irelands2gether.

com (accessed 18 April 2018); Andy Pollak, 'Nationalism by Numbers,' *The Irish Times*, Letter to the Editor, 9 June 2017; Sean Donlon, 'Sinn Féin Missing a Lifetime Opportunity to Set the Agenda,' *The Irish Times*, 1 August 2017; Bertie Ahern, quoted in John Manley, 'Border Poll Calls are Dangerous Says Ahern,' *Irish News*, 1 May 2017; and Fintan O'Toole, 'United Ireland Will Not Be Based on "50 Per Cent plus One"', *The Irish Times*, 15 August 2017.

23   'Peer: Tiny majority for united Ireland would spark civil war', *News Letter*, 18 October 2017, https://www.newsletter.co.uk/news/peer-tiny-majority-for-united-ireland-would-spark-civil-war-1-8201426 (accessed 18 April 2018).

24   Burke, 'Deepening the Unionist Veto'.

25   Comment made by Adams in response to a question during a debate on Northern Ireland at the World Economic Forum, 'Adams surprises with acceptance of need for consent on Irish unity', *The Irish Times*, 4 February 2002. Adams later retracted any such suggestion and indicates in Gerry Adams, *The New Ireland* (Dingle Brandon, 2005), that 50 per cent +1 is the test required.

26   Social Democratic and Labour Party, 'A United Ireland and The Agreement – A Better Way to a Better Ireland', 21 March 2005, p. 4, http://cain.ulst.ac.uk/issues/politics/docs/sdlp/sdlp210305unity.pdf (accessed 18 April 2018). See also, speech by Mark Durkan, then leader of the Social Democratic and Labour Party (SDLP), at the launch of the SDLP Unity Document, 'A United Ireland and The Agreement: A Better Way to a Better Ireland', Belfast Castle (21 March 2005), http://cain.ulst.ac.uk/issues/politics/docs/sdlp/md210305unity.htm (accessed 18 April 2018).

27   *Ibid.*

28   *Ibid.* (subject to a vote in the South also).

29   Sean Donlon, 'Sinn Féin missing a lifetime opportunity to set the agenda', *The Irish Times*, 1 August 2017, https://www.irishtimes.com/opinion/sinn-f%C3%A9in-missing-a-lifetime-opportunity-to-set-the-agenda-1.3172566 (accessed 18 April 2018).

30   Burke, 'Deepening the Unionist Veto'.

31   *Ibid.*

32   Emerson, 'Varadkar Tears up the Good Friday Agreement'.

33   Agreement, Constitutional Issues, Annex A, Schedule 1.

34   'Sinn Féin urges unity referendum within five years', *The Irish Times*, 1 April 2018, https://www.irishtimes.com/news/

politics/sinn-f%C3%A9in-urges-unity-referendum-within-five-years-1.3447391 (accessed 19 April 2018); John Manley, 'Sinn Féin call for border poll rejected by two governments', *Irish News*, 25 June 2016, http://www.irishnews.com/news/2016/06/25/news/sinn-fe-in-call-for-border-poll-rejected-by-two-governments-579054/ (accessed 19 April 2018).

35   Gerry Moriarty, 'SDLP calls for Border poll on united Ireland after Brexit negotiations', *The Irish Times*, 30 May 2017, https://www.irishtimes.com/news/politics/sdlp-calls-for-border-poll-on-united-ireland-after-brexit-negotiations-1.3101566 (accessed 19 April 2018).

36   *Ibid.*

37   Amanda Ferguson, 'Border poll could "erupt in violence", SDLP MLA warns', *The Irish Times*, 23 September 2017, https://www.irishtimes.com/news/politics/border-poll-could-erupt-in-violence-sdlp-mla-warns-1.3231955 (accessed 19 April 2018).

38   Bill White, 'Irish border poll: Sinn Féin need to be careful plus how would Naomi Long and Steven Agnew vote?' *Belfast Telegraph*, 7 November 2017, https://www.belfasttelegraph.co.uk/opinion/columnists/bill-white/irish-border-poll-sinn-fein-need-to-be-careful-plus-how-would-naomi-long-and-steven-agnew-vote-36297061.html (accessed 19 April 2018).

39   See Northern Ireland Act 1998, s. 98(1).

40   John F. Larkin QC, '*Miller* and Northern Ireland: The Northern Ireland Constitution Before the UK Supreme Court', Part II: Firing the Brexit Bullet – Who Pulls the Article 50 Trigger? (symposium), in Daniel Clarry (ed.), *The UK Supreme Court Yearbook,* vol. 8, *2016–2017 Legal Year* (Appellate Press, 2018), pp. 282–98, 287.

41   1921 Anglo-Irish Treaty, art. 11.

42   1920 Act s. 1(2).

43   Vienna Convention on the Law of Treaties 1969, art. 4.

44   *Ibid.*, arts 46 to 53.

45   *Ibid.*, art. 54(a).

46   *Ibid.*, art. 56.1(a).

47   *Ibid.*, art. 56.1(b).

48   *Ibid.*, art. 54(b).

49   Ian McTaggart Sinclair, *The Vienna Convention on the Law of Treaties* (Manchester University Press, 1984) p. 164.

50   Vienna Convention on the Law of Treaties 1969, art. 59.

51   *Ibid.*, art. 60.

52   *Ibid.*, art. 61.

53 *Ibid.*, art. 62.

54 *Ibid.*, art. 64.

55 McTaggart Sinclair, *The Vienna Convention*, p. 186.

56 Agreement, Strand One, Democratic Institutions in Northern Ireland, Relations with other institutions, para. 33.

57 *Ibid.*, Strand Three, British-Irish Intergovernmental Conference, para. 5.

58 Agreement, Constitutional Issues, para. 1(vi).

59 Vienna Convention on the Law of Treaties 1969, art. 62.

60 Bruno Bianchi, Review Note, *Termination of Treaties in International Law: The Doctrines of Rebus Sic Stantibus and Desuetude*, by Athanassios Vamvoukos, 198510 ASILS Int'l L.J. 263 (Clarendon Press, 1986), p. 265.

61 The 'rebus sic stantibus' doctrine.

62 [1973] ICJ Rep. 3.

63 McTaggart Sinclair, *The Vienna Convention*, p. 193.

64 British-Irish Agreement, art. 1 (iv).

65 'A New Framework For Agreement', 22 February 1995, para. 19, http://cain.ulst.ac.uk/events/peace/docs/fd22295.htm (accessed 19 April 2018).

66 Citing Vienna Convention on the Law of Treaties, art. 54.

67 Conor Donohue, 'The Northern Ireland Question: All Ireland Self-Determination post-Belfast Agreement' (2016) 47 VUWLR, p. 66, http://www.nzlii.org/nz/journals/VUWLawRw/2016/4.pdf (accessed 19 April 2018).

68 Social Democratic and Labour Party, *A United Ireland and the Agreement: A Better Way to a Better Ireland* (SDLP, 2005), http://cain.ulst.ac.uk/issues/politics/docs/sdlp/sdlp210305unity.pdf (accessed 19 April 2018).

69 Social Democratic and Labour Party, *A United Ireland through the Good Friday Agreement*, November 2003 (Belfast, 2003).

70 *Ibid.*, p. 3.

71 *Ibid.*, p. 5.

72 *Ibid.*

73 *Ibid.*, p. 4.

74 *Ibid.*, pp. 5–6.

75 *Ibid.*, p. 6.

76 *Ibid.*

77 Speech by Mark Durkan, 'A United Ireland and The Agreement'. See also SDLP, 'DUP would destroy Unionism's protections in a united Ireland – Durkan', Press Release, 15 November 2003,

and Gerry Moriarty, 'S.D.L.P. insists majority vote should secure united Ireland', *The Irish Times*, 22 March 2005.

78 Anne Campbell, 'Green Paper a red herring', *Daily Ireland*, 22 March 2005; Gerry Moriarty, 'Ahern compares SF plan to "snake-oil salesman"', *The Irish Times*, 22 March 2005, https://www.irishtimes.com/news/ahern-compares-sf-plan-to-snake-oil-salesman-1.425233 (accessed 19 April 2018).

79 Roy Garland, 'GFA must live on if unity is achieved', *The Irish News*, 17 November 2003, http://nuzhound.com/articles/irish_news/arts2003/nov17_GFA_must_live__RGarland.php (accessed 19 April 2018).

80 *Ibid.*

81 Matt Carthy, 'Turn desire for united Ireland into unstoppable momentum', 24 February 2018, http://www.sinnfein.ie/contents/48386 (accessed 19 April 2018).

82 Donohue, 'The Northern Ireland Question', pp. 67–8.

83 Agreement, Constitutional Issues, para. 1.

CHAPTER 5

1 Agreement, Declaration of Support, para. 5.

2 'SDLP Leader Colum Eastwood outlines his vision of Progressive Nationalism', http://www.sdlp.ie/site/assets/files/43036/colum_eastwood_outlines_progressive_nationalism.pdf (accessed 19 April 2018).

3 John Wilson Foster, 'Only a leap of faith can banish spectre of the endgame haunting us', *Belfast Telegraph*, 22 February 2017, https://www.belfasttelegraph.co.uk/opinion/news-analysis/only-a-leap-of-faith-can-banish-spectre-of-the-endgame-haunting-us-john-wilson-foster-35470285.html (accessed 19 April 2018).

4 John Wilson Foster, 'United Ireland campaign is based on a delusion', *The Irish Times*, 19 March 2018, https://www.irishtimes.com/opinion/united-ireland-campaign-is-based-on-a-delusion-1.3431695 (accessed 19 April 2018).

5 Jayne McCormack, 'Opinion split over Sinn Fein use of "Londonderry"', BBC News, 28 April 2018, http://www.bbc.com/news/uk-northern-ireland-politics-43906796 (accessed 8 May 2018).

6 That, in effect, is a return to the 1985 Anglo-Irish Agreement.

7   Explanatory Notes, Northern Ireland (Regional Rates and Energy) Bill (22 March 2018 (HL Bill 93)), para. 3, https://publications. parliament.uk/pa/bills/lbill/2017-2019/0093/18093en.pdf (accessed 19 April 2018).

8   Explanatory Notes, Northern Ireland Budget (Anticipation and Adjustments) Bill (21 March 2018 (HL Bill 92)), para. 3, https://publications.parliament.uk/pa/bills/lbill/2017-2019/0092/ 18092en.pdf (accessed 19 April 2018).

9   Peter Geoghegan, 'Brexiteers launch broadside at Northern Ireland peace deal', *Politico*, 22 February 2018, https://www. politico.eu/article/brexiteers-broadside-northern-ireland-peace-deal-good-friday-agreement/ (accessed 19 April 2018); Leigh Boobyer, '"Good Friday Agreement has Failed" Eurosceptics attack deal which stalls Brexit', *Express*, 23 February 2018.

10   Ian Jack, 'The Good Friday agreement is under attack: Can we really risk ditching it?', *The Guardian*, 23 February 2018, https:// www.theguardian.com/commentisfree/2018/feb/23/good-friday-agreement-irish-brexit-northern-ireland (accessed 19 April 2018), referencing Ruth Dudley Edwards, 'The collapse of power-sharing in Northern Ireland shows the Good Friday Agreement has outlived its use', *Daily Telegraph*, 15 February 2018, https:// www.telegraph.co.uk/politics/2018/02/15/collapse-power-sharing-northern-ireland-shows-good-friday-agreement/ (accessed 19 April 2018).

11   Nicola Sturgeon, 'Let's limit the Brexit damage by staying in the single market', *The Guardian*, 2 December 2017, https://www. theguardian.com/commentisfree/2017/dec/02/limit-brexit-harm-stay-single-market-theresa-may-confront-arch-brexiteers (accessed 19 April 2018).

12   Alex Kane, 'Belfast Agreement should be given last rites', *The Irish Times*, 4 December 2017, https://www.irishtimes.com/opinion/ alex-kane-belfast-agreement-should-be-given-last-rites-1.3314109 (accessed 19 April 2018).

13   Alex Kane, 'Bradley's job now is to take control and make decisions', *News Letter*, 26 March 2018, https://www.newsletter. co.uk/news/opinion/bradley-s-job-now-is-to-take-control-and-make-decisions-1-8431167 (accessed 19 April 2018).

14   Dan Keenan, 'NI parties must "engage with greater urgency"', *The Irish Times*, 30 June 2006, https://www.irishtimes.com/news/ ni-parties-must-engage-with-greater-urgency-1.1023950 (accessed 19 April 2018).

15 Government Information Services, 'Statement by the Taoiseach, Mr Bertie Ahern T.D.', 16 February 2000; Frank Millar, 'Blair and Ahern fail to agree on way forward', *The Irish Times*, 17 February 2000, https://www.irishtimes.com/news/blair-and-ahern-fail-to-agree-on-way-forward-1.245895 (accessed 19 April 2018).

16 Vienna Convention on the Law of Treaties 1969, art. 26.

17 Oliver Dörr and Kirsten Schmalenbach (eds), *Vienna Convention on the Law of Treaties: A Commentary* (Springer, 2012), p. v, https://link.springer.com/content/pdf/bfm%3A978-3-642-19291-3%2F1.pdf (accessed 8 April 2018).

18 Vienna Convention on the Law of Treaties 1969, art. 27.

19 Wilson Foster, 'Only a leap of faith can banish spectre of the endgame haunting us'.

20 'Union will only survive if UK is truly inclusive', *News Letter*, 9 March 2018, https://www.newsletter.co.uk/news/your-say/union-will-only-survive-if-uk-is-truly-inclusive-1-8408507 (accessed 19 April 2018).

21 James McLoone (ed.), *The British-Irish Connection* (Social Study Conference, 1985), p. 39.

22 'Offended by "curry my yoghurt"? Gregory Campbell thinks you need a "humour bypass"', *The Journal*, 27 November 2014, http://www.thejournal.ie/gregory-campbell-curry-my-yoghurt-1803414-Nov2014/ (accessed 19 April 2018).

23 '"Curry my yoghurt" DUP MP says he would treat Irish Language Act "like toilet paper"', *The Journal*, 22 November 2014, http://www.thejournal.ie/gregory-campbell-toilet-paper-1794090-Nov2014/ (accessed 19 April 2018).

24 'Arlene Foster regrets Sinn Féin "crocodiles" comment', *The Irish Times*, 9 March 2017, https://www.irishtimes.com/news/ireland/irish-news/arlene-foster-regrets-sinn-f%C3%A9in-crocodiles-comment-1.3004084 (accessed 19 April 2018).

25 Siobhán Fenton, 'The language debate resurrects the big question: How Irish is Northern Ireland?', *iNews*, 25 February 2018, https://inews.co.uk/opinion/debate-irish-language-resurrects-big-question-northern-ireland-british-irish/ (accessed 19 April 2018).

26 Feargal Mac Ionnrachtaigh, *Language, Resistance and Revival: Republican Prisoners and the Irish Language in the North of Ireland* (Pluto Press, 2013).

27 Nelson McCausland, 'Activist highlighted connection "between the struggle and revival of Irish language" – campaign central to the republican goal of "political reconquest"', *Belfast Telegraph*,

22 February 2018, https://www.belfasttelegraph.co.uk/opinion/columnists/nelson-mccausland/activist-highlighted-connection-between-the-struggle-and-revival-of-irish-language-campaign-central-to-the-republican-goal-of-political-reconquest-36629213.html (accessed 19 April 2018).

28 'The Guardian view on Northern Ireland talks collapsing: the lost language of power-sharing', *The Guardian*, 15 February 2018, https://www.theguardian.com/commentisfree/2018/feb/15/the-guardian-view-on-northern-ireland-talks-collapsing-the-lost-language-of-power-sharing?CMP=share_btn_fb (accessed 8 May 2018); see also ConservativeHome, https://www.conservativehome.com/thetorydiary/2018/02/the-prime-minister-is-not-the-reason-the-ulster-talks-collapsed.html (accessed 19 April 2018).

29 Wilson Foster, 'United Ireland campaign is based on a delusion'.

30 According to Maurice Fitzgerald, a correspondent to the *News Letter*, 'Irish is counter-productive in bid for a united Ireland and will divide the island even more', *News Letter*, 16 February 2018, https://www.newsletter.co.uk/news/your-say/irish-is-counter-productive-in-bid-for-a-united-ireland-and-will-divide-the-island-even-more-1-8380609 (accessed 19 April 2018).

31 John Wilson Foster, 'If you want to see true cost of an Irish Language Act, look to Canada', *Belfast Telegraph*, 9 June 2017, https://www.belfasttelegraph.co.uk/opinion/news-analysis/if-you-want-to-see-true-cost-of-an-irish-language-act-look-to-canada-35804226.html (accessed 19 April 2018).

32 European Charter for Regional or Minority Languages, Strasbourg, 21 April ECRML (2010) 4, https://www.coe.int/t/dg4/education/minlang/report/EvaluationReports/UKECRML3_en.pdf (accessed 19 April 2018).

33 St Andrews Agreement, para. 8.

34 *Ibid.*, Annex B, Human Rights, Equality, Victims and Other Issues.

35 Northern Ireland Act 1998, s. 20.

36 Northern Ireland (St Andrews Agreement) Act 2006, s. 15, http://www.legislation.gov.uk/ukpga/2006/53/section/15 (accessed 19 April 2018).

37 *Re Conradh na Gaeilge* [2017] NIQB 27. For a general discussion of the area, see Daithí Mac Sithigh, 'Official status of languages in the UK and Ireland', *Common Law World Review* (2018) 47(1), https://pure.qub.ac.uk/portal/files/141540053/Status_OA_Feb_2018.pdf (accessed 19 April 2018).

38   Welsh Language Act 1993.

39   Welsh Language (Wales) Measure 2011, 2011 nawm 1, http://
     www.legislation.gov.uk/mwa/2011/1/contents (accessed 19 April
     2018).

40   Administration of Justice (Language) Act (Ireland) 1737, enacted
     by the Old Irish parliament, http://www.legislation.gov.uk/aip/
     Geo2/11/6 (accessed 19 April 2018).

41   In re Administration of Justice (Language) Ireland Act (1737),
     Mac Giolla Catháin v. NICS [2009] NIQB 66; and on appeal
     [2010] NICA 24. See Seán Ó Conaill, 'The Irish Language and
     The Irish Legal System: 1922 to Present', https://orca.cf.ac.
     uk/58843/1/2014oconaillsPhd.pdf (accessed 19 April 2018).

42   See Verona Ní Dhrisceoil, 'Language conflict in Northern Ireland:
     revisiting the Irish language rights debate' (2013) *Public Law*
     693–701.

43   'O Muilleoir wants to end 279-year-old ban on Irish in courts in
     Northern Ireland', *Belfast Telegraph*, 16 December 2016, https://
     www.belfasttelegraph.co.uk/news/northern-ireland/o-muilleoir-
     wants-to-end-279yearold-ban-on-irish-in-courts-in-northern-
     ireland-35297937.html (accessed 19 April 2018).

44   Draft Agreement, para. 2.2.ii. See 'Full "Draft Agreement Text"',
     20 February 2018, http://eamonnmallie.com/2018/02/full-draft-
     agreement-text/ (accessed 19 April 2018).

45   'UUP leader Robin Swann says Irish language act would be
     "divisive"', BBC News, 21 October 2017, http://www.bbc.com/
     news/uk-northern-ireland-41697275 (accessed 19 April 2018).

46   'The Guardian view on Northern Ireland talks collapsing'. See also
     Stephen Gamble, 'Unionists unite over Irish act', *News Letter*, 31
     March 2018, https://www.newsletter.co.uk/news/unionists-unite-
     over-irish-act-1-8439245 (accessed 19 April 2018).

47   See sections on art. 8 and art. 25.4.6° of the Constitution, http://
     archive.constitution.ie/reports/crg.pdf (accessed 19 April 2018).

CHAPTER 6

1   Guidance – Devolution settlement: Northern Ireland, Cabinet
    Office and Northern Ireland Office, 20 February 2013, https://
    www.gov.uk/guidance/devolution-settlement-northern-ireland
    (accessed 19 April 2018).

2   Northern Ireland Act 1998, s. 85.

3   Northern Ireland Act 1998, s. 4(2).

4   Harry McGee, 'Varadkar proposed joint cabinet meetings with UK after Brexit', *The Irish Times*, 16 April 2018, https://www. irishtimes.com/news/politics/varadkar-proposes-joint-cabinet-meetings-with-uk-after-brexit-1.3462688 (accessed 29 April 2018).

5   A time-limited All-Island Civic Dialogue on Brexit was established by the Irish government. See https://merrionstreet.ie/en/EU-UK/ Consultations/ (accessed 19 April 2018); https://merrionstreet. ie/en/EU-UK/Consultations/Dialogue_Report_on_Brexit_ Compendium.pdf (accessed 19 April 2018).

6   Alan Day of UKIP, corresponding to the *News Letter*: 'Unionists missing opportunity to frame various narratives', 28 March 2018, https://www.newsletter.co.uk/news/opinion/unionists-missing-opportunity-to-frame-various-narratives-1-8436500 (accessed 19 April 2018).

7   See e.g. Report of the Law Enforcement Commission to the Minister for Justice of Ireland and the Secretary of State for Northern Ireland (Dublin and London, 1974) Prl. 3832 and Cmnd. 5627.

8   See, for an interesting discussion of the subject of regional or local judicial solutions, Thomas Buergenthal, 'Proliferation of International Courts and Tribunals: Is it Good or Bad?' (2001), 14 *Leiden Journal of International Law*, 267.

9   See Richard Humphreys, 'Articles 2 and 3 may copper-fasten partition', *Ireland on Sunday*, 29 March 1998.

10 See All-Party Oireachtas Committee on the Constitution, *Eighth Progress Report: Government* (Dublin, 2003), p. 77.

11 Good Friday Agreement, Validation, Implementation and Review Section, para. 7.

12 Art. 29.7.1°.

13 Simon Coveney, 'Brexit must not endanger the Good Friday agreement', *The Guardian*, 31 January 2018, https://www. theguardian.com/commentisfree/2018/jan/31/brexit-good-friday-agreement-britain-eu-ireland (accessed 19 April 2018).

14 See Northern Ireland Constitution Act 1973 (c. 36), and Northern Ireland Constitution (Amendment) Act 1973 (c. 69).

15 'New Northern Ireland flag should be created, says Lord Kilclooney', *News Letter*, 17 December 2013, https://www. newsletter.co.uk/news/new-northern-ireland-flag-should-be-created-says-lord-kilclooney-1-5753950 (accessed 19 April 2018).

16   Statute Law Revision Acts 2005, 2007, 2009, 2012, 2015 and 2016.

17   1 Will. & Mar. c. 6.

18   *Ibid.*, s. 3.

19   1 Will. and Mar. Sess. 2 c. 2.

20   Succession to the Crown Act 2013 (c. 20). See also previous private members bill, Succession to the Crown Bill 2005.

21   Succession to the Crown Act 2013 (c. 20), Explanatory Notes, s. 2, para. 17, http://www.legislation.gov.uk/ukpga/2013/20/notes/division/5 (accessed 19 April 2018).

22   1690 (c. 7).

23   4 Will. and Mar. (c. 1).

24   12 & 13 Will. 3. (c. 2).

25   *Ibid.*, s. 2.

26   2 Ann. (c. 5) (Ir.).

27   6 Ann. (c. 11).

28   *Ibid.*, art. 2.

29   1707 (c. 7).

30   *Ibid.*, s. 2.

31   10 Ann. (c. 10).

32   *Ibid.*, s. 9.

33   10 Geo. 4 (c. 7).

34   *Ibid.*, s. 12.

35   *Ibid.*, s. 16.

36   *Ibid.*, s. 18.

37   Explanatory Notes, Succession to the Crown Act 2013, Chapter 20, http://www.legislation.gov.uk/ukpga/2013/20/notes (accessed 29 April 2018).

38   1974 (c. 25).

39   See Thomas Smith (ed.), *The Laws of Scotland: Stair Memorial Encyclopaedia* (Law Society of Scotland, 1987), Vol. 5, p. 169.

40   Acts of Union of 1800, s. 1 of both Acts.

41   'SDLP Leader Colum Eastwood outlines his vision of Progressive Nationalism', http://www.sdlp.ie/site/assets/files/43036/colum_eastwood_outlines_progressive_nationalism.pdf (accessed 19 April 2018).

42   Matt Carthy, 'Turn desire for united Ireland into unstoppable momentum', 24 February 2018, http://www.sinnfein.ie/contents/48386 (accessed 19 April 2018).

43   See http://www.electoralcommission.org.uk/faq/voting-and-registration/who-is-eligible-to-vote-at-a-uk-general-election (accessed 19 April 2018).

44 Role – Northern Ireland Affairs Committee, http://www. parliament.uk/business/committees/committees-a-z/commons-select/northern-ireland-affairs-committee/role/ (accessed 19 April 2018).

45 Fifth Report of the Convention on the Constitution, Amending the Constitution to Give Citizens Resident Outside the State the Right to Vote in Presidential Elections at Irish Embassies, November 2013, https://www.constitution.ie/AttachmentDownload.ashx?mid= bf489ec7-9556-e311-8571-005056a32ee4 (accessed 9 April 2018).

46 Suzanne Lynch, 'Referendum to be held on granting Irish abroad voting rights', *Irish Times,* 12 March 2017, https://www. irishtimes.com/news/politics/referendum-to-be-held-on-granting-irish-abroad-voting-rights-1.3007413 (accessed 19 April 2018).

47 'Extension of Voting Rights for Irish Citizens Abroad in Irish Presidential Elections', Department of Foreign Affairs and Trade, 20 June 2017, https://www.dfa.ie/media/dfa/alldfawebsitemedia/ newspress/publications/ministersbrief-june2017/5--Voting-Rights-for-Irish-Citizens-Abroad-in-presidential-elections.pdf (accessed 19 April 2018).

48 'Government Sets Indicative Timetable for Referendums', 26 September 2017, https://merrionstreet.ie/en/News-Room/News/ Government_Sets_Indicative_Timetable_For_Referendums.html (accessed 19 April 2018).

49 *Dáil Debates*, vol. 1, col. 1949.

50 Although this might require the setting up of a 'vocational group or association or council' for the purposes of a direct election under Article 19 of the Constitution.

51 'The Working Group on Seanad Reform publishes its Report today', Department of the Taoiseach, https://www.taoiseach.gov. ie/eng/News/Government_Press_Releases/Working_group_on_ Seanad_Reform_.html (accessed 19 April 2018).

52 Speech of An Taoiseach, Leo Varadkar TD, to Seanad Éireann, 1 February 2018, https://www.taoiseach.gov.ie/eng/ News/Taoiseach's_Speeches/Speech_of_An_Taoiseach_Leo_ Varadkar_T_D_To_Seanad_Eireann_1_February_2018.html (accessed 19 April 2018).

53 See All-Party Oireachtas Committee on the Constitution, Seventh Progress Report: Parliament (Stationery Office, 2002).

54 Gerry Adams, 'North political momentum must be maintained', *The Irish Times,* 5 August 2005, https://www.irishtimes.com/opinion/

north-political-momentum-must-be-maintained-1.476748 (accessed 19 April 2018) and see Mark Brennock, 'Adams presses for North's MPs to have say in the Dáil', *The Irish Times*, 5 August 2005, https://www.irishtimes.com/news/adams-presses-for-north-s-mps-to-have-say-in-the-d%C3%A1il-1.476410 (accessed 19 April 2018).

55   Bertie Ahern, 'There was no deal over men's return', *The Irish Times*, 8 August 2005, https://www.irishtimes.com/news/there-was-no-deal-over-men-s-return-1.477414 (accessed 19 April 2018).

56   See Gerry Moriarty, 'SF admits Adams wrong on Dáil speaking rights', *The Irish Times*, 9 August 2005; Caoimhghín Ó Caoláin, 'Sinn Féin and Dáil speaking rights', Letter to the Editor, *The Irish Times*, 13 August 2005, citing the Report of the All-Party Oireachtas Committee on the Constitution, Seventh Progress Report: Parliament.

57   S.O. 84A(7)(a), http://www.oireachtas.ie/parliament/media/about/standingorders/Consolidated-version-of-all-the-D%C3%A1il-Standing-Orders-as-of--21-Nov-2017.pdf (accessed 19 April 2018).

58   All-Party Oireachtas Committee on the Constitution, Seventh Progress Report: Parliament.

59   *Ibid.*, pp. 50–1.

60   'These Sinn Féin MPs were at Leinster House today to demand speaking time', *Journal*, 15 June 2017, http://www.thejournal.ie/sinn-fein-mps-dail-3446422-Jun2017/ (accessed 19 April 2018).

61   Liam Reid, 'Empey opposes Dáil, Seanad role for MPs', *The Irish Times*, 2 August 2005, https://www.irishtimes.com/news/empey-opposes-d%C3%A1il-seanad-role-for-mps-1.475209 (accessed 19 April 2018).

62   Frank Millar, 'Tory warning on proposals for thirty-two-county "shadow" Dáil', *The Irish Times*, 5 August 2005, https://www.irishtimes.com/news/tory-warning-on-proposals-for-32-county-shadow-d%C3%A1il-1.476484 (accessed 19 April 2018).

63   Jim Duffy, 'Adams in Dáil could have the status of a British peer', *The Irish Times*, 13 August 2005, https://www.irishtimes.com/opinion/adams-in-d%C3%A1il-could-have-the-status-of-a-british-peer-1.479715 (accessed 19 April 2018).

64   The Constitution confers a right of audience on members of the Government to be heard in each House of the Oireachtas – art. 28.8.

65   Indeed, Article 30.4 provides merely that the Attorney shall not be a member of Government.

66   Just as the answering of parliamentary questions 'involves to such a degree the operation of internal machinery of debate of the House as to remain within the competence of Dáil Éireann to deal with exclusively', *per* O'Flaherty J., in *O'Malley* v. *An Ceann Comhairle* [1997] 1 IR 437 at p. 431. See also *Controller of Patents, Designs and Trade Marks* v. *Ireland* [2001] 4 IR 229.

67   All-Party Oireachtas Committee on the Constitution, Seventh Progress Report: Parliament, p. 50.

68   Joint Oireachtas Committee on European Affairs, Voting Rights of Irish Citizens Abroad, November 2014, https://www.oireachtas. ie/parliament/media/committees/euaffairs/archiveeuaffairs/Final-Voting-Rights-report_07112014.pdf (accessed 29 April 2018).

69   Donal O'Donnell, 'Constitutional Background to and Aspects of the Good Friday Agreement – A Republic of Ireland Perspective' (1999), 4 *Bar Review* 174.

70   All-Party Oireachtas Committee on the Constitution, Seventh Progress Report: Parliament, pp. 54–5.

CHAPTER 7

1   The phrase has been attributed to Hume by e.g. Garret FitzGerald, 'Difficult to imagine a more complex process of negotiations', *The Irish Times*, 5 November 1994, and seems to relate back to his speech to the SDLP party conference in 1993; see also John Hume, Speech to SDLP Annual Party Conference, 6 November 1999.

2   Conor Donohue, 'The Northern Ireland Question: All Ireland Self-Determination post-Belfast Agreement' (2016), 47 VUWLR, 61, http://www.nzlii.org/nz/journals/VUWLawRw/2016/4.pdf (accessed 19 April 2018), citing Code of Good Practice on Referendums, s. I.3.1.c.

3   'Political Comment: Persuading unionists on unity: How far would you go?' *Derry Now*, 18 March 2018, https://www. derrynow.com/news/political-comment-persuading-unionists-unity-far-go/213641 (accessed 19 April 2018).

4   'SDLP Leader Colum Eastwood outlines his vision of Progressive Nationalism', http://www.sdlp.ie/site/assets/files/43036/colum_eastwood_outlines_progressive_nationalism.pdf (accessed 19 April 2018).

5   'A better way forward is available', *Derry Journal*, 5 February 2018, https://www.derryjournal.com/news/opinion-a-better-way-forward-is-available-1-8364979 (accessed 19 April 2018).

6   Matt Carthy, 'Turn desire for united Ireland into unstoppable momentum', 24 February 2018, http://www.sinnfein.ie/contents/48386 (accessed 19 April 2018).

7   Wayne O'Connor, '"United Ireland discussions are premature" – Fianna Fail', *Independent*, 12 February 2018, https://www.independent.ie/irish-news/politics/united-ireland-discussions-are-premature-fianna-fail-36592546.html (accessed 19 April 2018).

8   Matt Carthy, 'Turn desire for united Ireland into unstoppable momentum', 24 February 2018, http://www.sinnfein.ie/contents/48386 (accessed 19 April 2018).

9   Houses of the Oireachtas, Joint Committee on the Implementation of the Good Friday Agreement Brexit and the Future of Ireland Uniting Ireland & Its People in Peace & Prosperity, August 2017, 32/JCIGFA/02, p. 15, http://www.oireachtas.ie/parliament/media/committees/implementationofthegoodfridayagreement/jcigfa2016/Brexit-and-the-Future-of-Ireland.pdf (accessed 19 April 2018).

10 John Wilson Foster, 'Memo to Michelle O'Neill: We're all "west Brits" now', *Belfast Telegraph*, 5 October 2017, https://www.belfasttelegraph.co.uk/opinion/news-analysis/memo-to-michelle-oneill-were-all-west-brits-now-36197130.html (accessed 19 April 2018).

11 See John Bowman, *De Valera and the Ulster Question 1917–1973* (Clarendon Press, 1982), pp. 335–7.

12 'Mary Lou McDonald: Intergovernmental Conference needed, not a shadow Assembly that gives "a veneer of accountability to direct rule"', 26 March 2018, https://sluggerotoole.com/2018/03/26/mary-lou-mcdonald-intergovernmental-conference-needed-not-a-shadow-assembly-that-gives-a-veneer-of-accountability-to-direct-rule/ (accessed 19 April 2018).

13 Social Democratic and Labour Party, 'A United Ireland and The Agreement – A Better Way to a Better Ireland', 21 March 2005, p. 4, http://cain.ulst.ac.uk/issues/politics/docs/sdlp/sdlp210305unity.pdf (accessed 19 April 2018).

14 See Bowman, *De Valera and the Ulster Question*, p. 318.

15 See Committee on the Elimination of Racial Discrimination, General Recommendation 30, Discrimination against Non-Citizens, 64th Session, 23 February to 12 March 2004, C.E.R.D/C64/Misc.11/rev.3: Committee on the Elimination of Racial

Discrimination, Consideration of reports submitted by State's parties under Article 9 of the Convention, concluding observations of the Committee on the elimination of racial discrimination, Ireland, 66th Session, 21 February to 11 March 2005, CERD/C/IRL/CO/2, 10 March 2005.

16　See Agreement, Constitutional Issues, para. 1(vi).

17　ECHR, art. 1.

18　Broadly it must be said that the courts have proceeded on the basis that non-nationals are entitled to most constitutional rights of citizens. See for example *N.V.H. v. Minister for Justice and Equality* [2017] IESC 35 [1984] ILRM 539 [1984] IR 268, *Rederij Kennemerland BV v. Attorney General* [1989] ILRM 821, *Re Article 26 and the Illegal Immigrants (Trafficking) Bill 1999* [2000] IESC 19 [2000] 2 IR 360, *Northampton County Council v. ABF* [1982] ILRM 194, *The State (McFadden) v. Governor of Mountjoy Prison* [1981] ILRM 113, *Finn v. Attorney General* [1983] IR 154, *The State (Kugan) v. O'Rourke* [1985] IR 658.

19　European Convention on Human Rights Act 2003.

20　William Binchy, 'McDowell creating divided Society – Do we really want two classes of children growing up side by side?', *The Irish Times*, 27 May 2004; see also Carol Coulter, 'Lawyers unite against referendum: amendment would create constitutional ambiguities, says group', *The Irish Times*, 20 May 2004.

21　See *Dáil Debates*, vol. 584 no. 3, 28 April 2004, http://oireachtasdebates.oireachtas.ie/debates%20authoring/debateswebpack.nsf/takes/dail2004042800001?opendocument (accessed 19 April 2018).

22　Electoral (Amendment) Bill 1983.

23　*In re Electoral (Amendment) Bill 1983* [1984] IR 268.

24　Ninth Amendment of the Constitution Act 1984, signed by the President on 2 August 1984.

25　Electoral (Amendment) Act 1985.

26　A provision now contained in the Electoral Act 1992, annotated by John T. O'Dowd (1992) *Irish Current Law Statutes Annotated* 23.

27　Art. 16.1.2°.ii, inserted by the Ninth Amendment of the Constitution Act 1984.

28　Art. 18.4.2°.

29　Agreement, Strand Three, Rights, Safeguards, and Equality of Opportunity, Comparable Steps by the Irish Government, para. 9.

30　Downing Street Declaration, 15 December 1993, para. 6.

31 National Archives, Department of the Taoiseach file ref. S230/15/12/0035C, 0037B, 0037C, 0043.

32 National Archives, Department of the Taoiseach file ref. S230/15/12/0035C Document ref. F303/SCO Rev. 1, dated May 1996.

33 National Archives, Department of the Taoiseach file ref. S230/15/12/0037C, Summary of Debate 24/2/95, Plenary Debate on Obstacles in the South to reconciliation. See also Mary Carolan, 'Ahern stands up for "historic" anthem', *Irish News*, 19 October 1995.

34 Art. 44.1.2°.

35 The Fifth Amendment of the Constitution Act 1972 was signed by President Éamon de Valera on 5 January 1973 and provided for the repeal of arts 44.1.2° and 44.1.3°, thereby deleting the special position of the Catholic Church and the recognition of other named churches.

36 Indeed, even Garret FitzGerald's account of the first divorce referendum does not mention Northern Ireland: *All in a Life* (Gill and Macmillan, 1991), pp. 625–31.

37 And arts 7, 8, 41 and 44 and the declarations in arts 12, 31 and 34. National Archives, Department of the Taoiseach file ref. S230/15/12/0035C, Document ref. F303/SCO Rev. 1, dated May 1996, p. 30.

38 John Rogers, 'Constitution Fails to Acknowledge Historic Problems', *The Irish Times*, 8 April 1998.

39 See Constitution Review Group, *Report* (Dublin, 1996), pp. 5–6, http://archive.constitution.ie/reports/crg.pdf (accessed 19 April 2018). For an interesting analysis of the Report, see Gerry Whyte, 'Discerning the philosophical premises of the Report of the Constitution Review Group: An Analysis of the recommendations on Fundamental Rights' (1998), 2 *Contemporary Issues in Irish Law and Politics*, 216.

40 Constitution Review Group, *Report.*, p. 5.

41 *Ibid.*

42 National Archives, Department of the Taoiseach file ref. S230/15/12/0035C, Document ref F303/SCO Rev 1, dated May 1996, pp. 31–2.

43 See Michael D. Higgins, 'Ahern misleading & confusing public on Eire/Ireland name change', Press Release, 28 June 2006, criticising the fact that Minister Ahern made comments suggesting that it

was proposed to change terminology used in press releases and website references as well.

44 As set out in arts 12.8.1°, 31.4 and 34.5.1° of the Constitution respectively. See Jamie McLoughlin, '"In the presence of Almighty God" – the human rights violations at the heart of the Irish Constitution', ILT 2017, 35(17), 230–5.

45 See United Nations Human Rights Committee, Concluding Observations of the Human Rights Committee: Ireland, 3 August 1993, CCPR/C/79/Add. 21, which referred in para. 15 to the oath for the President and judges only. The concerns about the oath, but only as regards judges, were referred to in the Committee's second report, United Nations Human Rights Committee, Concluding Observations of the Human Rights Committee: Ireland, 24 July 2000, A/55/40, paras 422–51. Para. 29(b) calls for '[r]eform of constitutional provisions requiring judges to make a declaration with religious references (art. 18)'.

46 Constitution Review Group, *Report*, pp. 33 (the President should be entitled to make either declaration or affirmation), & 130 (likewise for Councillors of State) and 179 (delete the references to God in the judicial oath).

47 Arts 41, 42 and 44.

48 Arts 15.3 and 18.7. See Anthony Whelan, 'Constitutional Democracy, Community and Corporatism in Ireland' (1995), *Irish Human Rights Yearbook*, 97, noting the particular influence on vocationalist thought of Pius XI's 1931 encyclical, *Quadragesimo Anno*, issued on the 40th anniversary of Leo XIII's *Rerum Novarum* of 1891.

49 Arthur Aughey, 'Obstacles to Reconciliation in the South', in Forum for Peace and Reconciliation, *Building Trust in Ireland: Studies Commissioned by the Forum for Peace and Reconciliation* (Blackstaff Press, 1996), pp. 1–52, at pp. 14–15.

50 *Ibid.*, pp. 28–9.

51 Brice Dickson, 'A Unionist Legal Perspective on Obstacles in the South to Better Relations with the North', *ibid.*, pp. 53–84.

52 *Ibid.*, p. 59.

53 National Archives, Department of the Taoiseach file ref. S230/15/12/0035C, Document ref F303/SCO Rev 1, dated May 1996, p. 30.

54 Dickson, 'A Unionist Legal Perspective on Obstacles', p. 61.

55 Annotated by Peter Duffy and Paul Stanley (1998) *Current Law Statutes*, 42.

56   Dickson, 'A Unionist Legal Perspective on Obstacles', p. 64.

57   *Ibid.*, p. 67.

58   *Ibid.*, p. 68.

59   *Ibid.*, p. 69.

60   *Ibid.* See art. 8 and art. 25.4.6°.

61   *Ibid.*

62   *Ibid.*, p. 70.

63   Art. 40.2.1°.

64   Dickson., 'A Unionist Legal Perspective on Obstacles', p. 71.

65   See National Archives, Department of the Taoiseach file ref. S230/15/12/0037C and 0043, the former file including a letter from Eason & Son Ltd., dated 27 February 1995, complaining about the burdens imposed by the censorship legislation, and the latter file includes material from the Campaign to Separate Church and State including a restatement of their policy document, 'Time to face up to "Rome Rule"'.

66   Wilson Foster, 'Memo to Michelle O'Neill: we're all "west Brits" now'.

67   British Council Ireland, *Through Irish Eyes; Irish Attitudes Towards the U.K.* (British Council Ireland, 2003).

68   See http://www.decadeofcentenaries.com/category/world-war-one/ (accessed 19 April 2018).

69   See http://meetings.derrycityandstrabanedistrict.com/documents/ g1067/Public%20reports%20pack%20Thursday%2029-Mar-2018%2016.00%20Derry%20City%20and%20Strabane%20 District%20Council%20Open.pdf?T=10 (accessed 19 April 2018).

70   As quoted partially in the following two reports: 'Unionists slam council vote on Armed Forces recruitment drives in schools put forward by former dissident republican', *Belfast Telegraph*, 30 March 2018, https://www.belfasttelegraph.co.uk/news/ northern-ireland/unionists-slam-council-vote-on-armed-forces-recruitment-drives-in-schools-put-forward-by-former-dissident-republican-36759269.html (accessed 19 April 2018) and Rebecca Black, 'Beattie slams SF backing of council motion to "ban" Army from recruiting in schools', *Belfast Telegraph*, 31 March 2018, https://www.belfasttelegraph.co.uk/news/northern-ireland/beattie-slams-sf-backing-of-council-motion-to-ban-army-from-recruiting-in-schools-36760181.html (accessed 19 April 2018).

71   The Earl of Longford and Thomas P. O'Neill, *Éamon De Valera* (Gill and Macmillan, 1970) p. 433.

72 Pat McArt 'Persuading unionists on unity: How far would you go?', *Derry Now*, 18 March 2018, https://www.derrynow.com/news/political-comment-persuading-unionists-unity-far-go/213641 (accessed 19 April 2018).

73 See Tim Pat Coogan, *De Valera: Long Fellow, Long Shadow* (Hutchinson, 1995) p. 640.

74 Denis Lehane and Liam O'Neill, 'Dev's grandson says republicans would be in favour of joining Commonwealth', *Examiner*, 27 November 1998.

75 Note the CRG suggested that Article 29.4.2° of the Constitution was unnecessary: see All-Party Oireachtas Committee on the Constitution, *Eighth Progress Report: Government* (Dublin, 2003) pp. 75–7.

76 Aughey, 'Obstacles to Reconciliation in the South', p. 38.

77 *Ibid.*, p. 39.

78 *Ibid.*, p. 36.

79 *Ibid.*

80 *Ibid.*, p. 39.

81 *Ibid.*, pp. 39–40, as suggested by Sean Farren of the SDLP at the Forum on 24 February 1995.

82 *Ibid.*, p. 40.

83 See Patsy McGarry, 'Independence possible without 1916, says Bruton', *The Irish Times*, 20 September 2004.

84 See Martin Frawley, 'Bid to make the 12th a holiday in the Republic', *The Sunday Tribune*, 12 June 2005.

85 Corey Kilgannon, 'Post "Troubles," Anti-British Banner Still Flies in St. Patrick's Parade', *New York Times*, 16 March 2018, https://www.nytimes.com/2018/03/16/nyregion/banner-st-patrick-parade-new-york-england.html (accessed 19 April 2018).

86 'A Dáil committee is talking to unionists to prepare for a possible united Ireland', *The Journal*, 17 February 2018, http://www.thejournal.ie/unionism-united-ireland-3849573-Feb2018/ (accessed 19 April 2018).

87 'A better way forward is available', *Derry Journal*, 5 February 2018, https://www.derryjournal.com/news/opinion-a-better-way-forward-is-available-1-8364979 (accessed 19 April 2018).

88 Gerry Adams, 'Uncomfortable Conversations: Building new Relationships', Speech on 17 September 2015 at launch of 'Uncomfortable Conversations' by Declan Kearney, http://www.sinnfein.ie/contents/36443 (accessed 29 April 2018).

89   Marie-Violaine Louvet, *Civil Society, Post-Colonialism and Transnational Solidarity: The Irish and the Middle East Conflict* (Springer, 2016), p. 150.

CONCLUSIONS

1   Agreement, Strand One, Relations with other institutions, para. 33.

2   Government of Ireland Act 1920 (10 & 11 Geo. 5 c. 67), s. 75.

3   Northern Ireland Act 1998 (c. 47), s. 5(6).

4   UK involvement in Ireland not mandated by the Agreement as it now stands could raise constitutional issues, but presumably any such issues will be anticipated and addressed in the international treaty between the two governments and the wording of any constitutional amendment required in the South to approve that treaty.

5   See http://www.oireachtas.ie/parliament/oireachtasbusiness/committees _list/good-friday-agreement/ (accessed 19 April 2018).

6   Walter Carruthers Sellar and Robert Julian Yeatman, *1066 and All That* (Methuen, 1931), p. 116, cited in Fintan O'Toole, Britain's Irish question becomes Ireland's English Question, *The Irish Times*, 21 October 2016, https://www.irishtimes.com/opinion/ fintan-o-toole-britain-s-irish-question-becomes-ireland-s-english-question-1.2838553 (accessed 19 April 2018).

7   'Alliance leader Naomi Long party conference address', *Belfast Telegraph*, 24 March 2018, https://www.belfasttelegraph. co.uk/news/northern-ireland/alliance-leader-naomi-long-party-conference-address-full-text-36740043.html (accessed 19 April 2018).

Index